Formal Object-Oriented
Speci... ...g Object-Z

Roger Duke and Gordon Rose

First published 2000 by
MACMILLAN PRESS LIMITED
Houndmills, Basingstoke, Hampshire RG21 6XS
and London
Companies and representatives throughout the world

ISBN 0-333-80123-7

A catalogue record for this book is available from the British
Library.

This book is printed on paper suitable for recycling and made
from fully managed and sustained forest sources.

10   9   8   7   6   5   4   3   2   1
09   08   07   06   05   04   03   02   01   00

Printed in Great Britain by
Antony Rowe Limited
Chippenham, Wiltshire

Contents

Preface   vii

1   Specification and object orientation   1
1.1   Formal specification   1
1.2   Object orientation   2
1.3   Getting started   3
1.4   Credit-card bank accounts: a case study   4
1.5   The Object-Z class construct   5
1.6   Object instantiation and interaction   12
1.7   Inter-object communication   18
1.8   Object aggregation   19
1.9   Inheritance   23
1.10   Polymorphism   29
1.11   Overview   31

2   Graphical presentation of specifications   33
2.1   Introduction   33
2.2   Class diagrams   33
2.3   Illustrating Object-Z composition   34
2.4   Illustrating inheritance   36
2.5   Selection from sets   37
2.6   Discussion   39

3   Local vs central control   41
3.1   Introduction   41
3.2   A magnetic key system: a case study   42
3.3   A local view   42
3.4   A central view   46

4   Distributed and mediated message passing   51
4.1   Introduction   51
4.2   Bingo: a case study   51

4.3	A buttons-toggling puzzle: a case study	55
4.4	Refinement to code	59

5 Dependency and information sharing — **63**
5.1	Introduction	63
5.2	Tic tac toe: a case study	63
5.3	Synchronising information	65
5.4	Centralising information	70
5.5	Collating information	74

6 Reliable behaviour — **79**
6.1	Introduction	79
6.2	The alternating-bit protocol: a case study	79
6.3	Complementary graphical diagrams	87
6.4	Discussion	93

7 Proving invariant properties — **95**
7.1	Introduction	95
7.2	Tic tac toe revisited	96
7.3	Alternating-bit protocol revisited	98
7.4	Safety and liveness	103

8 Polymorphic inheritance hierarchies — **105**
8.1	Introduction	105
8.2	Geometric shapes: a case study	106
8.3	Discussion	114

9 Class union — **117**
9.1	Introduction	117
9.2	Defining class union	117
9.3	Polymorphic core	118
9.4	Ginger Meggs: an example	119
9.5	A communications channel: an example	120
9.6	A telephone system: a case study	121
9.7	A mass transit railway: a case study	127

10 Object containment — **139**
10.1	Introduction	139
10.2	A file system: an example	140
10.3	Notation for object containment	142
10.4	Object containment in recursive structures	146
10.5	A retail chain: a case study	151

11 Computational systems — **161**
11.1	Introduction	161
11.2	A spreadsheet: a case study	161

12 Functional abstraction   **171**
12.1   Introduction   171
12.2   A virtual memory: a case study   171

13 Semantic issues of Object-Z   **183**
13.1   Introduction   183
13.2   Semantics of object identity   184
13.3   Informal semantics of composed operations   185
13.4   Formal semantics of composed operations   190
13.5   Semantics of inheritance   192

A   Background notation   **197**
A.1   Introduction   197
A.2   Predicate calculus   197
A.3   Sets   201
A.4   Relations   204
A.5   Functions   206
A.6   Sequences   207

B   Glossary of notation   **209**
B.1   Definitions and declarations   209
B.2   Logic   209
B.3   Sets   210
B.4   Numbers   211
B.5   Relations   211
B.6   Functions   211
B.7   Sequences   212
B.8   Class and other notation   212

C   Object-Z concrete syntax   **215**
C.1   Notation   215
C.2   Abbreviations   215
C.3   Productions   216

D   Further reading   **223**

Index   **225**

Preface

The objective of this book is to explore the technique of object-oriented formal specification using the Object-Z specification language.

The book has been written with two audiences in mind. It is suitable as a text-book for an advanced undergraduate or postgraduate course on formal specification, either on its own or within a course on object-oriented development methods. It is also aimed at the professional software engineer wanting an introduction to formal object-oriented specification and design. The book is primarily intended for the practitioner rather than for the theoretician. It aims to give a thorough and practical introduction to the technique of formal specification using the Object-Z notation.

Object-Z is based on the state-based formal specification language Z and provides specific constructs to facilitate specification in an object-oriented style. In particular, Object-Z has a class construct which encapsulates a single state schema with relevant operations. Each class can be examined and understood in isolation, and complex classes can be specified in terms of simpler classes through constructive techniques. The language provides facilities for defining class associations (class unions) not restricted to membership of inheritance hierarchies, and for containment which facilitates the specification of common object-reference structures. An operation, in addition to changing its object's state, may also invoke operations on one or more other objects which it can reference. Object-Z provides a range of composition operators to express such multiple communication.

Formal specification is only part of a software development process. Readers can incorporate the formal specification technique described in this book within their own development process. In particular, it is not necessary to discard existing development processes in order to include formal specification. The level of formality adopted can vary between projects and even within the one project. Safety critical aspects, for example, can be singled out for formal development, while other aspects might be developed informally.

The book focuses on formal specification intended for use within formal, object-oriented development. However, formal specification is strongly advocated for integration within informal or semi-formal development: that is, within the majority of current development processes. Abstracting away from inessential detail to focus on essential functionality forces the clarification of system issues. This is the essence of specification: without it, issues may be overlooked or confused in implementation detail and this may lead to expensive redesign and re-implementation. Unintended or incorrect functionality revealed at system test time, or in the extreme case revealed while in service, is serious. In safety-critical applications, manifestation of functional errors may be catastrophic.

The book does not attempt to present an overall formal development process. Other formal techniques such as refinement and verification are alluded to but a thorough discussion is beyond the scope of the book.

Approach taken

It is our view, based on teaching formal methods to students at all levels and to professional software engineers, that the central difficulty faced initially is not the comprehension of the mathematical notation, but its application to capture the key abstractions of data and functionality. Consequently, the approach taken is to illustrate concepts and techniques through carefully chosen case studies. These case studies demonstrate the features of the Object-Z language and, just as importantly, introduce and illustrate the issues of specification technique and architectural design, with particular emphasis upon specification patterns. Conventional wisdom recommends the separation of concerns. At the risk of being heretical, we believe that functionality and architectural design within object-oriented systems are inextricably intertwined: comprehension of the functionality of an object-oriented system is greatly assisted through sound architectural design.

Prerequisites

With the exception of Chapter 13, the book does not assume prior exposure to Z or to any other formal specification notation, nor does it assume familiarity with any particular object-oriented design process. However, it is assumed that the reader is familiar with basic set theory and predicate logic as taught in an undergraduate mathematics or computer science course. For those not familiar with this notation, Appendix A illustrates the required mathematical concepts of predicate logic and set theory. Readers who are unsure of their mathematical background are advised to first read this appendix. Other readers may wish to refer to this appendix as unfamiliar set or functional notation arises. Appendix B is a glossary of notation.

Structure of the book

Chapter 1 outlines our approach to object-oriented specification and design and introduces most features of the Object-Z notation: it is essential reading for an appreciation of the basics of Object-Z — the remainder of the book is built upon this chapter.

Chapter 2 illustrates the utility of graphical notation as a complement to aspects of Object-Z and discusses the limitations of such notation in formal development. Object-Z, like Z, is not a graphical notation, i.e. it does not describe a system as a graph comprising a variety of nodes and connections. Rather, an Object-Z specification consists of declarations, conditions and other constructs expressed in mathematical text. The graphical notation introduced in Chapter 2 is based on the Unified Modeling Language (UML). It is used from time to time in later chapters to complement the discussion of an Object-Z specification.

Chapters 3 to 6 and Chapters 8 to 12 develop the Object-Z notation by exploring commonly occurring patterns of specification and design. Although the Object-Z notation is developed progressively, it is possible for these chapters to be read out of order provided the reader is prepared to consult earlier chapters when unfamiliar notation arises. Chapters 9 and 10, however, introduce the important ideas and notation of class union and object containment which are used frequently later in the book.

Refinement of an Object-Z specification to an object-oriented implementation language, such as C++, Eiffel, Java or Smalltalk, is implied because the class structure of an Object-Z specification typically may be mapped directly to the class structure of an implementation. Although the book does not address formal refinement, Chapter 4 illustrates an informal conversion of an Object-Z specification to Java.

Chapter 7 looks at the issue of proving properties of specifications. This chapter relies for examples upon the case studies introduced in Chapters 5 and 6.

The book mostly reveals the semantics of Object-Z informally. Chapter 13, however, introduces a formal denotational semantics of object identity, operation composition and inheritance within Object-Z. Appendix C presents a concrete syntax for Object-Z.

For readers interested in pursuing issues raised in the book, some references for further reading are given in Appendix D. Technical papers that elaborate upon and extend the Object-Z notation beyond that presented in the book can be found at the home web page of the Software Verification Research Centre (SVRC) at `http://svrc.it.uq.edu.au/`.

The Object-Z specifications in this book were type checked using version 1 of the `wizard` type checker. This research version, which accommodates most Object-Z constructs, is freely available and may be down-loaded from the above SVRC web page.

Acknowledgments

This book would not have been possible without the collaboration of many colleagues. Those who have made a particular contribution include Steven

Atkinson, Cecily Bailes, Steven Butler, David Carrington, Jin Song Dong, David Duke, Alena Griffiths, Ian Hayes, Andrew Hussey, Wendy Johnston, Paul King, David Leadbetter, Anthony Lee, Andrew Lenart, Craig Mann, Carroll Morgan, Kinh Nguyen, Andreas Prinz, Udaya Shankar, Graeme Smith, Paul Swatman, Owen Traynor and Mark Utting. Specifically, we acknowledge the work of Jin Song Dong on class union and containment, the work of Alena Griffiths on the semantics of object identity, the work of Wendy Johnston on the `wizard` type checker and for using `wizard` to check our specifications, and the work of Graeme Smith on the semantics of composition operators. To these and to all who over the past few years have joined us in vigorously discussing the issues raised in this book we extend our sincere appreciation.

We acknowledge the financial support of the Overseas Telecommunications Corporation Australia, the Australian Research Council, and the School of Information Technology and the Software Verification Research Centre within the University of Queensland.

Roger Duke   Gordon Rose

Brisbane, Australia, October 1999

Specification and object orientation   1

1.1 Formal specification

Specification is one aspect of the overall process of engineering software, but it is a crucial aspect without which little confidence can be placed upon the accuracy and reliability of the software system created.

Formal specification is the process of creating precise (mathematical) models of a proposed system. The role of such models is to provide an unambiguous description of the functionality of the system. The specification is the ultimate reference for implementation, and is the basis for verification, i.e. for ensuring that the implementation satisfies the specification. The specification also provides a basis for the preparation of documentation and user-educational material. Thus the role of specification is central to a formal development method.

The motivation for formality in specification is that software engineering, like the classical engineering disciplines, should be built upon a formal mathematical foundation. The degree of formality considered adequate varies between systems and is influenced by the size, complexity and overall purpose of a system. Even within the one system, specifications at different levels of abstraction and formality are needed to meet the varying demands of those involved with the system. For example, if the nature of the interface and the rules of operation of a simple recreational computer game are adequately understood informally, a formal specification would not be needed to explain the game to a player. The implementor of the game, however, would need a detailed and possibly formal specification.

Safety critical software, such as that responsible for guiding aircraft or monitoring power stations, needs to behave exactly as intended, and it would be unprofessional to attempt the engineering of such software without producing a detailed and complete formal specification.

A specification is essentially an abstract model capturing some view of a system. Just as there may be a variety of different views, so there can be many relevant associated specifications. Consequently, when engineering a software system, specifications are constructed at different stages to reflect the way the various views evolve. For a typical software engineering project, the initial specification will be developed within the requirements analysis phase, and will reflect both the client's and engineer's perceptions of the system. At this stage, components in the specification directly model real-world entities. Later, concepts to directly model software (virtual) entities will be specified from the initial perceptions. At yet a later stage, these concepts will evolve further into a specification capturing low-level code detail.

Specifying a model of a system is not a new idea; it has always been at the centre of the scientific method. For example, Newton's model of planetary motion based on the inverse square law of gravitation is a formal specification that enables aspects of the behaviour of the solar system to be predicted. Although it is traditional to refer to the creation of such conceptual systems as mathematical modelling rather than specification, the idea is essentially the same.

There are, however, significant differences of detail that distinguish the formal specifications of software systems from the mathematical models of the physical world. Software systems are human artifacts that behave according to created laws, like the rules of chess, rather than to physical laws like those governing the motion of planets. Consequently, the mathematics used to specify and analyse software systems is not the calculus of continuity often used when modelling the physical world, but rather the predicate calculus and the related rules of logical inference. Although the rules governing a software system are generally much simpler in scope than the laws of physics, even a software system of moderate size may be governed by a large number of rules, the overall effect of which is often subtle and surprising. It is the need to handle such complexity that has propelled the development of formal methods within software engineering.

There is another difference between specifications of software systems and those of the physical world, and it is to do with the distinction between engineering and science. One purpose for creating a specification is as a basis for the construction of a software system. In this sense, a software specifier fulfils the role of the architect designing the system to be engineered. Although this architectural aspect of specification is central, it is important to appreciate that a specification plays a wider role within the overall software engineering process. It is the fundamental model through which the complex functionality and temporal behaviour of the system can be understood, analysed and communicated.

The primary aim of this book is to explore, using the Object-Z notation, the creation of object-oriented formal specifications of software-related systems.

1.2 Object orientation

The term *object orientation* refers not only to a particular approach to analysis and design or a particular coding style, but also to an underlying philosophic view of how systems can be conceived. Object orientation takes the view that a system can be realised as a collection of objects acting cooperatively. An object is an entity that communicates and cooperates with its environment through the sending and receiving of messages. An individual object encapsulates an internal state and a collection of operations (methods). The operations are invoked by messages that pass between the object and its environment: in response to a message, the object may change its state and send messages to other objects.

The objects of a system partition the total system space and individually assume responsibility for the integrity of their corresponding sub-space. A system's overall behaviour is therefore confined to cooperation within the pre-scribed individual behaviours of its constituent objects. This partitioning of space and responsibility is essential for development in the large.

In this book we take a class-based approach to the specification of object-oriented systems. An Object-Z class specifies both the states that are possible for an object of that class and the operations that such an object can undergo. Given that an object is in a particular state, the class specifies how that state may change and what communication takes place with the object's environment when it performs one of its operations. That is, an Object-Z class specifies the behaviour common to all objects of that class. To specify a system, it is necessary to identify its constituent objects and specify their classes and interaction.

The class-based approach to object orientation offers reuse of existing components by adaptation of their class definitions through the techniques of inheritance (defining a new class by modification/extension of an existing class or classes) and instantiation (defining a new class to include references to objects).

Assuming an object-oriented development process, there are two reasons for adopting object-oriented specification. Firstly, the nature of the specification is consistent with, and reinforces, the overall development process. Secondly, the specification captures the architectural aspects of the system, not just the functional aspects.

1.3   Getting started

The first task in creating a specification is to decide on its role. If the role is to describe the system from the point of view of the user, the specification would need to model the external interface of the system but could ignore internal aspects hidden from the user. If the role is to describe the system architecture to the software engineer responsible for coding the system, the specification would at least need to reflect the classes to be used in an implementation. If the role is to create a model in order to analyse behaviour and verify system safety and correctness, the specification would need to capture the system in detail.

In practice, deciding on the role of the specification is not simple because of the often conflicting needs of all those concerned. It is generally unreasonable to attempt to construct a single specification that can play all roles within the software process: instead, a suite of formally-related specifications is constructed, each evolving to satisfy a particular need. (To maintain the formal relationship between the several views as they evolve requires a formal refinement theory based on incremental class modification. Such considerations are outside the scope of the book.)

In getting started, the first specification should be at a high level of abstraction, i.e. should ignore as much lower-level detail as possible, and concentrate on the architectural and functional relationships between the main system components. Taking an object-oriented perspective, this means identifying the core objects within the system and defining these objects, and their inter-relationships, by specifying appropriate classes.

1.4   Credit-card bank accounts: a case study

To illustrate our approach to object-oriented specification, we construct and discuss a formal abstract model of a simple system consisting of a collection of credit-card accounts. In the process we introduce many aspects of Object-Z.

The aim of the specification is to capture the basic functionality of credit-card account objects and their interaction. Lower-level detail is ignored, even though such detail is essential in practice for the construction of a reliable, commercial system. Despite this lack of detail, the specification presented is sufficient for the purpose of illustrating key object orientation and specification issues. The specification is not unrealistic in that it is a valid high-level view that could be the first model produced within the overall development process.

Before formal specification can begin, an informal system view is needed. The level of detail of an initial informal view will strongly influence the level of abstraction adopted in the formal specification. For example, a customer wishing to operate a credit-card account, and the bank responsible for managing the account, may have quite distinct views as to which aspects are essential and which can be ignored. In this case study, we capture the functional and logical aspects of such accounts and ignore how credit-card accounts are managed within the banking system.

Taking a top-down approach to identify the essential components, the system is envisaged as a collection of credit-card account objects. Other objects, such as bank customers, are not modelled. Although a top-down approach informally identifies credit-card accounts as constituting the system, a bottom-up approach is needed to formally specify the exact nature of these objects and their interactions. First, the class of a credit-card account object in isolation is specified: this class encapsulates the details of the state of a credit card and the operations it can undergo. The operations specify the communication (inputs and outputs) that take place with the environment, without being specific about the nature of that environment, and the consequent effects upon the state.

Next, the class of the system is specified: this class declares that the system comprises a collection of credit-card account objects, together with operations to specify the actions that can take place within or between these objects.

Before writing the specification it must be decided whether the specification is to model the real-world objects or their software representation. We shall model virtual credit-card accounts as they would appear in a software system. The distinction in this simple example is not all that important as our view could be interpreted as an abstraction of either the real world or the software system. In general, however, the distinction affects the nature of the abstractions. For example, during the requirements analysis phase, the models are most likely abstractions of real-world entities which the client (user) can readily identify. During the coding phase, however, the models represent abstractions of the software entities that may have no real-world counterparts. The way that the relationships between levels of abstraction are formally maintained within the development process ultimately determines the correctness of the software system. This is one of the fundamental roles of formal specification and refinement.

We now consider the detail of a credit-card account. Informally the account is conceived as an object that records two numbers, one an integer denoting the current balance of the account (this balance is of course often negative, indicating that the account is overdrawn) and the other a natural number (a non-negative integer) denoting a fixed limit: the account cannot be overdrawn beyond this credit limit. (We shall ignore cents; i.e. all amounts are in whole dollars.) The balance will change as money is withdrawn or deposited, with the understanding that a withdrawal cannot overdraw the account beyond its set limit. In the model, withdrawal covers both cash withdrawals and purchases. Also, we suppose there is an operation to withdraw all the available funds which will overdraw the account to its limit. Finally, we suppose (somewhat unrealistically) that there are just three possible values for the credit limit: $1000, $2000 and $5000.

1.5   The Object-Z class construct

The above informal description is now expressed as a formal specification of a credit-card account object. The internal state of the object is determined by the current balance and credit limit. The operations (i.e. the procedures or methods) that the object can undergo are specified in terms of the inputs they accept, the outputs they generate and the state changes they produce. The Object-Z class construct shown in Figure 1.1 encapsulates this essential intertwining of state and operations. This example illustrates several aspects of Object-Z classes. (The notation used throughout this book for the fundamental mathematical concepts of predicates, sets, relations, functions and sequences is based on the mathematical toolkit developed for the Z specification language. For readers not familiar with this toolkit, Appendix A illustrates the notation. Appendix B is a glossary of all notation used in this book.)

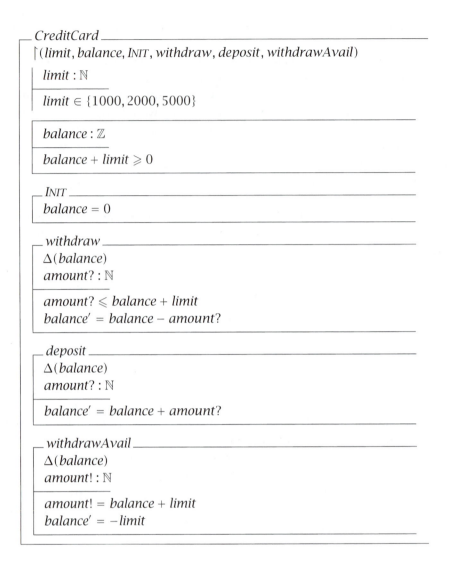

Figure 1.1: the class *CreditCard*

General structure

Syntactically, an Object-Z class is a named box inside of which are various constructs, including other unnamed and named boxes. In this case the class name is *CreditCard*. The class contains (in order) a visibility list, a constant definition, a state schema, an initial schema and three operation schemas.

In the following discussion each of these constructs is explored, both with respect to the class *CreditCard* specifically and with respect to Object-Z classes in general.

Visibility list

The visibility list

$$\upharpoonright(limit, balance, \textsc{Init}, withdraw, deposit, withdrawAvail)$$

lists those features (a technical term, defined later) that are visible to the environment of an object of the class *CreditCard*; effectively, it specifies the interface of such objects. The features listed are each defined within the body of the class; in this case their significance will be discussed as the class structure of *CreditCard* is unfolded.

   If a class has no explicit visibility list, as will often be the case in the examples in later chapters, all features are implicitly visible.

Constant definition

The following construct is an axiomatic definition (open schema box): it declares *limit* to be a constant natural number whose value is 1000, 2000 or 5000.

$$limit : \mathbb{N}$$
$$\overline{limit \in \{1000, 2000, 5000\}}$$

   Schemas in Object-Z (following the Z style) are divided into two parts: the top *declaration* part (above the horizontal dividing bar) contains the declarations of quantities pertinent to the schema, while the bottom *predicate* part contains a formula in first-order predicate logic involving the declared quantities and other quantities accessible to the schema. Each declaration of a quantity involves introducing an identifier and stating its associated type. The predicate imposes constraints upon the quantities it references beyond those constraints imposed by the declaration of types. Values of quantities which satisfy their types and result in a 'true' predicate value conform with the specification. Specifying 'true' itself for the predicate imposes no additional constraint: in that case the predicate part (and dividing bar) may be omitted.

   The value of the constant *limit* represents the magnitude of the credit limit beyond which the account cannot be overdrawn. For any particular credit-card account, the value of *limit* is constant; i.e. no operation changes it. However, note that two different credit-card account objects need not have the same value for *limit*. (In practice, there would be operations to alter the credit limit of an account: no such operations can be included in this model as *limit* is specified as a constant.)

   As *limit* is placed in the visibility list, the value of *limit* is visible to the environment and can be accessed directly by the environment without the need to first send the object a message. The environment could therefore use the value of *limit*, e.g. to decide whether or not to send a credit-card account object a message requesting that a given amount be withdrawn from the account.

State schema

The state schema is an unnamed box construct. In the class *CreditCard* it is:

$$\begin{array}{|l}
\hline
balance : \mathbb{Z} \\
\hline
balance + limit \geqslant 0 \\
\hline
\end{array}$$

Like the open schema box declaring constants, this schema is divided into two parts: the top part contains the declarations of the *state variables* of the class, and the bottom part contains a predicate involving the state variables and other accessible quantities. If there are no declared variables, the declaration part (and dividing bar) is omitted; similarly, if the predicate is 'true' the predicate part (and bar) is omitted. The state variables and constants of a class together constitute its *attributes*.

The state schema for *CreditCard* contains the declaration of just one state variable, namely

$balance : \mathbb{Z}$.

The value of this variable is an integer denoting the current balance of the account.

The predicate of the state schema of the *CreditCard* class,

$balance + limit \geqslant 0$,

is true if and only if the value of *balance* does not fall below the negative of *limit* (i.e. $-limit$). The specification insists that the state predicate be true; thus, the predicate of a state schema is called the *class invariant*.

A schema determines a set of valid *instances*, i.e. the set of all assignments of a value to each declared variable consistent with that variable's type and which satisfy the schema's predicate. For the state schema of *CreditCard*, an instance is valid when *balance* has as its value an integer number not more negative than $-limit$. A valid instance of the state schema is always maintained, i.e. the attributes are restricted to have values so that the class invariant is true initially and before and after every operation.

The attribute *balance*, like *limit*, is placed in the visibility list, i.e. its value is visible to the environment. (If an attribute is not placed in the visibility list it is hidden from the direct perusal of the environment. In such a case, the environment could only obtain the value of the attribute as an output of some operation.)

Initial schema

The initial schema, always named *INIT*, consists of a predicate which may involve the attributes and other accessible quantities. This predicate is conjoined with the class invariant to define the *initial condition*. An object is said to be in its *initial configuration* whenever the values of its attributes satisfy the initial condition.

For the *CreditCard* class, the initial schema is:

$$\begin{array}{|l}
\hline
\text{INIT} \underline{\hspace{6cm}} \\
\hline
balance = 0 \\
\hline
\end{array}$$

Logically conjoining the predicate of *INIT* (i.e. *balance* = 0) with the class invariant (i.e. *balance* + *limit* $\geqslant$ 0) results in the initial condition *balance* = 0: it implies that the value 0 is the balance of any credit-card account object in its initial configuration. As *INIT* is placed in the visibility list, the environment of any *CreditCard* object can observe whether or not the object is in its initial configuration.

It is important to appreciate that the initial schema simply defines a condition: it is not an operation of initialization. It is possible to specify an operation, say *reInitialize*, which, whenever applied, would put the state in its initial configuration. Also, it is possible for an object to revert to its initial configuration during its evolution by the application of operations (other than a specific re-initialize operation). For example, the balance of an account will be zero (its initial configuration) whenever the total withdrawals equals the total deposits.

Operation schemas

Each of the remaining three schemas in the *CreditCard* class, i.e.

$$\begin{array}{|l}
\hline
\text{withdraw} \underline{\hspace{4cm}} \\
\hline
\Delta(balance) \\
amount? : \mathbb{N} \\
\hline
amount? \leqslant balance + limit \\
balance' = balance - amount? \\
\hline
\end{array}
\qquad
\begin{array}{|l}
\hline
\text{deposit} \underline{\hspace{4cm}} \\
\hline
\Delta(balance) \\
amount? : \mathbb{N} \\
\hline
balance' = balance + amount? \\
\hline
\end{array}$$

$$\begin{array}{|l}
\hline
\text{withdrawAvail} \underline{\hspace{3cm}} \\
\hline
\Delta(balance) \\
amount! : \mathbb{N} \\
\hline
amount! = balance + limit \\
balance' = -limit \\
\hline
\end{array}$$

are *operation* schemas whose role is to specify the transitions a credit-card account object can undergo.

An operation will generally involve the passing of messages between the object and its environment, possibly accompanied by a change in the values of some of the class variables. Consequently, an operation schema will introduce a (possibly empty) set of *communication* variables used to pass information between the object and its environment, and will specify a relationship between the values of the attributes before and after the operation. (The 'before' and 'after' values of constants will of course be identical.) That is, the operation schemas specify message passing and consequent object evolution.

Consider the operation *withdraw*. This operation models the situation where a credit card is used to obtain funds for some purpose (e.g. to purchase goods, or to get cash).

The declaration part of *withdraw* begins with $\Delta(balance)$. In general, the Δ-list of an operation is a list of state variables whose values are subject to change by the operation. The value of any state variable not in the Δ-list implicitly remains unchanged when an object of the class undergoes the operation. For example, if *CreditCard* had another state variable, say v, its non inclusion in the Δ-list of *withdraw* would imply that v would remain unchanged whenever a *withdraw* operation were applied to a *CreditCard* object. (We shall see later, however, that when operations are combined, their Δ-lists are united so that only variables not in any of the combined operations' Δ-lists implicitly remain unchanged.) As constants cannot appear in Δ-lists, there is no mechanism to change them, i.e. their values persist. In the case of the operation *withdraw*, the Δ-list indicates that the value of *balance* may change.

Following the Δ-list, a communication variable *amount?* of type natural number is declared. As with Z, a communication variable ending in '?' or '!' denotes an input or output, respectively. Hence *amount?* denotes an input from the environment, i.e. the actual value to be withdrawn is supplied by the environment.

An operation schema has access to the unprimed attributes and the primed state variables. As with Z, an unprimed quantity denotes its value before an operation, while a primed quantity denotes its value afterwards.

The predicate of an operation relates the unprimed (before) values of the attributes, the primed (after) values of the state variables and the communication variables (i.e. *limit*, *balance*, *balance'* and *amount?* for operation *withdraw*). For *withdraw* the predicate states that

- the input natural number value *amount?* denoting the amount to be withdrawn must not exceed *balance + limit* (i.e. the maximum funds available if the credit card is not to be overdrawn beyond its credit limit);

- the value of the balance after the operation (*balance'*) is equal to the value of the balance before the operation (*balance*) minus the amount withdrawn (the supplied value *amount?*).

For predicates in schemas there is an implicit logical conjunction ($\wedge$) between lines, i.e. the predicate of the schema *withdraw* is logically equivalent to

$$amount? \leqslant balance + limit \quad \wedge \quad balance' = balance - amount?.$$

Because the class invariant must always hold, to determine the effect of an operation the schema predicate is conjoined with the class invariant (to ensure the invariant is true before the operation) and with the class invariant with each state variable replaced by its primed version (to ensure the invariant is true after the operation). For *withdraw*, this gives the schema

$$balance, balance' : \mathbb{Z}$$
$$amount? : \mathbb{N}$$

$$balance + limit \geqslant 0$$
$$balance' + limit \geqslant 0$$
$$amount? \leqslant balance + limit$$
$$balance' = balance - amount?$$

which represents the overall effect of the operation on a credit-card account object.

Logically, the condition $amount? \leqslant balance + limit$ is redundant as it can be deduced from the other conditions, i.e. it could have been omitted from the predicate of *withdraw* without logical consequence. To clarify to a reader the intention of an operation it is quite common to include such redundant conditions in the predicate of a schema, even if logically they can be deduced from the class invariant or from other conditions. In this case, the redundant condition is something that must hold before the *withdraw* operation can occur: it is explicitly included to ensure the precondition of the operation is clear.

An attempt to give a value to *amount?* in excess of *balance + limit* would violate the specification of *withdraw*. In Object-Z, operation *withdraw* is said to be *inapplicable* for such values of *amount?*. There is no notion of operation 'failure' or of 'forcing' an operation — an object cannot undergo an evolution step specified by an inapplicable operation. If a state is reached where every operation is inapplicable, the object cannot evolve further.

The operation *deposit* is structurally similar to *withdraw*; it models the situation where a natural number value supplied by the environment (*amount?*) is deposited into the account. As a result the balance of the account is increased by this amount (*balance' = balance + amount?*). This operation is always applicable: if the class invariant is true, adding a natural number to the balance will ensure it remains true.

Finally, consider operation *withdrawAvail*; it models the situation where the total amount currently available (i.e. *balance + limit*) is withdrawn and output to the environment as a natural number (*amount!*). The balance is adjusted accordingly (i.e. *balance' = -limit*) and as a result the account becomes overdrawn to the maximum permitted. Notice the distinction in terms of communication with the environment between the operations *withdraw* and *withdrawAvail*. For *withdraw* the amount to be withdrawn needs to be supplied by the environment, while for *withdrawAvail* the amount withdrawn is calculated by the credit-card account object itself and the environment informed. Notice also that the physical flow of cash is not modelled, only the information specifying the amounts, e.g. *withdraw* has an input but no output.

As all three operations are in the visibility list, the environment will have direct access to these operations (see Section 1.6).

The *features* of a class are *INIT* (if it has an initial schema) and the names of its attributes and operations.

Notice that the specification of an object involves a 'black-box' view of the object's environment with respect to communication. It is not appropriate for the specification of a credit-card account object to be explicit as to the origin of input required for the operations *withdraw* and *deposit*, or the destination of output generated by the operation *withdrawAvail*. By leaving such details unspecified, a credit-card account object can be placed into any cooperative environment.

1.6   Object instantiation and interaction

Continuing a bottom-up approach to system specification, once the fundamental objects (in this case, credit-card accounts) have been modelled, the next task is to model a system consisting of a collection of such objects. The specification will capture not only the way objects behave as individual and independent entities within the system, but also the way they can interact.

In the last section, the Object-Z class construct was introduced to model abstractly the functionality of individual objects. In this and the next two sections we will see how object-oriented systems can also be modelled using the Object-Z class construct: attributes are declared to identify objects, and operations are defined to specify object interaction.

Within the context of the credit-cards case study, the task is to model a banking system consisting of a collection of credit-card accounts. In general, such a system would consist of an indeterminate, or even variable, number of such accounts. However, before considering in detail the general case (in Section 1.8), we shall first construct a small system consisting of two distinct credit-card account objects, c_1 and c_2, together with a suite of operations to withdraw and deposit amounts to either account, or transfer various amounts between accounts, etc. Suppose also that there is an operation to replace one account by a new account (e.g. if the plastic card in the real world that is used to confirm customer identity is lost or stolen). This small system, although unrealistic as a model of an actual banking system, will enable us to introduce and clarify issues to do with object identity, instantiation and interaction. It is specified by the Object-Z class *TwoCards* in Figure 1.2.

Objects as attributes

The declaration

$$c_1, c_2 : CreditCard$$

in the state schema of the class *TwoCards* introduces two attributes, c_1 and c_2, whose values are identities of objects of the class *CreditCard*, i.e. identities of

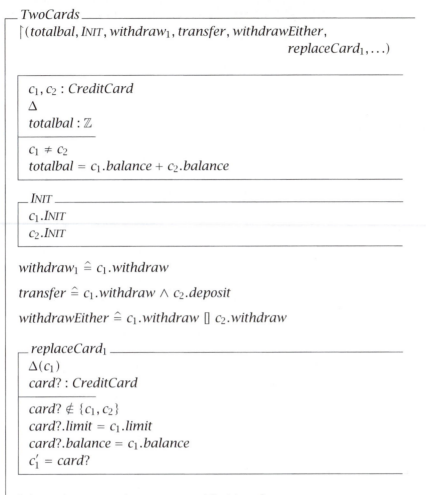

Figure 1.2: the class *TwoCards*

credit-card account objects.

It is important to distinguish between the state of an object and its identity. The state of an object is an instance of the state schema of the object's class, whereas the identity of an object uniquely identifies that object, distinguishing it from all other objects of its or any other class. This identity is invariant in that it does not change, regardless of how the state of the object evolves. In Object-Z, the values of attributes like c_1 and c_2 are object identities.

The predicate

$$c_1 \neq c_2$$

indicates that the values of c_1 and c_2 are distinct, i.e. that they identify distinct objects of the class *CreditCard*. The states of the credit-card account objects so identified, however, may well be identical.

Throughout this book attributes such as c_1 and c_2 will be informally referred to as objects, although technically it is understood that their values only identify objects.

Secondary variables

All of the state variables discussed so far, both in this class and in *CreditCard*, are *primary*: their values can only change via those operations whose Δ-lists explicitly include them. The variable *totalbal*, however, denoting the sum of the balances of the credit-card accounts c_1 and c_2, is declared to be *secondary*. Syntactically, the declarations of secondary variables (if any) appear below a Δ separator placed in the declaration part of the state schema. The values of secondary variables ultimately depend on constants and primary variables and will generally change as the values of the primary variables change. In particular, a secondary variable is subject to change every time an operation is performed. Indeed, this motivates the use of the Δ separator before the declaration of the secondary variables — although not listed explicitly, secondary variables are included implicitly in every Δ-list.

The quantities on which a secondary variable ultimately depend need not necessarily belong to the same object as that of the secondary variable. For example, the value of *totalbal* of a *TwoCards* object depends on the *balance* attribute of the objects identified by the primary variables c_1 and c_2 according to the predicate

$$totalbal = c_1.balance + c_2.balance.$$

The expressions $c_1.balance$ and $c_2.balance$ appearing in the above predicate are syntactically valid as *balance* is in the visibility list of class *CreditCard*. The general rule is that an expression *ob.feature* is syntactically valid if and only if *feature* is in the visibility list of the class of the object *ob*. If *feature* is an attribute of the class of *ob*, the expression *ob.feature* evaluates to the value of this attribute in the object identified by the value of *ob*.

Notice that there is no requirement that the values of $c_1.limit$ and $c_2.limit$ be the same.

Initial schema

The predicates

$$c_1.INIT \quad \text{and} \quad c_2.INIT$$

in the initial schema of *TwoCards* indicate that an object of class *TwoCards* is in its initial configuration if and only if the referenced credit-card account objects are distinct and each is in their initial configuration. In general, an expression *ob.INIT* is a predicate that evaluates to true if and only if the state of the object identified by the value of *ob* is in its initial configuration.

Promoting operations

The expression

$$withdraw_1 \mathrel{\widehat{=}} c_1.withdraw$$

defines an operation *withdraw*$_1$ in the class *TwoCards* in terms of the operation *withdraw* of the class *CreditCard* applied to the credit-card account object c_1, i.e. the effect of the operation *withdraw*$_1$ is to apply the *withdraw* operation on the object c_1 (the symbol '$\widehat{=}$' indicates that what appears on the right defines the operation denoted by the identifier on the left). Operation *withdraw*$_1$ is said to *promote* the *withdraw* operation of c_1 to be an operation of *TwoCards*. The operation *withdraw*$_1$ receives from the environment an input *amount?* of type $\mathbb{N}$ and transforms the internal state of the object c_1 subject to the conditions imposed by the *withdraw* operation of the *CreditCard* class, i.e.

$$amount? \leqslant c_1.balance + c_1.limit$$
$$c_1.balance' = c_1.balance - amount?,$$

adopting here the convention that expressions *ob.att* and *ob.att'* denote the value of the attribute *att* of object *ob* before and after the operation, respectively.

Because the object c_2 is not referenced by the operation *withdraw*$_1$, its internal state will not be changed by the application of *withdraw*$_1$ to an object of the *TwoCards* class. Similarly, as there is no Δ-list involving variables declared in *TwoCards* associated with *withdraw*$_1$, the values of the primary variables (i.e. c_1 and c_2) are also unchanged whenever the operation is applied to a *TwoCards* object. This implies that c_1 and c_2 identify the same objects after *withdraw*$_1$ as they did before.

The secondary variable *totalbal*, however, will be changed by *withdraw*$_1$ if the operation changes c_1's *balance* (which will be the case if *amount?* > 0). In general, all that can be asserted about a secondary variable is that it may assume any value consistent with the constraints imposed upon it. This is in contrast to a primary variable — its value can only change via an operation which contains the variable in its Δ-list.

In general, an expression of the form *ob.op*, where *op* is a visible operation in the class of the object *ob*, denotes *operation application*. In operation application the communication variables of *op* become the communication variables of *ob.op*. The effect is to transform the internal state of *ob* according to the specification of *op*.

The conjunction operator

The operation expression

$$transfer \mathrel{\widehat{=}} c_1.withdraw \wedge c_2.deposit$$

defines the operation *transfer* in terms of the Object-Z conjunction operator '$\wedge$'. The understanding is that the individual *withdraw* and *deposit* operations for objects c_1 and c_2, respectively, proceed independently except that the same input value *amount?* is passed to both, i.e. the single natural number *amount?* is the input to both operations. The conjunction operator is commutative and associative; it conjoins the constraints on the component operations, equating variables (including communication variables) with the same name. In this case, after the *transfer* operation, $c_1.balance$ is reduced by, and $c_2.balance$ increased by, the value *amount?*, i.e. the quantity *amount?* is effectively transferred from account c_1 to account c_2. The operation is only applicable if the operation *withdraw* is applicable for object c_1, i.e.

$$amount? \leqslant c_1.balance + c_1.limit.$$

Compare this operation with a hypothetical *withdrawAvailBoth* defined by

$$withdrawAvailBoth \mathrel{\widehat{=}} c_1.withdrawAvail \wedge c_2.withdrawAvail.$$

This operation is only applicable if

$$c_1.balance + c_1.limit = c_2.balance + c_2.limit,$$

because the outputs *amount!* from both components would be equated under conjunction. To construct an operation *withdrawAvailBoth* that outputs the available funds of the credit-card accounts c_1 and c_2 as two individual values, renaming of a communication variable is required, e.g.

$$withdrawAvailBoth \mathrel{\widehat{=}} c_1.withdrawAvail$$
$$\wedge$$
$$c_2.withdrawAvail[other!/amount!].$$

In this case the output from the *withdrawAvail* operation applied to c_2 is renamed from *amount!* to *other!*, and hence it is distinguished from the output *amount!* from the *withdrawAvail* operation applied to c_1. The overall effect of this operation is that two output values, *amount!* and *other!*, are passed to the environment, where

$$amount! = c_1.balance + c_1.limit$$
$$other! = c_2.balance + c_2.limit.$$

The choice operator

The operation expression

$$withdrawEither \mathrel{\widehat{=}} c_1.withdraw \;[\!]\; c_2.withdraw$$

defines the operation *withdrawEither* in terms of the Object-Z choice operator ' $[\!]$ '. The understanding is that a choice is made between the component operations.

The choice operator is subject to the following conditions:

- The communication variables of both components must be the same, and these become the communication variables of the composite operation. In the case of *withdrawEither*, there is only one such variable, the input *amount?* of type $\mathbb{N}$.

- If neither component operation is applicable, the composite operation is not applicable. For example, this would be the case with *withdrawEither* if

$$amount? > c_1.balance + c_1.limit \;\wedge$$
$$amount? > c_2.balance + c_2.limit.$$

- If only one component operation is applicable, the choice operator selects and applies that operation. For example, in the case of *withdrawEither*, suppose that

$$amount? \leqslant c_1.balance + c_1.limit \;\wedge$$
$$amount? > c_2.balance + c_2.limit;$$

then $c_1.withdraw$ is selected.

- If both component operations are applicable (i.e. their preconditions are satisfied), one of the component operations is selected. For example, in the case of *withdrawEither* suppose that

$$amount? \leqslant c_1.balance + c_1.limit \;\wedge$$
$$amount? \leqslant c_2.balance + c_2.limit;$$

then either $c_1.withdraw$ is selected or $c_2.withdraw$ is selected.

When a choice construct is a sub-expression and both components are applicable, the choice is angelic in the sense that it is not locally preselected but delayed to facilitate the applicability of the overall operation expression. The semantics of choice is based on disjunction as discussed in Chapter 13.

There is no communication between the component operands of a choice construct.

Replacing objects

The operation *replaceCard*$_1$ models the replacement of the credit-card account c_1 by a new credit-card account, but with the same limit and balance as the original account. A credit-card account object *card?*, distinct from c_1 or c_2, is input from the environment and replaces the object c_1. Unlike the other operations in this class discussed so far, as c_1 appears in the Δ-list, the value of this attribute (i.e. an object identity) is subject to change. Also, the secondary variable *totalbal* is subject to change, as it appears implicitly in every Δ-list, including that of *replaceCard*$_1$. (In fact, as *card?.balance* = c_1.*balance*, the value of *totalbal* will not change.)

1.7   Inter-object communication

The conjunction and choice operators, as illustrated by the operations *transfer* and *withdrawEither*, respectively, in the previous section, do not involve the communication of information between objects. In this section, an operator for modelling inter-object communication, namely parallel '||' is introduced.

The parallel operator

To illustrate this operator, consider the class *TwoCardsExtended* which is like *TwoCards* specified in Figure 1.2 but defines an extra operation *transferAvail*. This operation models the transfer of all the available funds of account c_1 into account c_2.

$$\begin{array}{l} \underline{\textit{TwoCardsExtended}} \\ \quad \upharpoonright(\ldots, \textit{transferAvail}, \ldots) \\[4pt] \quad \text{[features as before]} \\[4pt] \quad \textit{transferAvail} \mathrel{\hat{=}} c_1.\textit{withdrawAvail} \parallel c_2.\textit{deposit} \\ \end{array}$$

The operation definition

$$\textit{transferAvail} \mathrel{\hat{=}} c_1.\textit{withdrawAvail} \parallel c_2.\textit{deposit}$$

defines the operation *transferAvail* as a composition using the Object-Z parallel operator '||'. This operator behaves like the Object-Z conjunction operator, but also enables inter-object communication between the components by equating any input to one of the components of || with any output from the other component that has the same base name (i.e. the inputs and outputs are denoted by the same identifier apart from the ? and ! endings). The equated inputs and outputs are hidden, i.e. the communication is internalised between the components and does not involve external communication with the environment. Inter-object communication via the parallel operator can be in either direction, so that it is even possible for communication in both directions in the one operation. Communication variables that are not hidden as a result of internal communication are treated as in operation conjunction and represent external communication with the environment.

In the case of the operation *transferAvail*, the operation *withdrawAvail* of the class *CreditCard* is applied to the object c_1, resulting, as we have seen, in an output *amount*! of type $\mathbb{N}$, with the balance of c_1 reduced to the overdraft limit. In parallel, the *CreditCard* operation *deposit* is applied to the object c_2. This operation requires an input *amount*? of type $\mathbb{N}$ and has the effect that the balance of c_2 is increased by *amount*?.

Because the input — *amount*? — for the $c_2.deposit$ component is denoted by an identifier with the same base name as the output — *amount*! — from the $c_1.withdrawAvail$ component, the values of these communication variables are equated and hidden. The overall effect, therefore, of the *transferAvail* operation is that the funds available in credit-card account object c_1 are transferred into the credit-card account object c_2.

The parallel operator, like conjunction, is commutative, but it is not associative because of the hiding mechanism. When there is no inter-object communication, $\|$ is identical to $\wedge$. There is a second version of $\|$ (namely $\|_!$) which hides only the input of each communicating input-output pair. It is described in Chapter 12.

1.8   Object aggregation

The *TwoCards* class specified in Section 1.6 involved the instantiation of just two credit-card account objects. In this section we consider the more general case of systems consisting of an indeterminate and variable number of objects of a given class.

As an illustration we shall specify a banking system consisting of an aggregate of credit-card account objects, each with the same limit on the magnitude of the overdraft permitted. This somewhat unrealistic constraint is included for illustrative purposes. (The term 'aggregate' is used consistently throughout the book to refer to a set of objects; this is in contrast to the more general usage of an aggregate as an arbitrary grouping.)

The number of credit-card account objects in the aggregate is not fixed: a new initialised account object can be added to the aggregate and any account object in the aggregate can be removed. Each account object in the aggregate can independently perform its *withdraw*, *deposit* or *withdrawAvail* operation. Furthermore, suppose there is an operation in the system so that given any two account objects in the aggregate, the available funds of the first can be transferred to the second.

An Object-Z specification of this system is given by the class *CreditCards* in Figure 1.3. (In this class the *add* and *delete* operations are placed side by side to save space. In Object-Z specifications, schemas in classes are often placed side by side for this reason; no other significance is implied by this layout.)

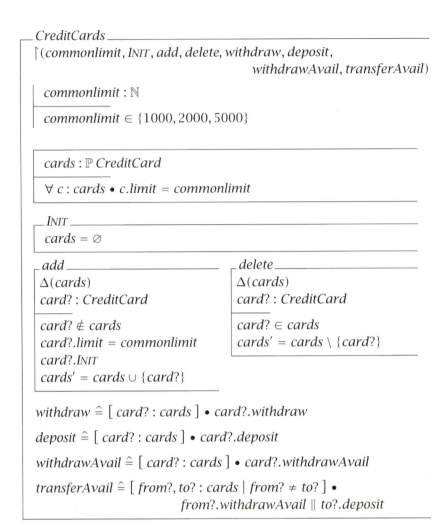

Figure 1.3: the class *CreditCards*

Aggregates as attributes

The declaration

$$cards : \mathbb{P}\,CreditCard$$

in the state schema of the class *CreditCards* introduces the attribute *cards* whose value is a set of identities of objects of the class *CreditCard*. The set *cards* varies in size; initially it is empty (*cards* = ∅ is the predicate of the initial schema) and identities of credit-card account objects can be added to, or removed from, the set (see below).

A set such as *cards* will be informally referred to as a set of objects, although technically it is a set of object identities.

The predicate

$$\forall\, c : cards \bullet c.limit = commonlimit$$

requires that the value of *limit* for each object in the set *cards* be the same and equal to the value of the constant *commonlimit*.

Adding and deleting objects

The schema *add* specifies the addition of a new credit-card account object to the set *cards*. The new object is declared as an input (*card?*) of class *CreditCard* (to be precise, the input *card?* identifies the object to be added). The predicate for this operation requires that the input object

- is not already in the aggregate (*card?* $\notin$ *cards*);

- has the common limit on the magnitude of the overdraft permitted (*card?.limit = commonlimit*);

- is in its initial configuration (*card?.INIT*), i.e. the balance of the credit-card account is 0;

- is added to the aggregate (*cards'* = *cards* $\cup$ {*card?*}).

The application of *add* to an object of the *CreditCards* class provides for change to *cards* only; i.e. *add* will change the set *cards* by adding the object identity *card?*, but the internal state of existing elements of *cards* will remain unchanged. Because *cards* is initially empty and the predicate

$$card?.limit = commonlimit$$

is satisfied by each object added to the set *cards*, and because the value of *limit* is constant for each credit-card account object, the predicate

$$\forall\, c : cards \bullet c.limit = commonlimit$$

can be omitted from the state schema without affecting the definition of the class. This is another example of a redundant predicate included to improve readability. Alternatively, given the class invariant, the predicate *card?.limit = commonlimit* could be omitted from the operation. However, care is required in removing class invariants because the subsequent addition of an operation may invalidate the reasoning which established that the class invariant was redundant.

The schema *delete* specifies the deletion of an object from the set *cards*. The object to be deleted is identified by the input *card?*, where this object is in the aggregate (*card?* $\in$ *cards*), and is removed (*cards'* = *cards* \ {*card?*}).

It is important to emphasise that Object-Z does not address the creation or destruction of objects per se: it is asserted that objects always exist. This

profusion is not reflected in an object-oriented programming language implementation where objects are created as required and usually destroyed when
no longer accessible.

To illustrate this point, suppose the *add* operation is applied to an object,
say *ccs*, of class *CreditCards*: the identity of the object added is passed to *ccs*
via *add* as an input — as all objects are assumed to pre-exist, the operation does
not create the object so identified. A credit-card account object deleted from
ccs.cards by *delete* may remain accessible via other objects in the system —
even if there is no such reference, the object is assumed to remain in existence:
it is not destroyed.

Selecting objects

To withdraw or deposit funds using the *CreditCards* system, the particular
credit-card account object is selected and the appropriate operation is applied
to it. This is specified by the definitions

$$withdraw \mathrel{\widehat{=}} [\, card? : cards \,] \bullet card?.withdraw$$
$$deposit \mathrel{\widehat{=}} [\, card? : cards \,] \bullet card?.deposit$$

where the schema $[\, card? : cards \,]$ simply specifies the selection by the environment of the particular credit-card account object from the set *cards*. Compare this, for example, with the promotion

$$withdraw_1 \mathrel{\widehat{=}} c_1.withdraw$$

defined in the class *TwoCards* in Section 1.6; there the relevant object (i.e. c_1) is
named directly. For aggregates of objects, such as the set *cards*, a set member
is selected not by its name but by its object identifier.

The semantics of the *withdraw* operation in the class *CreditCards* is that
card? and *amount?* are input from the environment. The object *card?*, which
is required to be in the aggregate *cards*, undergoes its *withdraw* operation, i.e.

$$amount? \leqslant card?.balance + card?.limit$$
$$card?.balance' = card?.balance - amount?$$

The application of *withdraw* to an object of the class *CreditCards* changes
the state of no object in *cards* other than the identified *card?*. Furthermore,
as *cards* does not appear in a Δ-list it is unchanged, i.e. after the operation the
set *cards* identifies the same credit-card account objects, even although one of
them (i.e. *card?*) has had its state updated.

Similarly, *deposit* involves the inputs *card?* and *amount?*, and the object
card? in the aggregate *cards* undergoes its *deposit* operation.

The final operation definition of the *CreditCards* class,

$$transferAvail \mathrel{\widehat{=}} [\, from?, to? : cards \mid from? \neq to? \,] \bullet$$
$$from?.withdrawAvail \parallel to?.deposit$$

involves the schema

$$[\ from?, to? : cards \mid from? \neq to?\ ]$$

whose role is simply to specify the selection from the set *cards* of two distinct credit-card account objects between which funds transfer is to occur. The semantics in this case is the same as the *transferAvail* operation of the *TwoCards* class in Section 1.6, the only distinction being that now the objects are not selected by name but by input from the environment. The application of *transferAvail* to an object of the class *CreditCards* changes no object in *cards* other than those identified by *from?* and *to?*, nor does it change attribute *cards*.

The general syntactic structure for promoting operations when there are aggregates of objects is of the form

$$SelectObjects \bullet OperationExpression$$

where *SelectObjects* is a schema for specifying one or more objects of the aggregate to be selected, and *OperationExpression* is an operation expression involving the application of appropriate operations to the selected objects. Semantically, the schema to the left of the dot '•' enriches the environment in which the expression to the right of the dot is interpreted.

1.9 Inheritance

Within object-oriented programming languages, inheritance allows the code of existing classes to be reused in the coding of a new class. When constructing a formal specification using the Object-Z notation, inheritance can play a similar role: it enables the specification of features of existing Object-Z classes to be reused when creating a new Object-Z class. In this section we explore the inheritance mechanism in Object-Z whereby the features of an inherited class (the *superclass*) are merged with the features of the new inheriting class (the *subclass*).

As in programming languages, inheritance in formal specification is more than just feature reuse. It enables class inheritance hierarchies to be constructed that capture key structural and architectural design aspects of the system being modelled. Indeed, it has been argued that inheritance should only be used when the behaviour of objects of a subclass is formally related to the behaviour of objects of the superclass, i.e. that inheritance should conform to some notion of subtyping.

In Object-Z no such subtype restrictions are imposed on inheritance, although good specification style may suggest that preservation of behavioural properties be a factor when designing inheritance hierarchies. This aspect of inheritance will be emphasised in later chapters.

In this section we consider two examples of single inheritance, i.e. where the subclass inherits just one other class. The more complex multiple inheritance, i.e. where the subclass inherits more than one other class, is discussed in Chapter 8.

Class extension

The first example uses inheritance to extend an existing Object-Z class with additional features. This example also introduces the sequential composition operator.

Consider an object that has the same operations as a credit-card account, but in addition has an operation where a withdraw can be confirmed by producing as an output the value of the remaining funds available. Such an object could be used like any credit-card account object, but with this enhanced functionality to confirm withdrawals.

When specifying the enhanced credit-card account object, use can be made of the class *CreditCard*, as that class already specifies much of the enhanced object. This reuse is achieved through the mechanism of inheritance: the new class *CreditCardConfirm* inherits the class *CreditCard*.

  ┌─ *CreditCardConfirm* ──────────────────────────

  │ $\upharpoonright$ (*limit, balance*, INIT, *withdraw, deposit, withdrawAvail,*

  │   *withdrawConfirm*)

  │ *CreditCard*

  │   ┌─ *fundsAvail* ──────────────────────────

  │   │ *funds*! : $\mathbb{N}$

  │   ├────────────────────────────

  │   │ *funds*! = *balance* + *limit*

  │ *withdrawConfirm* $\hat{=}$ *withdraw* $\mathbin{\substack{\circ \\ 9}}$ *fundsAvail*

The class *CreditCardConfirm* is a subclass of *CreditCard* or, alternatively, *CreditCard* is a superclass of *CreditCardConfirm*. Inheriting *CreditCard* implies that the features of *CreditCard* become features of *CreditCardConfirm*. However, the visibility list is not inherited — this enables a new interface to be defined.

A semantically equivalent specification of the class *CreditCardConfirm* is given by the flat version (i.e. with all the features expressed explicitly rather than implicitly through inheritance) in Figure 1.4.

The class *CreditCardConfirm* defines explicitly two operations, *fundsAvail* and *withdrawConfirm*, that are not inherited from *CreditCard*. The *fundsAvail* operation is not in the visibility list of the *CreditCardConfirm* class, indicating that it is not directly available to the environment of any object of this class. It is defined only so that it can be applied within *CreditClassConfirm* in the definition of the visible operation *withdrawConfirm*, i.e. *fundsAvail* is an *auxiliary* operation.

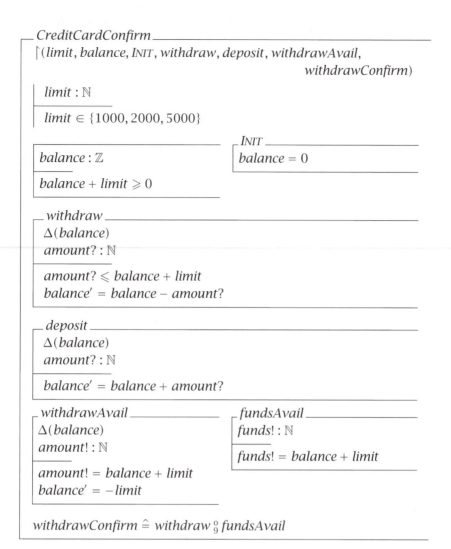

Figure 1.4: flat version of the class *CreditCardConfirm*

The sequential composition operator

The *withdrawConfirm* operation, defined by

$$withdrawConfirm \mathrel{\widehat{=}} withdraw \mathbin{\overset{\circ}{,}} fundsAvail,$$

uses the Object-Z sequential composition operator '$\overset{\circ}{,}$'. The effect of this operation is to apply the operation *withdraw* (i.e. withdraw some *amount?*) and then apply on the resulting state the *fundsAvail* operation (i.e. output *funds!* whose value gives the funds now available). The overall consequence, therefore, of applying *withdrawConfirm* is to withdraw some amount from the account and output the value of the available funds that remain in the account.

It is important to appreciate that the *withdrawConfirm* operation, like all operations in Object-Z, is atomic. The informal description may be temporal (i.e. this happens, then that, etc.), but an operation always defines a relationship between the values of the state variables after the operation with the values beforehand. Formally, there is no notion of the time taken to effect the change in values, nor any notion of some changes happening before others. The formal requirement is that an intermediate state exist for each sequential composition. The semantics of sequential composition is based on relational composition as discussed in Chapter 13.

More on sequential composition

Although not required in this example, the sequential composition operator also facilitates inter-object communication. Given the operation expression $op_1 \, \mathring{,} \, op_2$, outputs from op_1 and inputs to op_2 with the same base name are equated and hidden from the environment, i.e. the inter-object communication supported by the sequential composition operator is like that for the parallel operator except that the communication is in one direction only (left-to-right). Because communication is unidirectional, $\mathring{,}$ is non-commutative, and because the communication is hidden, like $\|$, it is non-associative. Sequential chains are interpreted left-associatively.

Sequential composition behaves like forward relational composition compounding constituent relationships via the existence of an intermediate state. In contrast, parallel composition is based on conjunction which does not involve an intermediate state.

Conjoining features

As a second example of inheritance, consider a credit-card account where a count is kept of the number of withdrawals made. (This tally may be needed for setting charges or taxes for the account; these considerations will not be of concern here.) Such an object can be specified by the class *CreditCardCount*:

$$
\begin{array}{l}
\underline{\text{\textit{CreditCardCount}}} \\
\upharpoonright (\textit{limit}, \textit{balance}, \textsc{init}, \textit{withdraw}, \textit{deposit}, \textit{withdrawAvail}) \\[4pt]
\textit{CreditCard} \\[4pt]
\begin{array}{ll}
\underline{} & \underline{\textsc{init}} \\
\textit{withdrawals} : \mathbb{N} & \textit{withdrawals} = 0 \\
\end{array} \\[8pt]
\underline{\textit{withdraw}} \\
\Delta(\textit{withdrawals}) \\
\underline{} \\
\textit{withdrawals}' = \textit{withdrawals} + 1 \\
\end{array}
$$

The semantics of this class is determined by conjoining the features defined explicitly with those inherited from *CreditCard*.

- The state schema is determined by conjoining the explicit state schema

$$\begin{array}{|l}\hline withdrawals : \mathbb{N} \\\hline\end{array}$$

with the state schema of *CreditCard* to give

$$\begin{array}{|l}\hline balance : \mathbb{Z} \\ withdrawals : \mathbb{N} \\\hline balance + limit \geqslant 0 \\\hline\end{array}$$

i.e. the declarations are merged and the predicates are conjoined. This is only defined (as in Z) if there are no type clashes: if a variable is declared in both schemas its type must be the same. The role of the attribute *withdrawals* is to keep count of the number of times the *withdraw* operation has been applied.

- The initial schema is determined by conjoining the explicit initial schema

$$\begin{array}{|l}\hline \text{INIT} \\\hline withdrawals = 0 \\\hline\end{array}$$

with the initial schema of *CreditCard* to give

$$\begin{array}{|l}\hline \text{INIT} \\\hline balance = 0 \\ withdrawals = 0 \\\hline\end{array}$$

- The operation *withdraw* is determined by conjoining the explicit operation schema

$$\begin{array}{|l}\hline \text{withdraw} \\\hline \Delta(withdrawals) \\\hline withdrawals' = withdrawals + 1 \\\hline\end{array}$$

with the inherited operation schema *withdraw* of *CreditCard*. The conjunction of two operation schemas is similar to schema conjunction, but with the additional property that the Δ-list of the resulting schema is the union of the Δ-lists of the component schemas. In this case the operation *withdraw* of *CreditCardCount* is semantically equivalent to the operation:

```
┌─ withdraw ─────────────────────────────────────────────
│ Δ(balance, withdrawals)
│ amount? : ℕ
├────────────────────────────────────────────────────────
│ amount? ⩽ balance + limit
│ balance' = balance − amount?
│ withdrawals' = withdrawals + 1
└────────────────────────────────────────────────────────
```

Operation renaming and redefinition

The implicit merging of operation schemas illustrated in the *CreditCardCount*
class could have been made explicit by using renaming as follows:

```
┌─ CreditCardCount ──────────────────────────────────────
│ ⎾(limit, balance, INIT, withdraw, deposit, withdrawAvail)
│
│ CreditCard[oldWithdraw/withdraw]
│ ┌────────────────────────┐   ┌─ INIT ─────────────────
│ │ withdrawals : ℕ        │   │ withdrawals = 0
│ └────────────────────────┘   └────────────────────────
│
│ ┌─ incrementCount ───────────────────────────────────
│ │ Δ(withdrawals)
│ ├────────────────────────────────────────────────────
│ │ withdrawals' = withdrawals + 1
│ └────────────────────────────────────────────────────
│
│ withdraw ≙ oldWithdraw ∧ incrementCount
└────────────────────────────────────────────────────────
```

Appending [*oldWithdraw*/*withdraw*] to the name *CreditCard* indicates that
the *withdraw* operation of *CreditCard* is renamed *oldWithdraw* when it is inherited, i.e. the operation *oldWithdraw* in *CreditCardCount* is:

```
┌─ oldWithdraw ──────────────────────────────────────────
│ Δ(balance)
│ amount? : ℕ
├────────────────────────────────────────────────────────
│ amount? ⩽ balance + limit
│ balance' = balance − amount?
└────────────────────────────────────────────────────────
```

The name *withdraw* is now available for a new operation in *CreditCardCount*.
(Any feature can be renamed when a class is inherited.) In effect,

$$withdraw \mathbin{\widehat{=}} oldWithdraw \wedge incrementCount$$

redefines *withdraw*.

This *withdraw* is semantically identical to the *withdraw* operation defined
by implicit conjunction in the previous version of *CreditCardCount*. Notice
that the operations *incrementCount* and *oldWithdraw* are not placed in the

visibility list of *CreditCardCount*: they are used only in the redefinition of *withdraw*.

Figure 1.5 illustrates the inheritance hierarchy constructed in this section, where the arrow denotes *inherits*, i.e. both of the classes *CreditCardConfirm* and *CreditCardCount* inherit the class *CreditCard*.

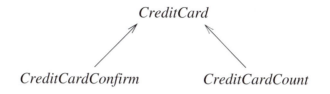

Figure 1.5: credit-card account inheritance hierarchy

1.10 Polymorphism

Object-oriented polymorphism allows the strict typing of objects to be relaxed. Within an object-oriented programming language for example, polymorphism allows an object to be in any one of a given collection of classes. The effect upon such an object of receiving a message will generally depend upon the actual class to which the object belongs, and this is determined only at run-time.

In an Object-Z formal specification, polymorphism is similar in so far as it also allows the type of an object to be relaxed. All the object declarations encountered so far in this chapter (e.g. the declaration of the objects c_1, c_2 and *card?* in the class *TwoCards* in Figure 1.2, or the set *cards* in the class *CreditCards* in Figure 1.3) are such that the class of each object is uniquely determined. In this section we shall see how to declare in Object-Z an object whose class may be any one of the classes in a specified inheritance hierarchy.

The consequences of such a polymorphic declaration differ from those for an object-oriented programming language as there is no notion of run-time associated with an Object-Z specification. If *ob* is an object declared polymorphically, the semantics of an expression such as *ob.feature* will depend upon the actual class of *ob*.

As an illustration, consider a new system of credit-card accounts similar to that specified by the class *CreditCards* in Figure 1.3 but this time consisting of an aggregate of objects from any of the classes *CreditCard*, *CreditCardConfirm* or *CreditCardCount*. Such a general system can be specified by the Object-Z class *GenCreditCards* in Figure 1.6.

The declaration *cards* : $\mathbb{P}\downarrow CreditCard$ indicates that the value of the attribute *cards* is a set of identities of objects of the class *CreditCard* or of any subclass of *CreditCard*, i.e. the class of an object in the set *cards* is not specified uniquely but may be any class which inherits (directly or indirectly) *CreditCard* (see Figure 1.5). Similarly, the input communication variables *card?*, *from?* and

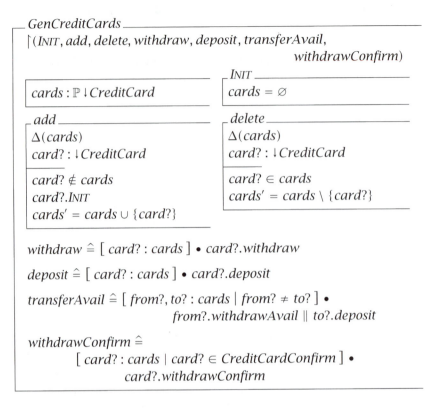

Figure 1.6: the class *GenCreditCards*

to? can each take a value that identifies an object of the class *CreditCard* or of any of its subclasses.

Operations *withdraw*, *deposit* and *transferAvail* can be applied to the object *card?* regardless of the class of the object identified by *card?*, although the actual effect of the operation on the object will in general depend upon its class (e.g. only if the class of *card?* is *CreditCardCount* will there be a variable *card?.withdrawals* to be incremented).

Operation *withdrawConfirm*, however, is only applicable if *card?* identifies an object of class *CreditCardConfirm*.

Signature compatibility

A declaration such as $a : \downarrow A$ is polymorphic in that a may refer to an object of class A or any of its subclasses, i.e. of any class in the inheritance hierarchy rooted at A. However, in order for an expression *a.feature*, where *feature* is a feature in A, to be statically well-formed regardless of the class of a within the hierarchy, the following signature compatibility conditions must apply:

- each attribute in the visibility list of A must be an attribute in the visibility list of each subclass of A;

- if *INIT* is in the visibility list of A it must also be in the visibility list of each subclass of A; and

- each operation name in the visibility list of A must be an operation name in the visibility list of each subclass of A, and this operation in the subclass must have the same communication interface as in A, i.e. the input and output variables must be identically named and typed.

These conditions hold for the inheritance hierarchy in Figure 1.5.

A class inheritance hierarchy that is suitable for polymorphic declarations in that it satisfies the above rules for signature compatibility is said to be a *polymorphic hierarchy*. Notice that even if an inheritance hierarchy is polymorphic, there is no guarantee that an object of a subclass will behave like an object of a superclass. For example, the *withdraw* operation for an object of the class *CreditCardCount* involves an action (i.e. incrementing *withdrawals*) not specified for an object of the class *CreditCard*.

In this section, polymorphism has been restricted to polymorphic inheritance hierarchies: such hierarchies are discussed further in Chapter 8. In Chapter 9 polymorphism is generalised to apply to arbitrary collections of classes.

1.11   Overview

In this chapter we have explored some of the key concepts associated with the construction of object-oriented, state-based formal specifications. The broad architectural approach is to first partition the system into component objects, specify them in isolation, and then specify how they interact to create a system with the desired properties. Using the Object-Z notation, classes are created to specify objects, with the system itself being envisaged as an object which encapsulates attributes identifying other objects together with operations that specify the way these objects behave and communicate. Objects which are directly referenced from the system object may, in turn, reference further objects.

Typically, a specification is developed iteratively through a series of approximations. Classes are conjectured conceptually from requirements (a top-down procedure) and the classes are then specified in sufficient detail to synthesise an approximation to the system (a bottom-up procedure). Comparison of the approximation with the requirements then provides insight for modification and further development of the class specifications, the way the system is partitioned into objects, and the means of inter-object communication.

Issues guiding the specification process include clarity of functionality, directness of relationships between reality and the abstraction (the specification), and ease of refinement towards a given implementation language. Furthermore, in the case of safety-critical systems, the ability to identify and isolate safety-critical components is an important consideration. In formally-verified systems, the chosen specification must provide a suitable basis for reasoning within the given environment. Each of these issues will be discussed in subsequent chapters.

Object-oriented concepts such as instantiation, aggregation, object identity, inheritance and polymorphism were introduced in this chapter within the context of Object-Z specifications. In the chapters that follow, these and related object-oriented specification issues are explored further.

Graphical presentation of specifications 2

2.1 Introduction

Mathematical expression dominates formal specification. However, some parties associated with a development project may prefer to see various aspects projected graphically rather than mathematically. Graphical diagrams can be useful complementary aids to communication between those involved in the development.

This chapter presents graphical diagrams which relate to selected aspects of formal specification introduced in Chapter 1 as a complementary aid to the presentation of formal specifications. Later chapters include further examples of graphical illustrations complementing formal text.

The graphical notation used in the book is based on the Unified Modeling Language (UML), a comprehensive graphical notation for describing object-oriented systems. The UML notation is the property of Rational Software Corporation — http://www.rational.com. We have drawn on only a portion of UML, namely Class Diagrams, Object Diagrams, State Diagrams and the 'swimlanes' version of Activity Diagrams, and we have introduced an additional graphical element primarily to facilitate the illustration of Object-Z operational composition.

The diagrams are graphs in that they comprise nodes and arcs which conform to prescribed graphical shapes and line forms. In most diagrams, the actual size and position of graphical elements is unimportant as the topology carries the essential associations. Swimlane diagrams are an exception, however, in that the alignment of nodes in rows and columns is important. Like UML, we use varying degrees of detail so that only the information pertinent to a particular projection is shown.

2.2 Class diagrams

Figure 2.1 shows a UML-like class diagram which projects the attribute declarations and operation headings of the class *CreditCard* specified in Section 1.5.

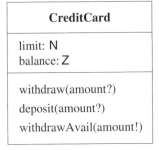

Figure 2.1: features of class *CreditCard*

This diagram is a graph comprising just one node, the class *CreditCard*. A class is represented as a solid outline rectangle partitioned into three compartments: the top compartment holds the class name, the central compartment holds the attribute declarations and the bottom compartment holds the operation headings with the names of the communication variables included as a parameter list.

As a presentational device, Figure 2.1 is a useful summary of the features of the class *CreditCard*. In order to focus on the essential, the attribute or operation compartments, or both, of a class node may be omitted. Some later diagrams use this abridgment. Also, omission of the types of attributes or the parameter list of operations is justified in some projections.

Figure 2.2 illustrates an abridged class diagram for the class *TwoCards* specified in Section 1.6.

2.3 Illustrating Object-Z composition

Diagrams are particularly helpful in illustrating operational composition. Figure 2.3 relates to class *TwoCardsExtended* in Section 1.7. The figure omits the card replacement operation to enhance the focus on composed operations.

Operation *transferAvail* is the parallel composition of card c_1's operation *withdrawAvail* and card c_2's operation *deposit*. The shield-like symbol is not within UML: it is introduced primarily to accommodate operational composition in Object-Z. The operations to be composed (the operands) are attached to the straight edge of the shield, the result of the composition is attached to the rounded edge, and the kind of composition is indicated on the shield. Compositional direction is implicit in the shape of the shield symbol.

Showing parameter lists in the illustration of composed operations is important as it provides a useful visual check on conformity with respect to the kind of composition. Thus for *transferAvail*, as the output *amount!* of c_1's *withdrawAvail* matches the input *amount?* of c_2's *deposit*, these quantities are equated and hidden resulting in no parameter for *transferAvail* as shown by its empty list.

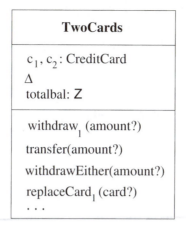

Figure 2.2: features of class *TwoCards*

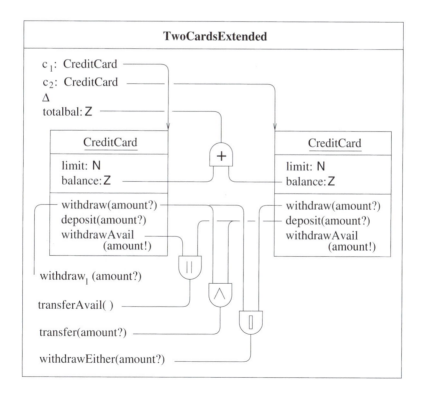

Figure 2.3: objects and composed operations in *TwoCardsExtended*

For the conjunction *transfer*, the parameter *amount?* is common to the constituent *withdraw* and *deposit* operations and the resultant *transfer* operation. For the choice *withdrawEither*, the parameters of each constituent component and of the result are identical as required. Figure 2.3 also shows that the operation $withdraw_1$ is simply the promotion of c_1's *withdraw* operation.

The shield symbol indicating summation and its associated lines illustrate the dependence of the secondary variable *totalbal* on the sum of the balances of the individual cards.

To distinguish between the representations of classes and objects, UML recommends bold font for class names and plain font underscored for object headings: we follow that convention.

Figure 2.3 is a graph within a node (the node *TwoCardsExtended*). The arcs represent references to the nested cards, the data flow constituting the secondary variable *totalbal*, and the linkages forming the composed operations. To avoid line confusion, no horizontal line is drawn to separate the attributes of *TwoCardsExtended* from its operations.

2.4 Illustrating inheritance

Inheritance hierarchies are illustrated by linking the derived class nodes to the parent class node by lines directed to the parent with an open triangular arrow as shown in Figure 2.4. The figure shows the derivation of *CreditCardConfirm* and *CreditCardCount* as specified in Section 1.9.

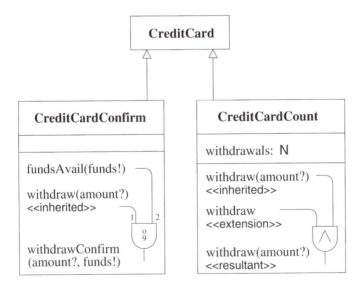

Figure 2.4: derivation by inheritance

Figure 2.4 illustrates within class *CreditCardConfirm* the sequential composition of the inherited operation *withdraw* (with input *amount?*) and the local operation *fundsAvail* (with output *funds!*) resulting in *withdrawConfirm* with input *amount?* and output *funds!*. As no parameters match, there is no hiding and therefore the resultant parameter list comprises all the parameters of the constituent operations. The numbers '1' and '2' on the shield indicate the order of sequential composition.

Figure 2.4 abridges the node for *CreditCard* to just its name compartment as the purpose of the figure is to show the inheritance hierarchy and the extensions effected by the two derivations.

The 'stereotype' «inherited» indicates inheritance without modification. The stereotype is a UML feature which provides for the introduction of user-defined keywords: they are distinguished textually by enclosure in matching double angle brackets.

Stereotype «extension» indicates modification of an inherited operation by the local extension of the same name to produce a resultant operation also of the same name, distinguished by the stereotype «resultant» . Operation *withdraw* of *CreditCardCount* provides an example.

2.5   Selection from sets

Figure 2.5 projects the description of the operation *transferAvail* of the class *GenCreditCards* defined in Section 1.10.

The attribute *cards* is a set of references to objects of class *CreditCard* or any descendant, namely the classes *CreditCardConfirm* and *CreditCardCount*, as indicated by the declaration *cards* : $\mathbb{P} \downarrow CreditCard$.

The source and destination cards for the transfer are selected by the input parameters *from?* and *to?* respectively. The selection role in UML is termed 'qualification' as it qualifies the association between a collection and a selection from it. We enclose constraints, such as *from?* ≠ *to?*, in brackets rather than in braces (UML notation) to avoid confusion with braces in Object-Z notation which enclose set denotations. Similarly, we avoid other UML syntax which would clash with Object-Z text.

It is noted that *from?* and *to?* are parameters of the *transferAvail* operation as the parallel composition of *from?*'s *withdrawAvail* with *to?*'s *deposit* has the environment enriched by

$$[\, from?, to? : cards \mid from? \neq to? \,].$$

Figure 2.6 illustrates the promotion to *GenCreditCards* level of the operations *withdraw*, *deposit* and *withdrawConfirm* of the card selected by *card?*. Selection *card?* joins the parameter list of the promoted operations.

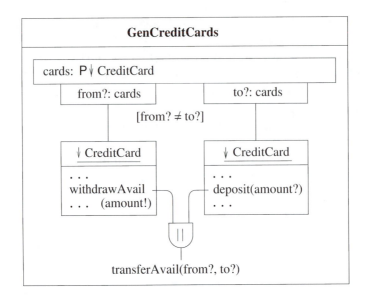

Figure 2.5: the *transferAvail* operation of *GenCreditCards*

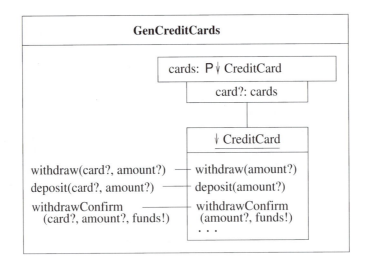

Figure 2.6: promotion of the selected card's operations

2.6   Discussion

The UML-like graphical diagrams in this and later chapters provide a useful complementary aid for presenting Object-Z specifications. These diagrams can aid communication between the diversity of interested parties involved in a development project. Diagrams are also useful in the presentation of user-educational material.

However, graphical notation is primarily descriptive: it is at most semi-formal and therefore cannot provide an adequate basis for formal procedures, such as proofs of correctness or refinement by mathematical transformation. Such procedures are conducted in mathematical notation.

Local vs central control 3

3.1 Introduction

In most object-oriented systems various associations exist between the underlying objects: a prime responsibility of the system is to record and maintain these associations. For example, in a library system each book is associated with the reader currently borrowing the book. As the library system evolves the association between books and readers is constantly updated.

An important architectural issue is where to record the object associations in the system, and which objects should control and maintain them. There are two broad approaches to this issue: information about an association can be distributed throughout the system and recorded and maintained locally, or information can be managed centrally in an appropriate database.

In the local approach to the software architecture for a library system, each (virtual) book object directly references the (virtual) reader object representing the current borrower of the book. A book object maintains this association in response to appropriate messages received from its environment (i.e. the book's class contains the necessary methods).

In contrast, in the central approach the system maintains a database object that captures the association between books and readers. Messages are sent to the database object when information about a book or reader is required, or an association needs updating.

Whether in practice to adopt a local or central architecture depends upon the nature of the software system being constructed. It can be argued in the case of the library system that the local approach is more 'object oriented' in some sense, but the issues are generally not clear-cut.

In this chapter we consider the architectural and functional implications of both approaches from the viewpoint of formal specification. Indeed, one of the advantages of constructing a formal specification is that it brings the architectural issues into focus and establishes a framework in which these issues can be discussed and resolved.

3.2   A magnetic key system: a case study

For reasons of security, an organisation has decided to implement a system whereby each employee is issued with a magnetic key to access (unlock) certain rooms. Access rights will in general depend upon an employee's status and responsibilities; thus, as an employee's role changes, operations are needed to modify the access rights associated with that employee's key.

Informal description

- There is a set of keys and a set of rooms. As a simplification, it will be assumed that the sets of keys and rooms are fixed, i.e. neither keys nor rooms are added to or removed from the system. Furthermore, although each key is issued to an employee, as the association between keys and rooms is at the heart of this system, employees need not be modelled.

- Each key has access rights to a subset of rooms. In general, a key will be able to unlock some rooms but not others. However, the model should allow for the possibility that some keys may be able to unlock all the rooms (master keys) while other keys can unlock no room.

- When a key is inserted into a room's lock, access is granted (i.e. the room unlocks) if and only if the key has access rights to that room.

- The access rights of a key may be changed, i.e. there are operations to add a room to or remove a room from the set of rooms a key can access.

In modelling this system, it must be decided whether information about the access association between keys and rooms is distributed locally among the key and room objects themselves, or stored in a central database. To distinguish between the local and central views, both are modelled below.

3.3   A local view

In this model the system consists of key and room objects, with each key containing information about which rooms it can access.

A key

A key object is specified by the class *Key* in Figure 3.1. (Classes in this and following case studies often have their visibility list omitted. In such circumstances all features will be assumed to be visible.)

The attribute *rooms* denotes the set of rooms which a key can access. The type *Room* is a class (defined below), so *rooms* is a set of references to room objects. When refined to an implementation, *rooms* would probably be concretely realised as a list of codes for distinguishing rooms, but at this level of abstraction such a distinction can be captured by using the identities of the

```
┌─ Key ──────────────────────────────────────────────────────────┐
│  ┌─────────────────────────────┐  ┌─ INIT ───────────────────┐  │
│  │ rooms : ℙ Room              │  │ rooms = ∅                │  │
│  └─────────────────────────────┘  └──────────────────────────┘  │
│  ┌─ extendAccess ──────────────┐  ┌─ rescindAccess ──────────┐  │
│  │ Δ(rooms)                    │  │ Δ(rooms)                 │  │
│  │ rm? : Room                  │  │ rm? : Room               │  │
│  ├─────────────────────────────┤  ├──────────────────────────┤  │
│  │ rm? ∉ rooms                 │  │ rm? ∈ rooms              │  │
│  │ rooms' = rooms ∪ {rm?}      │  │ rooms' = rooms \ {rm?}   │  │
│  └─────────────────────────────┘  └──────────────────────────┘  │
│  ┌─ accessGranted ─────────────┐  ┌─ accessDenied ───────────┐  │
│  │ rm? : Room                  │  │ rm? : Room               │  │
│  ├─────────────────────────────┤  ├──────────────────────────┤  │
│  │ rm? ∈ rooms                 │  │ rm? ∉ rooms              │  │
│  └─────────────────────────────┘  └──────────────────────────┘  │
└────────────────────────────────────────────────────────────────┘
```

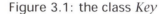

Figure 3.1: the class *Key*

room objects themselves, without the need to specify what such identities are, or how they would be represented in a real system. Initially, the set *rooms* is empty, i.e. a key can access no room.

The operations *extendAccess* and *rescindAccess* model, respectively, the addition of a room to, and the removal of a room from, those accessible by the key. Information as to which room is to be added or removed (*rm?*) is supplied by the environment. By placing these operations in the *Key* class, a key object takes responsibility for maintaining its association with the rooms it can access.

The operations *accessGranted* and *accessDenied* model the situation where a given room (*rm?*) is checked to see whether or not the key has access rights to that room. In this model these operations need to be placed in the *Key* class as only a key object knows which rooms it can access. Consequently, a key object assumes control over granting or denying permission when it attempts to access a room.

A room

A room object is specified by the class *Room* in Figure 3.2. The attribute *locked* of type boolean denotes whether or not a room is locked. Initially, a room is locked.

The operation *supplyId* results in a room sending its identity as output to the environment. This operation uses the reserved word *self* to denote the identity of an actual room object. To be specific, if *r* : *Room* is declared, then in any application *r.op* all occurrences of *self* in the operation *op* are replaced by the identity of the object *r*. For example, the application *r.supplyId*

```
┌─ Room ─────────────────────────────────────────────────────────────┐
│ ┌──────────────────────────┐  ┌─ INIT ──────────────────────────┐   │
│ │ locked : 𝔹               │  │ locked                          │   │
│ └──────────────────────────┘  └─────────────────────────────────┘   │
│ ┌─ supplyId ───────────────┐                                        │
│ │ rm! : Room               │                                        │
│ ├──────────────────────────┤                                        │
│ │ rm! = self               │                                        │
│ └──────────────────────────┘                                        │
│ ┌─ unlock ─────────────────┐  ┌─ lock ──────────────────────────┐   │
│ │ Δ(locked)                │  │ Δ(locked)                       │   │
│ ├──────────────────────────┤  ├─────────────────────────────────┤   │
│ │ locked                   │  │ ¬ locked                        │   │
│ │ ¬ locked'                │  │ locked'                         │   │
│ └──────────────────────────┘  └─────────────────────────────────┘   │
└─────────────────────────────────────────────────────────────────────┘
```

Figure 3.2: the class *Room*

is equivalent to the following schema:

```
┌──────────────────────────────┐
│ rm! : Room                   │
├──────────────────────────────┤
│ rm! = r                      │
└──────────────────────────────┘
```

The identifier *Room* is used in two distinct contexts in this class, i.e. it is overloaded. It not only denotes the name of a class, but also denotes a type in the declaration *rm!* : *Room* within operation *supplyId*. As a type, it denotes the entire set of identities of objects of the class *Room*.

The operations *unlock* and *lock* model the unlocking and locking of a room, respectively.

The magnetic key system

The magnetic key system consists of a set of keys and a set of rooms, together with the operations that can be performed on and between these objects. This system is specified by the class *KeySystem* in Figure 3.3.

The attributes *keys* and *rooms* denote the sets of key and room objects in the system. The class invariant captures the restriction that a key can only access the rooms of the system. Initially, all keys and rooms are in their initial state, i.e. each key can access no room and each room is locked.

The operations *extendAccess* and *rescindAccess* denote the selection by the environment of a key ($k?$) and the performance of the same-named operation by that key.

The operation *lock* is specified in terms of the distributed choice operator and can only occur if some room is unlocked. It denotes the selection of a

```
__KeySystem_____

  _____   __INIT_____
   keys : ℙ Key                          ∀ k : keys • k.INIT
   rooms : ℙ Room                         ∀ r : rooms • r.INIT
  _____  _____
   ∀ k : keys • k.rooms ⊆ rooms
  _____


   extendAccess ≙ [ k? : keys ] • k?.extendAccess

   rescindAccess ≙ [ k? : keys ] • k?.rescindAccess

   lock ≙ ⫿ r : rooms • r.lock

   insertKey ≙ [ r? : rooms; k? : keys ] •
                     r?.supplyId
                     ‖
                     (k?.accessGranted ∧ r?.unlock
                     ▯
                     k?.accessDenied)
_____
```

Figure 3.3: the class *KeySystem*

room from among those rooms that are unlocked, and the performance of *lock* by that room. The selection is internal, capturing the idea that the selection of which unlocked room to lock is made at the discretion of the system. In practice, *lock* would be implemented to occur at some specified time (e.g. 10 seconds) after a room is unlocked, but this level of detail is not modelled here.

Distributed operators are particularly useful when specifying operations that involve an arbitrary number of objects. In this case, distributed choice is used so that an internal selection can be made between all unlocked rooms. The conjunction and sequential composition operators can also be distributed. Examples are given in Sections 4.2 and 5.5, respectively.

The final operation, *insertKey*, captures what happens when the environment nominates that key *k*? is inserted into the lock of room *r*?.

Consider the case when the room is initially locked. The room supplies its identity (*rm*!) and either access is granted (*rm*? ∈ *k*?.*rooms*) and the room unlocks or access is denied (*rm*? ∉ *k*?.*rooms*). Because the output *rm*! of *r*?.*supplyId* has the same base name as the input *rm*? of the choice operation, their values are equated and hidden. By the semantics of *self*, the output *rm*! from *r*?.*supplyId* identifies the room object *r*?. Notice that precisely one of the component operations of the choice operator is applicable.

In the case when the room is initially unlocked, the operation is applicable only if access is denied.

Discussion

The model specified here lacks symmetry between the keys and rooms: a key object knows about the rooms it can access, but a room object has no information about the keys that can access it. The system could equally as well have been modelled by specifying rooms that know which keys can access them, while specifying keys with no room information. Indeed, a symmetric model could have been constructed so that keys know about the rooms they can access, and at the same time rooms know about the keys that can access them. Although such a model may well have the aesthetic satisfaction of symmetry, it can be criticised in that information is unnecessarily duplicated. Furthermore, there would be an overhead in maintaining the consistency of information as the system evolves.

The suitability of a local model in practice would be influenced by how the model is actually implemented. If the magnetic keys were 'smart' then the functionality as specified in the class *Key* could become part of the physical key itself. If this design was implemented it would have the advantage that whenever a key is inserted into a room's lock, access rights could be checked on the spot without the need to refer to any other object in the system. A disadvantage, however, would be that such smart keys would need to have read-write memory and would be relatively expensive to produce. Furthermore, the updating of access rights would be difficult as it would require the keys to be recalled and modified.

3.4   A central view

In this section the key system is modelled by specifying a central database object containing all access information.

Keys and rooms

A key object now has no attributes and only one operation, *supplyId*, whereby a key can send its identity as output to the environment.

$$
\begin{array}{|l}
\hline
\_Key \rule[-0.2ex]{0pt}{2ex}_____ \\
\quad \begin{array}{|l}
\hline
\_supplyId_____ \\
\;\; key! : Key \\
\hline
\;\; key! = self \\
\hline
\end{array} \\
\hline
\end{array}
$$

The *Room* class is identical to that specified in Section 3.3 in the previous model.

The database

A database object (of class *DataBase*) takes responsibility for recording and maintaining the access association between keys and rooms. It also takes control for granting or denying permission when a key attempts to access a room.

DataBase

access : Key ↔ Room	**INIT** access = ∅

extendAccess
Δ(access)
key? : Key
rm? : Room

¬ (key? <u>access</u> rm?)
access' =
    access ∪ {key? ↦ rm?}

rescindAccess
Δ(access)
key? : Key
rm? : Room

key? <u>access</u> rm?
access' =
    access \ {key? ↦ rm?}

accessGranted
key? : Key
rm? : Room

key? <u>access</u> rm?

accessDenied
key? : Key
rm? : Room

¬ (key? <u>access</u> rm?)

The attribute *access* is a relation between keys and rooms, i.e. for any key *k* and room *r* the predicate *k* <u>access</u> *r* is true if and only if *k* has access rights to *r*. Initially *access* is the empty relation, i.e. no key has any access rights. (Relational notation is defined in Appendix A.)

Each of the four operations *extendAccess*, *rescindAccess*, *accessGranted* and *accessDenied* play a role similar to that played by the operations of the same name in the *Key* class defined in Section 3.3 in the previous model, only now both the key (*key?*) and room (*rm?*) in question must be supplied to the database by its environment. Responsibility for updating access rights (operations *extendAccess* and *rescindAccess*) and for checking these rights (operations *accessGranted* and *accessDenied*) is now vested in the database object.

The magnetic key system

In this model the key system consists of a set of keys, a set of rooms and a database (see Figure 3.4).

As before, the attributes *keys* and *rooms* denote the sets of key and room objects. The attribute *db* denotes the (central) database. The class invariant ensures that only information about the keys and rooms of the system is contained in the database. Initially the rooms and the database are in their initial state (a key has no attributes and hence no initial state).

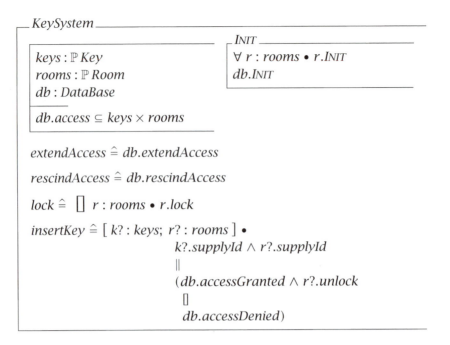

Figure 3.4: the class *KeySystem* (centralised version)

Operations *extendAccess* and *rescindAccess* are now just the promotions to the system of the database operations of the same name. The operation *lock* is unchanged from the previous model.

The operation *insertKey* involves the key and room in question supplying their identities (*key*! and *rm*!) to the database which checks for access rights. Assuming a locked room, either the key has access rights (*db.accessGranted*) and the room is unlocked or access is denied (*db.accessDenied*). The input required by the database (*key*? and *rm*?) is identified with the previous outputs and hidden. Again, assuming an initially locked room, precisely one of the component operations of the choice operator will be applicable. A graphical representation of this operation in the style of Chapter 2 is given in Figure 3.5.

Discussion

In this model there is no need for either the keys or rooms to be 'smart'. As all information about access rights is stored in the central database, in any implementation updating would be straightforward. Furthermore, it would be relatively easy to add extra functionality, e.g. to keep track of the rooms accessed by a particular key. However, as all the checking of access rights is done centrally, the rooms would need to be in physical communication with the database so as to pass key and room identities. This model has the aesthetic satisfaction of symmetry with respect to keys and rooms without the need to

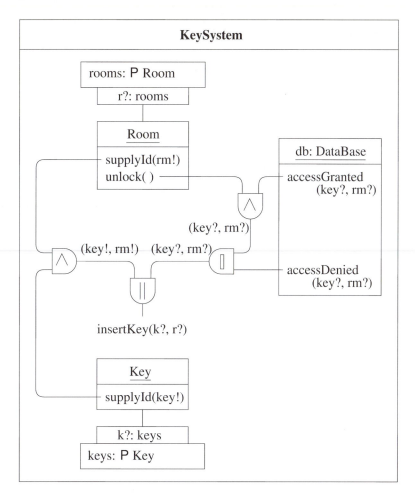

Figure 3.5: the operation *insertKey*

duplicate information.

Our comparison between the local and central models has so far been based on the view that the classes *Key* and *Room* model the actual physical objects. In fact, a local model could be implemented by interpreting these classes as specifying virtual software objects. In this case objects of these classes could be easily created and maintained: the actual physical keys and rooms would not need to be smart but could simply pass as required relevant information to their virtual counterparts. Even adopting the symmetric local model, i.e. where the virtual keys know about the virtual rooms they can access and the virtual rooms know about the virtual keys that can access them, does not impose a serious overhead despite the duplication of information, as consistency of information is now a software problem. In this case the virtual local view has a nice object-oriented property: it associates functionality and control with the objects directly involved.

Distributed and mediated message passing 4

4.1 Introduction

In object-oriented systems it often happens that some object sends a common message to a number of other objects. For example, a bank may send the message 'calculate charges' to each of its accounts, or a student may send a common email to each of the other students in their class. In both of these examples, a message is distributed to each object in some given collection. In this chapter we look at how distributed message passing can be captured within an Object-Z specification.

A common pattern associated with distributed message passing involves the introduction of a *mediator* object. A message for distribution is first passed to the mediator object. This object has links to all relevant objects in the system and hence is able to distribute the message to the appropriate receiver objects, i.e. the mediator object acts like a message-clearing house. The existence of a mediator considerably reduces the inter-object links required in the system, as other objects need only communicate with the mediator. Furthermore, the mediator is able to maintain the inter-object links efficiently as the system evolves. This chapter discusses the formal specification of the architecture and functionality of a system with a mediator object, and demonstrates the informal refinement of this architecture to Java code.

4.2 Bingo: a case study

The game of bingo involves a collection of players each allocated a set of numbers. An announcer calls out numbers in some arbitrary order and the first player to have all their numbers called is the winner.

The main issue of interest in this case study is how to specify formally the distributed message passing that occurs when the announcer calls a number. From an object-oriented point of view, the number-call message from the announcer object is distributed to all the player objects.

Informal description

- There is a set of players each of whom is initially allocated a set of 16 numbers in the range $1..99$. The sets allocated to any two players may have numbers in common, but must not be identical.

- There is an announcer who from time to time calls individual numbers in the range $1..99$ in arbitrary order, with no number being called more than once.

- When all of the numbers allocated to a player have been called, that player can shout 'bingo'. The first player to do so is the winner.

A player

A player object is specified by the class *Player*:

```
┌─ Player ─────────────────────────────────────────────────
│  ┌──────────────────────────┐   ┌─ INIT ─────────────────
│  │ remain : ℙ(1..99)        │   │ #remain = 16
│  └──────────────────────────┘   └────────────────────────
│  ┌─ hearCall ───────────────┐   ┌─ shoutBingo ───────────
│  │ Δ(remain)                │   │ shout! : Player
│  │ n? : 1..99               │   ├────────────────────────
│  ├──────────────────────────┤   │ remain = ∅
│  │ remain' = remain \ {n?}  │   │ shout! = self
│  └──────────────────────────┘   └────────────────────────
└──────────────────────────────────────────────────────────
```

The attribute *remain* denotes the set of numbers that remain to be called, i.e. those numbers that were allocated to the player but have yet to be called by the announcer. Initially, *remain* contains 16 numbers.

The operation *hearCall* corresponds to the player hearing the latest number called ($n?$) and removing it from *remain* if it had been allocated to the player. Notice that if the number called is not in *remain*, this set is unaltered.

The operation *shoutBingo* can only occur when all the numbers allocated to the player have been called. In an actual game, the player shouts 'bingo', but as this is done only so that the winning player can be identified, in the model here the player is identified directly by having the output (*shout!*) take the value *self*.

The announcer

The announcer is modelled by the class *Announcer* in Figure 4.1. The boolean attribute *active* denotes whether or not the game is in progress. Initially *active* is *true*, and only becomes *false* when one of the players completes the game. This attribute is associated with the announcer to model the fact that this person takes responsibility for controlling the game, albeit with the cooperation of the players.

Announcer

active : $\mathbb{B}$	INIT
remain : $\mathbb{P}(1 \mathinner{.\,.} 99)$	active
	remain $= 1 \mathinner{.\,.} 99$

callOut
$\Delta(remain)$
$n! : 1 \mathinner{.\,.} 99$

active
$n! \in remain$
$remain' = remain \setminus \{n!\}$

stopCalling
$\Delta(active)$
$shout? : Player$

active
$\neg\ active'$

Figure 4.1: the class *Announcer*

The attribute *remain* in this class denotes those numbers in the set $1 \mathinner{.\,.} 99$ that have not yet been called. Initially *remain* is the entire set $1 \mathinner{.\,.} 99$.

The operation *callOut* corresponds to the announcer calling any remaining number. This can occur only if the game is active and not all numbers have been called. Notice that the order in which the numbers are called is not specified.

The operation *stopCalling* corresponds to the announcer receiving as input the identity of a player (*shout?*) who has completed the game. The game is active before the operation, but becomes inactive afterwards.

The bingo system

The game of bingo involves a set of player objects and an announcer object, denoted by the attributes *players* and *announcer* respectively. It is specified by the class *Bingo* in Figure 4.2.

Initially, each player and the announcer are in their initial states, i.e. each player has 16 numbers and the announcer is active but has not yet called any numbers. Furthermore, distinct players initially have distinct sets of numbers.

The operation *numberCalled* models distributed message passing and is illustrated in Figure 4.3: the number called by the announcer is passed to all of the players. It involves the operation *announcer.callOut*, whereby the announcer calls out a number, in parallel with the distributed conjunction operation

$$\bigwedge p : players \bullet p.hearCall,$$

whereby each player hears the number called. This distributed conjunction is equivalent to

$$p_1.hearCall \wedge p_2.hearCall \wedge \cdots \wedge p_k.hearCall$$

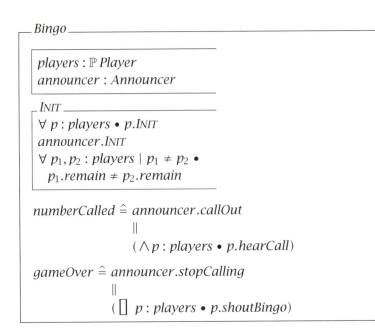

$$
\begin{array}{|l}
\hline
\textit{Bingo} \underline{\hspace{7cm}} \\
\hline
\begin{array}{|l}
\hline
\textit{players} : \mathbb{P}\;\textit{Player} \\
\textit{announcer} : \textit{Announcer} \\
\hline
\end{array} \\
\begin{array}{|l}
\hline
\textit{INIT} \underline{\hspace{3cm}} \\
\forall\, p : \textit{players} \bullet p.\textit{INIT} \\
\textit{announcer.INIT} \\
\forall\, p_1, p_2 : \textit{players} \mid p_1 \neq p_2 \bullet \\
\quad p_1.\textit{remain} \neq p_2.\textit{remain} \\
\hline
\end{array} \\
\\
\textit{numberCalled} \;\hat{=}\; \textit{announcer.callOut} \\
\qquad\qquad \| \\
\qquad\qquad (\textstyle\bigwedge p : \textit{players} \bullet p.\textit{hearCall}) \\
\\
\textit{gameOver} \;\hat{=}\; \textit{announcer.stopCalling} \\
\qquad\qquad \| \\
\qquad\qquad (\textstyle\Box\; p : \textit{players} \bullet p.\textit{shoutBingo}) \\
\hline
\end{array}
$$

Figure 4.2: the class *Bingo*

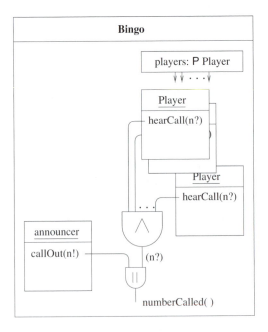

Figure 4.3: the *numberCalled* operation of *Bingo*

where $p_1, p_2, \ldots, p_k$ are the players. As the input $n?$ to each *hearCall* operation in this conjunction is denoted by the same identifier, these inputs are all equated; hence the result of the distributed conjunction is that each player hears the same number. Furthermore, because the output $n!$ from *announcer.callOut* has the same base name (n) as the common input to the players, $n?$ is equated to $n!$ and both are hidden, with the overall result that the number called by the announcer is distributed to and heard by each player.

The operation *gameOver* is specified using the parallel and distributed choice operators and can only occur if some player has completed the game. If the operation does occur, the player to shout is selected non-deterministically from among those who have completed the game. This models the situation where several players may have completed the game but it is the first one to shout 'bingo' who is the winner. The output *shout!* of *p.shoutBingo* is equated to the input *shout?* of *announcer.stopCalling* and both are hidden, i.e. the announcer identifies the player concerned and stops the game.

4.3   A buttons-toggling puzzle: a case study

A simple puzzle that can be played on a computer consists of 16 square toggle buttons arranged on a board in a 4 by 4 array. A toggle button may be in one of two states: *hollow* or *solid*. Clicking (with the mouse) on any button toggles it and each of its horizontal and vertical neighbours between hollow and solid. (Buttons in the centre of the board have 4 neighbours; those at an edge have 3; those at a corner have just 2.) Initially all the buttons are hollow and the aim of the puzzle is to reach a state where all the buttons are solid. Figure 4.4 illustrates a typical intermediate state that could be reached while attempting to solve the puzzle. Hollow toggle buttons are shown in white, solid toggle buttons in black.

Figure 4.4: the buttons-toggling puzzle

The issue of distributed message passing arises in this case study when the mouse is clicked on a button: the message 'toggle' is sent not just to the button directly identified by the mouse, but also to each neighbouring button.

The specification presented here uses a mediator to facilitate this message passing. Section 4.4 presents a refinement of the specification to Java code.

Initial abstractions

Before modelling the board of toggle buttons and the way they interact, it is useful to establish a data structure of board positions so that the buttons can be easily referenced. As the board consists of 16 positions, one possible labelling of these positions is to use natural numbers as in Figure 4.5.

0	1	2	3
4	5	6	7
8	9	10	11
12	13	14	15

Figure 4.5: the board positions

Hence define $Posn == 0..15$.

The 'neighbour' relationship between grid positions can now be expressed in terms of the corresponding coordinates.

$$
\begin{array}{|l}
neigh : Posn \leftrightarrow Posn \\
\hline
\forall\, i,j : Posn \bullet \\
\quad i \; neigh \; j \; \Leftrightarrow \\
\quad\quad i - j \in \{-4, 4\} \\
\quad\quad \vee \\
\quad\quad (i - j \in \{-1, 1\} \wedge i \; div \; 4 = j \; div \; 4)
\end{array}
$$

(Here $div : \mathbb{N} \times \mathbb{N}_1 \to \mathbb{N}$ denotes integer division.) The relation $neigh$ captures the idea that two board positions are neighbours when they are adjacent either horizontally or vertically, i.e. the corresponding squares have an edge in common.

Define the global type $Style$ to model the two possible states of a toggle button.

$$Style ::= hollow \mid solid$$

A global type is available to each class in a specification (in fact, it is only used in the class $ToggleButton$ in this simple specification).

A toggle button

A toggle button is modelled by the class:

$$
\begin{array}{l}
\underline{\text{ToggleButton}} \\[4pt]
\begin{array}{|l}
\hline
\begin{array}{|l}
\hline
\textit{style} : \textit{Style} \\
\hline
\end{array}
\qquad
\begin{array}{|l}
\hline
\text{I\scriptsize{NIT}} \\
\hline
\textit{style} = \textit{hollow} \\
\hline
\end{array}
\\[10pt]
\begin{array}{|l}
\hline
\textit{toggle} \\
\Delta(\textit{style}) \\
\hline
\textit{style}' \neq \textit{style} \\
\hline
\end{array}
\qquad
\begin{array}{|l}
\hline
\textit{isSolid} \\
\hline
\textit{style} = \textit{solid} \\
\hline
\end{array}
\\
\hline
\end{array}
\end{array}
$$

A toggle-button object has an attribute *style* of type *Style*: this will be used to indicate whether it is hollow or solid. Initially the button is hollow. If the operation *toggle* is performed the style of the button alternates between hollow and solid.

Notice that there is no attribute to record the position of a toggle button: it is not the concern of the button to know where on the board it may be placed, or which buttons are its neighbours. Also, at this level of abstraction the shape of a toggle button is immaterial: the fact that in an implementation a button is actually square is not relevant to the functionality and architecture being specified.

The buttons puzzle

The buttons puzzle is specified by the class *ButtonsPuzzle* in Figure 4.6. The attribute *board* is a function that associates a toggle button with each position in the set *Posn*. The arrow '$\rightarrowtail$' indicates that *board* is a one-one total function, i.e. a unique toggle button is associated with each of the 16 positions. The secondary variable *buttons* is this set of 16 toggle buttons. The secondary variable *posn* is the inverse of the function *board* (the symbol '~' denotes relational inverse). That is, *posn* is a one-one partial function that associates with each toggle button its position on the board.

The operation *toggleButtonAndNeighbours* takes as its input one of the board's buttons (*b*?) and toggles both this button (*b?.toggle*) and, using the distributed conjunction operator, each neighbouring button:

$$\wedge\, b : \textit{buttons} \mid \textit{posn}(b) \; \underline{\textit{neigh}} \; \textit{posn}(b?) \bullet b.\textit{toggle}$$

Notice how the function *posn* and the relation *neigh* are used to select the neighbours of *b*?.

The operation *puzzleSolved* is applicable if all the buttons on the board are solid (i.e. if the puzzle is solved). However, even it does occur, the state is unchanged and afterwards the operation *toggleButtonAndNeighbours* is still applicable and button toggling can continue. This is consistent with a physical array of buttons with no 'lock-on-all-solid' mechanism. Compare this with the

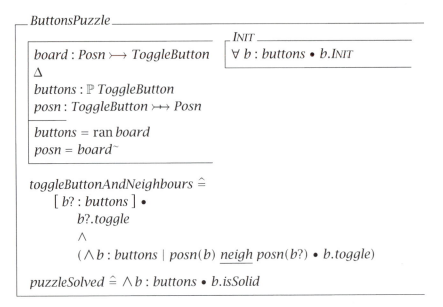

Figure 4.6: the class *ButtonsPuzzle*

gameOver operation for the bingo game in Section 4.2: once this operation is performed the game stops.

Discussion

In this specification, a buttons-puzzle object acts both as a system object whose attribute *board* identifies the toggle-button objects in the system, and as a mediator for passing messages between the buttons. When a button is selected for toggling, the buttons-puzzle object ensures that the neighbours of the selected button are also sent the message *toggle*. In this model a button has no direct reference to any of the other buttons.

It would have been possible to have specified a *ToggleButton* class having attributes to record an associated grid position and to reference buttons in neighbouring positions. However, not only would this architecture result in a multitude of inter-object references, the button would have become highly specialised to this particular application making it less reusable in other contexts.

Notice that it is possible to solve this puzzle: starting from the initial state, click on the buttons in positions 1, 7, 8 and 14.

4.4   Refinement to code

This section illustrates informally the refinement of the Object-Z specification of the buttons-toggling puzzle to code implemented in the Java object-oriented programming language. In particular, we shall see how the pattern of mediated message passing underlying the specification is mirrored in code.

Java is used as the implementation language as its established library of classes means that the translation of predicates into code can be done without recourse to low-level detail. The refinement closely follows the functionality, architecture and class structure of the specification. However, a knowledge both of the basic syntax of Java and its AWT library of graphical classes is needed to fully appreciate the details of the code. (See for example, the book by Horstmann and Cornell listed in Appendix D.) The processes of the refinement to Java given below could be emulated in other object-oriented programming languages.

Code for the toggle-button class

The *ToggleButton* class specified in Section 4.3 can be refined to the Java class ToggleButton whose code is given in Figure 4.7. This class inherits the library class Canvas.

Each aspect of the specification of the Object-Z class *ToggleButton* has a direct counterpart in the Java class ToggleButton.

For example, the boolean instance variable hollow mirrors the attribute *style* in the specification and plays the same role: its value, *true* or *false*, determines respectively whether the button is hollow or solid. The method toggle implements the operation *toggle* in the specification: its effect is to toggle the button's style. The method isSolid implements the operation *isSolid*: it returns *true* if and only if the button is solid.

However, there are aspects of the code not derived directly from the specification. For example, unlike the specification, the implementation needs to be explicit about the shape of a button, and this is captured by the method paint which sets a button to be a 48 pixels by 48 pixels rectangle (i.e. a square).

Also, the instance variable mediator was not required in the specification. Its role in the code is to reference the mediator object that has responsibility for distributing messages to other buttons (see below for further discussion on this issue). This reference is needed by the method mousePressed which, when the mouse is pressed on the button, sends to the mediator object the message toggleButtonAndNeighbours with the button itself as argument. As we shall see in the code for the class ButtonsPuzzle, when the mediator object receives this messages it sends the message toggle to the button that sent the message (i.e. the button self) and to each of the button's neighbours. That is, the button and all of its neighbours are toggled.

The constructor method sets the value of the variable mediator to be the object passed as argument when the button is first created.

```java
import java.awt.*;
import java.awt.event.*;

public class ToggleButton extends Canvas {

 // instance variable
 private boolean hollow = true;
 private ButtonsPuzzle mediator;

 // constructor
 public ToggleButton (ButtonsPuzzle med) {
    mediator = med;
    addMouseListener(new MouseAdapter() {
        public void mousePressed(MouseEvent evt) {
            mediator.toggleButtonAndNeighbours(ToggleButton.this);
        }
    });
 }

 public void paint (Graphics g) {
    // draw button
    if (hollow) g.drawRect(1, 1, 48, 48);
    else g.fillRect(1, 1, 48, 48);
 }

 public void toggle ( ) {
    // toggle the button
    hollow = !hollow;
    repaint();
 }

 public boolean isSolid ( ) {
    return !hollow;
 }}
```

Figure 4.7: code for the ToggleButton class

Code for the buttons-puzzle class

The *ButtonsPuzzle* class specified in Section 4.3 can be refined to the Java class
ButtonsPuzzle whose code is given in Figure 4.8. This class inherits the library class Applet.

In this code the instance variable board mirrors the attribute of the same
name in the specification. It is set to be an array of integers of length 16, which
is a way of implementing a function such as *board* in Java. In the method init
a unique toggle button is created for each of the 16 possible positions. That
is, the code creates the functional relationship between positions and buttons

```java
import java.applet.*;
import java.awt.*;

public class ButtonsPuzzle extends Applet {

  // instance variables
  private ToggleButton [] board = new ToggleButton[16];

  public void init ( ) {
     for (int i=0; i<16; i++) {
      board[i] = new ToggleButton(this);
      add(board[i]);
     }
  }

  public void paint (Graphics g) {
     for (int i=0; i<16; i++)
      board[i].setBounds(50*(i%4), 50*(i/4), 50, 50);
  }

  public void toggleButtonAndNeighbours (ToggleButton but) {
     but.toggle();
     int butPosn = posn(but);
     for (int i=0; i<16; i++)
      if (neigh(butPosn, i)) board[i].toggle();
     if (puzzleSolved())
      showStatus("Puzzle solved. Congratulations!");
     else showStatus("Puzzle not solved. Keep trying!");
  }

  public int posn (ToggleButton but) {
     int index = 0;
     while (!(board[index] == but)) index++;
     return index;
  }

  public boolean neigh (int i, int j) {
     return
      i-j == 4
      || j-i == 4
      || ((i-j == 1 || j-i == 1) && i/4 == j/4);
  }

  public boolean puzzleSolved ( ) {
     boolean result = true;
     for (int i=0; i<16; i++)
      result = result && board[i].isSolid();
     return result;
}}
```

Figure 4.8: code for the ButtonsPuzzle class

to mirror its declaration in the specification.

Also, as each button is created, its mediator variable is set to be this, i.e. the object of the class ButtonsPuzzle itself. Hence, just as in the specification the mediator was the object referencing all the toggle-button objects in the system, the mediator in the implementation is the object responsible for creating all the toggle-button objects of the system.

The secondary variables *buttons* and *posn* used in the specification to select the neighbours of a given button are not declared as variables in the implementation as the selection is performed by direct computation. For example, the relation *neigh* defined in the specification is implemented by the method neigh, but whereas the specification of *neigh* simply states a condition that must be true if two coordinate positions are neighbours, the implementation directly computes the boolean equivalent, i.e. it returns *true* if and only if the two given positions are neighbours.

Similarly, the inverse function *posn* defined in the specification is implemented by the method posn. This method returns the position of the given toggle button.

The method toggleButtonAndNeighbours: aButton is an implementation of the operation of the same name defined in the specification. First the identified button is sent the message toggle, and then this message is sent to each of the neighbouring buttons. In the implementation, the puzzle is checked to see if it has been solved, and an appropriate message displayed, every time a toggle button is pressed by the mouse. The method puzzleSolved is used to do this checking; this method is a direct implementation of the operation of the same name in the specification.

Discussion

The implementation of the buttons-toggling puzzle closely follows the specification. In particular, the implementation of a mediator object for distributed message passing is architecturally similar to the specification. Furthermore, the predicates in the specification are translated more or less directly into code. The implementation, however, requires that functions and relations be directly calculated, whereas the specification can be declarative.

In the implementation, each button object has a variable mediator. This was not needed in the specification because the button identified for toggling (*b*?) was simply input directly to the mediator by the environment. In the implementation, this button is identified by the mouse, and the information has to be passed to the mediator object: to do this each button needs to reference the mediator object.

The *INIT* schema in each Object-Z class is not an operation; it simply gives the condition (predicate) for an object of that class to be in its initial state. In the code, however, this is implemented by an appropriate constructor method that sets the instance variables to take the required initial values.

The implementation of the button-toggling puzzle presented here can be executed as a Java applet on any Java-enabled web browser.

Dependency and information sharing **5**

5.1 Introduction

A crucial aspect of any object-oriented system is the way components depend upon each other for the sharing of information. As we have seen frequently in earlier chapters, one way to model the flow of information is through inter-object message passing. In this chapter we consider another approach: the declaration of variables to enable information to be shared between objects without the need for direct message passing. Such variables effectively create information dependencies between objects: whenever one object changes, these changes are recorded by other objects.

This approach to inter-object communication is illustrated through the specification of the game of tic tac toe. Two contrasting views of this game are considered, each of which involves subdividing the system into spheres of influence with separate objects taking responsibility for managing information within each sphere. Global consistency of information is maintained both by dependencies between the objects and by modelling the synchronous evolution of objects through the use of the conjunction and parallel operators.

Finally, the chapter extends the tic tac toe game to consider the (somewhat fanciful) idea of a tic tac toe tournament involving a master playing several opponents. The tournament illustrates the inverse of distributed message passing discussed in Chapter 4.

5.2 Tic tac toe: a case study

The game of tic tac toe (or noughts and crosses as it is often called) involves two players and a 3-by-3 board. As a comparative study, the game is modelled from two distinct perspectives.

The first perspective looks at the game as played traditionally with pencil and paper: the board is drawn on the paper and the players record their moves by placing marks directly onto the paper. In the specification (Section 5.3) the players have responsibility for ensuring the rules of the game are followed.

Information about the current state of the game is shared by creating a dependency between each player and the board.

The second perspective corresponds to the situation where the game is played on a computer. The two players communicate their moves to the board via the keyboard or mouse. In this specification (Section 5.4) the machine displays the board and takes responsibility for ensuring the game is played within the rules. Indeed, the specification presented here could form the basis for such an implementation. As before, information about the current state of the game is shared by creating a dependency between each player and the board.

Informal description

- The game involves two players and a board. For convenience the players will be called *black* and *white*.

- The board consists of 9 positions in a 3-by-3 array.

- Initially the board is clear, i.e. all board positions are unoccupied.

- The players take turns to move, where a move consists of a player occupying an unoccupied board position, thereby adding to their collection of occupied positions.

- The first player whose occupied positions include three positions in a vertical, horizontal or diagonal line (i.e. three in a line) is the winner.

- The game is drawn if all positions are occupied and no player has three in a line.

Global abstractions

Before modelling the player and board objects and the way they interact, it is useful to establish a data structure so that the board positions can be easily referenced and the notion of 'three in a line' can be formally specified. As the board consists of 9 positions in a 3-by-3 array, one possible labelling of the positions is shown in Figure 5.1. Hence define $Posn == 0 .. 8$.

0	1	2
3	4	5
6	7	8

Figure 5.1: the board positions

The aim of the game is to occupy a set of board positions that include three in a line. As the board is small, it is easy to specify this precisely by simply listing all cases. Hence a boolean function *inLine* can be defined by:

$$inLine : \mathbb{P}\, Posn \rightarrow \mathbb{B}$$

$$\forall\, ps : \mathbb{P}\, Posn \,\bullet$$
$$\quad inLine(ps) \Leftrightarrow$$
$$\qquad \exists\, s : \{\{0,1,2\},\{3,4,5\},\{6,7,8\},\{0,3,6\},$$
$$\qquad\qquad \{1,4,7\},\{2,5,8\},\{0,4,8\},\{2,4,6\}\} \,\bullet\, s \subseteq ps$$

For any set *ps* of board positions, *inLine*(*ps*) is true if and only if *ps* contains 3 positions in at least one of the 3 horizontal, 3 vertical or 2 diagonal lines.

Also, the following global data type is needed to specify the outcome of a game:

$$Result ::= black\_wins \mid white\_wins \mid draw$$

5.3 Synchronising information

In this section the traditional game of tic tac toe as played with pencil and paper is specified. The board is drawn on the paper and has the passive role of simply recording the positions currently occupied by the players. Control of the game resides with the players themselves who agree upon whose turn it is, the validity of moves and the game's outcome.

Both players need to have information about the current positions occupied both by themselves and the other player, and this is obtained from the board. As the board is passive, it cannot send messages to the players; rather, each player accesses the board through an attribute that identifies the board.

The model presented here captures not just perceptions about the flow of information but also perceptions about the control of the game.

The passive board

The board, specified by the class *PassiveBoard* in Figure 5.2, is passive in that it does no more than record and update the positions occupied by the players.

The attributes *bposn* and *wposn* denote the set of board positions occupied by the players black and white, respectively, and initially neither player occupies any position.

The operations *addToBlack* and *addToWhite* specify what happens when a new position is occupied, respectively, by black or white. A position *p*? is input and added to the respective set of positions already occupied by the player. Notice that no checking is done by the board to ensure that the position *p*? is unoccupied, or that the players move in turn, or that the game is not over. Ensuring these things will be the responsibility of the players and we want the

$\underline{\quad PassiveBoard}$

| $bposn, wposn : \mathbb{P}\ Posn$ | $\underline{INIT}$ $bposn = \varnothing$ $wposn = \varnothing$ |

$\underline{\quad addToBlack}$
$\Delta(bposn)$
$p? : Posn$

$bposn' = bposn \cup \{p?\}$

$\underline{\quad addToWhite}$
$\Delta(wposn)$
$p? : Posn$

$wposn' = wposn \cup \{p?\}$

Figure 5.2: the class *PassiveBoard*

specification to capture this. For example, the condition

$$bposn \cap wposn = \varnothing$$

could have been added as a class invariant, but this would make it less clear that
the players, not the board, have responsibility for maintaining this condition.

The active players

In specifying the player classes, a general class *ActivePlayer* containing the
features common to both players is first defined (in Figure 5.3). Then specific
subclasses *PlayerBlack* and *PlayerWhite* are defined.

The attribute *board* of the class *ActivePlayer* identifies the board in order
to ascertain its current state and to make a move (i.e. update its state). In
order to refer to the board's state, expressions *board.bposn* and *board.wposn*
are available to a player as all features of the *PassiveBoard* class are visible.
To facilitate this, secondary variables *bposn*, *wposn* and *free* are defined in
the class *ActivePlayer*. These secondary variables add nothing to the state of
ActivePlayer, but simply record available information in a more convenient
form, enabling the other secondary variable *over* to be easily defined. Notice
that, unlike the primary attributes *board* and *turn*, these secondary variables
are not encapsulated by a player object: their values will change whenever the
state of the identified board changes. Hence information about the current
state of the board is always available to a player. Both *bposn* and *wposn* will
initially be empty as the board is then in its initial state.

Attribute *turn* indicates whether or not it is the player's turn to move next.
Its initial value is not specified. The secondary variable *free* denotes the set of
board positions that have not yet been occupied by either player, i.e. are free
to be occupied; initially all positions are free. The boolean secondary variable
over is true if and only if the game is over, i.e. either player has occupied three
board positions in a line, or no free positions remain; initially *over* is *false*.

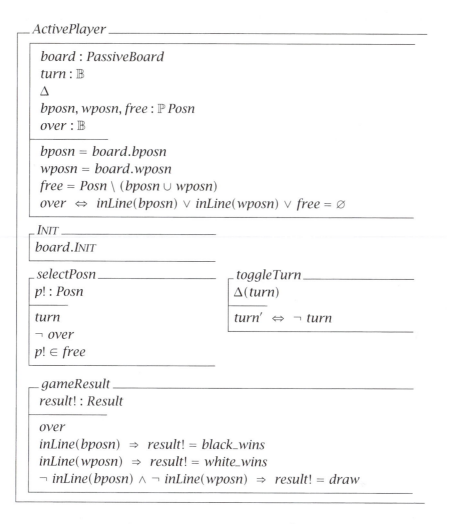

Figure 5.3: the class *ActivePlayer*

The operation *selectPosn* is an example of a partial operation; it models the conditions that must apply for the player to select the next position to occupy, i.e. it is a player's turn, the game must not be over, and there must be an unoccupied (free) position to select. The position selected, *p!*, is designated as an output as it is information that needs to be passed to the board when this partial operation is composed (in the specific player classes below) with other operations to specify the player making a move.

Notice that the player takes responsibility for checking that the selection of the next position to occupy is valid.

Operation *toggleTurn* denotes the changing (*true* to *false*, or vice versa) of the value of the attribute *turn*. This operation will later be composed with the *selectPosn* operations to ensure that the players move alternately.

Operation *gameResult* specifies what happens at the completion of the game. The game ends when either player occupies three positions in a line, in which case the successful player is the winner, or when all board positions are occupied and neither player has three in a line, in which case the game is drawn.

Specific player classes can be defined by inheriting the class *ActivePlayer*.

PlayerBlack

$\upharpoonright$(*board*, *turn*, INIT, *toggleTurn*, *move*, *gameResult*)

ActivePlayer

move $\hat{=}$ (*selectPosn* $\wedge$ *toggleTurn*) $\|$ *board.addToBlack*

In this class, the operation *move* specifies a move by black. It can occur only if the conditions specified in *selectPosn* hold. The effect of the operation is that it is no longer black's turn to move (*toggleTurn*) and a new board position is added to those occupied by black (*board.addToBlack*).

Notice that because the operation *selectPosn* is not applicable if the game is over, when the game is over either it is drawn or there is exactly one winner. A formal proof of this is given in Chapter 7.

The visibility of *board* is required so that at the system level it can be checked that both players are identifying the same board object. Likewise, the attribute *turn* is visible so that it can be checked that at the start of the game it is exactly one player's turn to move. On the other hand, the operation *selectPosn* is not visible as it is only used internally to define *move*.

The class *PlayerWhite* is similar.

PlayerWhite

$\upharpoonright$(*board*, *turn*, INIT, *toggleTurn*, *move*, *gameResult*)

ActivePlayer

move $\hat{=}$ (*selectPosn* $\wedge$ *toggleTurn*) $\|$ *board.addToWhite*

The tic tac toe game

The game can now be defined by the class *TicTacToe* in Figure 5.4 in terms of the players black and white. Both players identify the same board object (identified by the secondary variable *board*) ensuring that they are indeed playing on the same board. Again, this secondary variable adds no information to the state of the class and could be omitted if the class invariant is replaced by

$$bplayer.board = wplayer.board$$

It was included to add clarity to the specification: it makes the role of the board less obscure.

```
┌─ TicTacToe ──────────────────────────────────────────────────────────┐
│  ┌───────────────────────────────┐  ┌─ INIT ─────────────────────────┐│
│  │ bplayer : PlayerBlack         │  │ bplayer.INIT                   ││
│  │ wplayer : PlayerWhite         │  │ wplayer.INIT                   ││
│  │ Δ                             │  │ bplayer.turn ≠ wplayer.turn    ││
│  │ board : PassiveBoard          │  └────────────────────────────────┘│
│  ├───────────────────────────────┤                                    │
│  │ bplayer.board = board         │                                    │
│  │ wplayer.board = board         │                                    │
│  └───────────────────────────────┘                                    │
│                                                                       │
│  blackMove ≙ bplayer.move ∧ wplayer.toggleTurn                        │
│                                                                       │
│  whiteMove ≙ wplayer.move ∧ bplayer.toggleTurn                        │
│                                                                       │
│  gameResult ≙ bplayer.gameResult ∧ wplayer.gameResult                 │
└───────────────────────────────────────────────────────────────────────┘
```

Figure 5.4: the class *TicTacToe*

Initially, both players are in their initial states, i.e. the board is clear. It is either (but not both) black's turn or white's turn to move: the decision as to who moves first is not specified. The operation *blackMove* involves black making a move (*bplayer.move*) while at the same time white changes its attribute *turn* (*wplayer.toggleTurn*), i.e. it will be white's turn next. The operation *whiteMove* is defined similarly.

Finally, the operation *gameResult* requires the consensus of both players. Operations *bplayer.gameResult* and *wplayer.gameResult* have identical specifications, and in particular have identical output (*result!*). Logically, it would have been sufficient when specifying *gameResult* to have included just one (either would do) of the components of the conjunction. Both are included, however, to indicate that both players agree on whether the game has been won or drawn, and if won, by whom.

Discussion

This view of tic tac toe corresponds closely to our perceptions of the game as it is played traditionally. The specification captures the reality that the board has no role other than to record the moves — all the responsibility for ensuring the game is played according to the rules resides with the players. However, the information recorded by the board needs to be shared with the players so that they can make correct moves: to this end, in the class *ActivePlayer* the variable *board* and the secondary variables *bposn* and *wposn* are defined, enabling a player to have direct access to the state of the board. Note that this is achieved in the specification without recourse to direct message passing from the board to the player.

Although the specification of the board captures information about the positions occupied by players, it does not contain information about which player is to move next. To ensure the players maintain a consistent view, operation conjunction is used (e.g. in the operation *blackMove*) so that the *turn* attribute of each player is toggled every time either player makes a move. Effectively, operation conjunction is being used to emulate the flow of information between the players and ensure they remain synchronised.

5.4 Centralising information

In contrast to the perceptual view in Section 5.3, the model presented in this section assigns effective control of the system to the board, not the players. It is the board that has operations to ensure that players make moves within the rules of the game, and it decides when the game is over.

As before, both players need to have information about the current positions occupied both by themselves and the other player, and again this is modelled by each player having an attribute that directly identifies the board. The global definitions *Posn*, *inLine* and *Result* are as defined in Section 5.2.

The active board

Figure 5.5 specifies the class *ActiveBoard*. The class begins with the declaration of the local type *Colour*: the colours *black* and *white* enable the board to distinguish between the two players. This type is available when specifying features of the class, but is not available outside the class. The attributes *bposn* and *wposn* denote the set of board positions as previously defined.

The operation *addToBlack* specifies the effect on the board of a successful move by black, i.e. it is black's turn to make a move, the game is not over, and the input position (*p?*) representing the position black wishes to occupy is free. The outcome is that the selected position is added to those occupied by black and it becomes white's turn to move. The operation *addToWhite* is defined similarly.

The operation *rejectBlack* occurs if any of the preconditions for the operation *addToBlack* fail. This operation models the effect of black attempting to make an invalid move. The operation *rejectWhite* is defined similarly.

The operation *considerBlack* is always applicable and specifies the effect of black attempting to make a move by sending an input position (*p?*) to the board. Either the move is accepted by the board (operation *addToBlack*) or the move is rejected (operation *rejectBlack*). At any time, exactly one of the component operations will be applicable. Operation *considerWhite* is defined similarly.

Compare this class with those defined in Section 5.3: *ActiveBoard* has the control previously invested in the class *ActivePlayer*.

Figure 5.5: the class *ActiveBoard*

A player

A player is an object of the class *Player*:

```
┌─ Player ──────────────────────────────────────────────────────┐
│  ┌──────────────────────────────┐  ┌─ selectPosn ─────────────┐ │
│  │  board : ActiveBoard         │  │  p! : Posn               │ │
│  └──────────────────────────────┘  └──────────────────────────┘ │
└───────────────────────────────────────────────────────────────┘
```

This class has one variable, *board*, identifying a board object, and one operation, *selectPosn*, whereby a selected board position is output. This operation corresponds to the player making a choice (internally) about which position to next occupy and passing this choice to the environment (in fact, as we shall see, the choice is passed to the board), i.e. as far as this class is concerned, the position selected when a player makes a move is arbitrary.

The unspecified assumption is that as information about the state of the board is visible (through the variable *board*), each player can make use of this information when deciding upon their next move. However, there is nothing to stop a player attempting to make an incorrect move, and in this model the board would detect and reject it.

The tic tac toe game

The tic tac toe game can now be modelled by the class *TicTacToe*:

```
┌─ TicTacToe ──────────────────────────────────────────────────┐
│  ┌──────────────────────────────┐  ┌─ INIT ──────────────────┐ │
│  │  bplayer : Player            │  │  board.INIT             │ │
│  │  wplayer : Player            │  └─────────────────────────┘ │
│  │  board : ActiveBoard         │                              │
│  ├──────────────────────────────┤                              │
│  │  bplayer ≠ wplayer           │                              │
│  │  bplayer.board = board       │                              │
│  │  wplayer.board = board       │                              │
│  └──────────────────────────────┘                              │
│                                                                │
│  blackMove ≙ bplayer.selectPosn ∥ board.considerBlack          │
│                                                                │
│  whiteMove ≙ wplayer.selectPosn ∥ board.considerWhite          │
│                                                                │
│  gameResult ≙ board.gameResult                                 │
└────────────────────────────────────────────────────────────────┘
```

The attributes *bplayer*, *wplayer* and *board* identify the player black, player white and board objects, respectively. When the game starts the board is clear and it is not specified which player has first move.

The operation *blackMove* corresponds to the player black selecting a position in parallel with the board considering it, i.e. either the board accepts the move and updates accordingly (its *addToBlack*), or the board rejects the move (its *rejectBlack*). The operation *whiteMove* is defined similarly.

Finally, the operation *gameResult* is the promotion to the system of the same-named board operation.

Discussion

The specification of tic tac toe in this section presents a conceptual model similar to one which may have been developed by a software engineer wishing to implement the game on a computer. The board is conceived not just as a device for displaying (on the screen) the moves made so far, but as encapsulating the functionality and control of the game. In this model the players are active as they need to pass to the board information about the next move they wish to make. However, all checking and control becomes the responsibility of the board. A player can even attempt to occupy a position already occupied, or make a move when it's the other player's turn. The board will detect and prevent such moves.

Conceptually, a player still has access to information about the board, and this is captured in the specification by the variable *board* declared in the class *Player*. Secondary variables *bposn* and *wposn* could have been defined in this class and used to place conditions upon the position selected by a player when making a move. In a computer implementation of the game, no such restrictions could be placed upon a player — the computer cannot control the key presses or mouse moves — and we want the specification to capture this. Indeed, only the class *ActiveBoard* would be implemented: this class models the virtual board object, whereas the class *Player* models real-world objects.

In terms of the software development process, the specification in Section 5.3 is an initial perceptual model capturing a real-world view. Typically such models enable the software engineer to analyse and validate the functionality, architecture and control of an existing system. The specification in this section is a refined conceptual model capturing a view of the software system to be constructed. Typically such models form the basis for implementation and verification. Relating the conceptual model to the real-world view reveals how the proposed software system will affect the control and functionality of the system.

The use of global abstractions such as the type *Posn* and the function *inLine* greatly shortens and simplifies the specification of the classes. Furthermore, as these abstractions are defined globally, in some cases they can be modified without affecting the internal specification of the classes. For example, an alternative view of the game is captured by the a 'magic square' abstraction as shown in Figure 5.6. With this abstraction the notion of three in a line corresponds precisely to having three distinct numbers whose sum is 15. Hence define the set *Posn* and the function *inLine* as follows:

Posn $== 1 .. 9$

6	1	8
7	5	3
2	9	4

Figure 5.6: 'magic square' view of tic tac toe

$$inLine : \mathbb{P}\,Posn \rightarrow \mathbb{B}$$

$$\forall\,ps : \mathbb{P}\,Posn \bullet$$
$$\quad inLine(ps) \Leftrightarrow$$
$$\qquad \exists\,p, q, r : ps \bullet \#\{p, q, r\} = 3 \;\wedge\; p + q + r = 15$$

Taking this abstraction, the specification of the classes remains unaltered.

5.5 Collating information

Imagine a tic tac toe tournament involving a master tic tac toe player and several opponents playing concurrently. The situation is summarised in Figure 5.7. Each opponent is assigned white and is allocated a board on which to play. The master is assigned black, and at any time can make a move on any board, provided it is black's turn to move on that board.

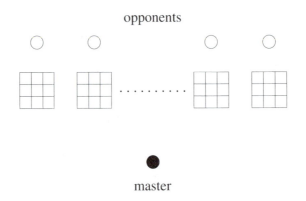

opponents

master

Figure 5.7: a tic tac toe tournament

Information about the state of each game needs to be shared between the master and the opponent. In the specification which follows, this is modelled by creating a dependency between each opponent and the board on which they are playing, and between the master and each board. The specification also illustrates how Object-Z can be used to model situations involving the collation of information from aggregates of objects. This situation is the inverse of distributed message passing discussed in Chapter 4: rather than an object sending a message *to* each object in a given collection, it involves the collation of information *from* each object.

The specification of the tournament is based on the active-board/player variant as given in Section 5.4.

A tournament board

To begin, the boards on which the tournament is played are modelled as objects of the class *TournBoard*:

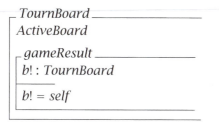

A tournament board is an *ActiveBoard* extended so that when the operation *gameResult* occurs, in addition to the result being output (*result!*, as inherited from *ActiveBoard*), the identity of the board is also output (*b!*). This is needed to distinguish between the outcomes for the games of distinct opponents.

The master

The master is modelled as an object of the class *Master*:

Master
boards : $\mathbb{P}$ TournBoard

selectPosn
p! : Posn
b! : TournBoard

b! $\in$ boards

The master is like a player, but rather than identifying a single board, has an attribute *boards* whose role is to identify the set of opponent's boards upon which the tournament is played. Furthermore, when the operation *selectPosn* occurs, in addition to the board position to be occupied being output (*p!*), the identity of the board upon which the move is to be made is also output (*b!*).

The opponents

Each opponent is like a player as in Section 5.4 except that the board referenced is now a tournament board.

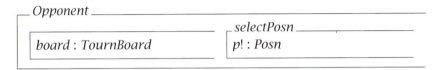

The tournament

The class of the tournament is now specified in Figure 5.8. It consists of a master and a set of opponents. The set of boards associated with the master is the set of boards associated with the opponents. Furthermore, the boards are distinct — no two opponents share a board.

If the operation *masterMove* occurs, the master selects a position $p!$ and board $b!$ (i.e. operation *master.selectPosn*) in parallel with the selected board $b?$ considering the selected position $p?$, i.e. the board either adds this position to the set already occupied by the master or, if the move is invalid, rejects it (see Section 5.4). By the semantics of the parallel operator, inputs $b?$ and $p?$ are identified with the board $b!$ and position $p!$ output by the master, i.e. the required move is attempted on the board selected by the master.

Compare this with the operation *opponentMove* whereby some opponent *op* makes a move. In this case the position selected by *op* is considered by *op*'s board *op.board*. The use of the distributed choice operator to specify this operation ensures that any opponent, when ready, can make the move without prompting from the environment.

The final operation, *tournamentResult*, leads to the overall outcome of the tournament being output. Some care is required in specifying this operation: each board has an operation *gameResult* which outputs the outcome (*result!*) of the game played on that board ($b!$), but what is required here is that all these results are collated to give an overall outcome. It is the role of the operation *insertResult* to facilitate this. It accepts the outcome (*result?*) for a given board ($b?$) and adds the ordered pair ($b?, result?$) to the function *results*.

The operation *tournamentResult* can now be defined by first taking the distributed sequential composition

$$\overset{0}{\underset{9}{}} \; b : boards \bullet b.gameResult \parallel insertResult$$

whereby each board b in the tournament in turn outputs the outcome of its game ($b!$ and *result!* from the operation *b.gameResult*) to the *insertResult* operation. This distributed composition is only applicable if *gameResult* is applicable for every board, i.e. if the tournament is over. Finally, the operation *outputResults* passes to the environment the value of the function *results* which now consists of the collation of the results of all the games, i.e. the overall outcome.

$\qquad$ *TicTacToeTournament* $_____$
$\upharpoonright$ (*INIT*, *masterMove*, *opponentMove*, *tournamentResult*)

$\rule{7cm}{0.4pt}$

master : *Master*
opponents : $\mathbb{P}$ *Opponent*
results : *TournBoard* $\nrightarrow$ *Result*
Δ
boards : $\mathbb{P}$ *TournBoard*

$\rule{3cm}{0.4pt}$

master.boards = {*op* : *opponents* • *op.board*}
$\forall\, op_1, op_2$: *opponents* •
$\quad op_1 \neq op_2 \;\Rightarrow\; op_1.board \neq op_2.board$
boards = *master.boards*
dom *results* $\subseteq$ *boards*

$\rule{8cm}{0.4pt}$

$\_$ *INIT* $_____$
$\forall\, b$: *boards* • *b.INIT*
results = $\varnothing$

$\rule{5cm}{0.4pt}$

masterMove $\;\widehat{=}\;$ *master.selectPosn*
$$\|$$
$$([\, b? : boards \,] \bullet b?.considerBlack)$$

opponentMove $\;\widehat{=}\;$ $\square$ *op* : *opponents* •
$$op.selectPosn \parallel op.board.considerWhite$$

$\_$ *insertResult* $_____$
Δ(*results*)
b? : *TournBoard*
result? : *Result*

$\rule{3cm}{0.4pt}$

results′ = *results* $\cup$ {*b?* $\mapsto$ *result?*}

$\_$ *outputResults* $_____$
results! : *TournBoard* $\nrightarrow$ *Result*

$\rule{3cm}{0.4pt}$

results! = *results*

tournamentResult $\;\widehat{=}\;$
$$\quad (^{\,\circ}_{9}\; b : boards \bullet b.gameResult \parallel insertResult)$$
$$^{\,\circ}_{9}$$
$$\quad outputResults$$

Figure 5.8: the class *TicTacToeTournament*

Hence the overall effect of the *tournamentResult* operation is to collate information from a collection of objects. In this operation, all inter-object communication is hidden, with just the final output *results!* being passed to the environment. Generally, as sequential composition is not commutative, the order within a distributed sequential composition needs to be specified, e.g. by having a total order on the quantification set. In this case, however, the order of collation does not affect the result and therefore need not be specified.

Despite the indefinite number of boards, and that sequential composition is involved, the operation *tournamentResult* is atomic. The sequential chain is similar to a chain of forward relational compositions.

Discussion

As for the specifications in Sections 5.3 and 5.4, information about the state of each board is shared with the master and the opponent playing on that board by creating information dependencies using direct object references. However, an opponent does not and need not have information about the other games in the tournament.

The sequential nature of the operation *tournamentResult* arises because information about the outcome of each game in the tournament is expressed as an output, and these outputs need to be collated. However, had the class *ActiveBoard* been specified so that the status of the game was included as part of the state, the specification of the operation *tournamentResult* could have been captured declaratively. For example, suppose the *ActiveBoard* class had a visible attribute *status* of type

$$Status ::= active \mid black\_wins \mid white\_wins \mid draw$$

where *status* = *active* initially and remains *active* until the outcome of the game has been decided. (The operations *addToBlack* and *addToWhite* would need to be modified to ensure that *status* = *active* beforehand and remains *active* afterwards if and only if the move does not end the game.)

Using this attribute, the operation *tournamentResult* in the tournament system class could be specified as

```
┌─ tournamentResult ────────────────────────────────────────
│  results! : TournBoard ⇸ Status
├────────────────────────────────────────────────────────
│  ∀ b : boards • b.status ≠ active
│  results! = {b : boards • (b, b.status)}
└────────────────────────────────────────────────────────
```

This operation can occur only if each game in the tournament has been completed (i.e. *status* is not *active*). It outputs to the environment the set of all ordered pairs (*b*, *b.status*) where *b* identifies a tournament board and *b.status* gives the outcome of the game played on that board.

Reliable behaviour   6

6.1   Introduction

The aim of any software development project is to construct a system exhibiting some specific behaviour in the belief that such a system will be able to solve a particular real-world problem. The behaviour of an object-oriented system ultimately depends on the behaviour of the underlying objects and the way they are composed to form the system. Indeed, the skill of object-oriented development is in designing the underlying objects and the architecture of their composition so as to achieve the intended behaviour.

This chapter illustrates the specification of a system which achieves its intended behaviour despite the inclusion of some unreliable components. The example chosen is a communications protocol that faithfully conveys a stream of input messages to a remote location despite an unreliable communications medium, i.e. the input stream is reproduced without loss, replication, permutation or corruption. The particular protocol is the 'alternating-bit' protocol, the simplest member of a family of protocols known as the 'cyclic-redundancy' protocols.

6.2   The alternating-bit protocol: a case study

Informal description

- Messages are submitted to a transmitter for transmission to a remote receiver via a 'noisy' communication channel that can corrupt messages.

- When the transmitter accepts a message for transmission, it first tags the message with either a 0 or a 1 and transmits the tagged message to the receiver. Periodically, the tagged message is retransmitted until an acknowledgment is returned to the transmitter from the receiver to confirm that the message has been received successfully. The transmitter is then ready to accept the next message for transmission, this time tagging it with the alternate tag (i.e. if a message is tagged with a 0, the next message is tagged with a 1, and the message after that with a 0, and so on, hence the name alternating-bit protocol).

- Tagged messages pass to the receiver via a tagged-message channel. It is assumed that any tagged message that is corrupted in transmission can be detected and removed (e.g. by using a redundant code). The overall result is that tagged messages can, in effect, be lost while in the message channel. The message channel behaves like a queue in that it is able to convey several tagged messages at the one time, up to its maximum queuing capacity.

- At each stage, the receiver knows the tag of the next tagged message it is expecting. If an uncorrupted tagged message arrives with the expected tag the message is accepted, otherwise the tagged message is rejected. Periodically, as an acknowledgment of receipt, the receiver sends back to the transmitter the tag of the last tagged message accepted (i.e. not rejected).

- Tags as acknowledgments pass to the transmitter via an acknowledgment channel. As with the message channel, tags can be corrupted in transmission, and corrupted tags can be detected and removed, with the overall result that acknowledgment tags can, in effect, be lost. The acknowledgment channel may also convey several tags at the one time, up to its maximum queuing capacity.

The flow of messages and acknowledgments in the system is shown in Figure 6.1. In constructing an object-oriented formal specification of this communication system, the transmitter, receiver, message channel and acknowledgment channel will be modelled as objects, with the flow of messages and acknowledgments modelled in terms of inter-object communication.

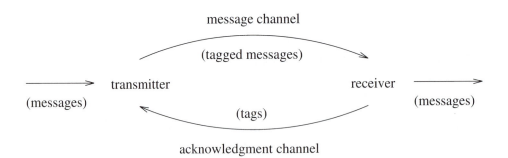

Figure 6.1: the communication system

Global types

The following three global types are needed in the specification:

$Tag == \{0, 1\}$

$[Msg]$

$TagMsg == Tag \times Msg.$

   The type *Tag* denotes the set $\{0, 1\}$ of possible tags that can be associated with messages. The type *Msg* denotes the set of all possible messages that the environment may wish to be transmitted. Placing this set in square brackets indicates that it is a given type with no further structure, i.e. the exact nature of messages for transmission is not relevant at this level of abstraction. The type *TagMsg* denotes the set of all possible tagged messages that can be sent by the transmitter.

The transmitter

A transmitter object is specified by the class *Trans*:

```
┌─ Trans ─────────────────────────────────────────────────────
│  ┌──────────────────────────┐  ┌─ INIT ──────────────────┐
│  │ current : ℙ TagMsg       │  │ current = ∅             │
│  │ tag : Tag                │  │ tag = 0                 │
│  ├──────────────────────────┤  └─────────────────────────┘
│  │ #current ⩽ 1             │
│  │ current ≠ ∅  ⇒           │
│  │    ∃ m: Msg •            │
│  │      current = {(tag, m)}│
│  └──────────────────────────┘
│  ┌─ transMsg ───────────────┐  ┌─ retrans ───────────────┐
│  │ Δ(current, tag)          │  │ tm! : TagMsg            │
│  │ m? : Msg                 │  ├─────────────────────────┤
│  │ tm! : TagMsg             │  │ tm! ∈ current           │
│  ├──────────────────────────┤  └─────────────────────────┘
│  │ current = ∅              │
│  │ tag′ = 1 − tag           │
│  │ tm! = (tag′, m?)         │
│  │ current′ = {tm!}         │
│  └──────────────────────────┘
│  ┌─ accAck ─────────────────┐  ┌─ rejAck ────────────────┐
│  │ Δ(current)               │  │ t? : Tag                │
│  │ t? : Tag                 │  ├─────────────────────────┤
│  ├──────────────────────────┤  │ current = ∅ ∨ t? ≠ tag  │
│  │ current ≠ ∅              │  └─────────────────────────┘
│  │ t? = tag                 │
│  │ current′ = ∅             │
│  └──────────────────────────┘
└──────────────────────────────────────────────────────────────
```

The attribute *current* is a set that is either empty or contains exactly one tagged message (as *#current* $\leqslant$ 1). If *current* is empty, the previous message has been sent and acknowledged successfully and the transmitter is ready to accept from the environment the next message for transmission. If *current* is not empty, it contains the tagged message that has been transmitted one or more times and for which the transmitter is awaiting acknowledgment of successful receipt.

The attribute *tag* denotes the tag component of the last tagged message to be transmitted (or retransmitted). In the case when *current* is not empty, i.e. this set contains the last transmitted tagged message, the value of *tag* is the same as the tag component of this tagged message. The class invariant explicitly captures this requirement. Initially, *current* is empty and *tag* is 0.

The operation *transMsg* can occur if and only if *current* is empty. A new message (*m?*) is accepted from the environment, tagged, and the tagged message (*tm!*) is output (transmitted). The value used to tag the new message is that which was not used to tag the previous message, i.e. as *tag* records the tag value of the previous message, the value $1 - tag$ tags the new message. Also, the value of *tag* changes to this new value, i.e. $tag' = 1 - tag$, and so maintains the invariant that the value of *tag* is that used to tag the message currently being transmitted. The new tagged message is therefore (tag', *m?*). (The first message to be accepted will be tagged with a 1, as the initial value of *tag* is 0.) Finally, a copy of this tagged message is placed in the set *current* ready for retransmission.

The operation *retrans* can occur whenever the set *current* is not empty. The tagged message (*tm!*) contained in the set is retransmitted; no attribute changes value, i.e. the state of the transmitter is unchanged. As modelled here, this operation can occur at any time when *current* is not empty. In practice, retransmission would occur only after a prescribed time delay.

The accept-acknowledgment operation *accAck* applies when *current* holds a tagged message awaiting acknowledgment (i.e. *current* $\neq \varnothing$) and a matching acknowledgment tag is received by the transmitter (i.e. $t? = tag$).

The reject-acknowledgment operation *rejAck* applies if *current* is empty (i.e. the most recent message has already been successfully acknowledged) or when there is an acknowledgment mismatch ($t? \neq tag$) which arises if a resent acknowledgment arrives after a new message has been transmitted.

The receiver

The receiver is an object of the class *Rec* in Figure 6.2. The attribute *exptag* denotes the value of the tag component of the next tagged message expected by the receiver. Initially *exptag* is 1 because, as was observed above, the first message to be transmitted is tagged with 1.

The operation *accMsg* occurs when a tagged message (*tm?*) is received whose tag component (*first*(*tm?*)) is equal to the expected tag. In this case, the tagged message is accepted as correct and the message component of the

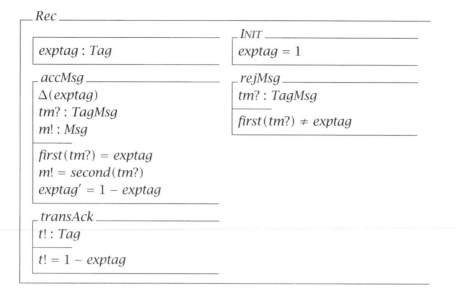

Figure 6.2: the class *Rec*

tagged message (*second*(*tm*?)) is output back to the environment (*m*!). (The functions *first* and *second* extract the first and second component respectively from an ordered pair.) Finally, the value of the expected tag is changed to the alternate value (*exptag*' = 1 − *exptag*) in expectation of the next message.

The second operation, *rejMsg*, occurs when a tagged message (*tm*?) is received whose tag is not equal to the expected tag. In this case the tagged message is rejected as not the expected one, no message is output to the environment, and the state of the receiver is unchanged. Note: the rejection of a message is based on tag mismatching. It is assumed that tagged messages which are corrupted are not even considered; as we will see, corruption is modelled as loss in the transmission medium.

The final operation, *transAck*, can occur at any time and results in the value of the tag component of the last accepted tagged message being output. As we will see, this value is passed to the acknowledgment channel to be returned to the transmitter. As *exptag* is the value of the tag of the next expected tagged message, the tag of the last accepted tagged message must have been 1−*exptag*, so it is this value that is output. As modelled here, this operation can occur at any time. In practice, acknowledgments would be sent at regular intervals.

The message and acknowledgment channels

Both the message and acknowledgment channels act like queues that can also lose messages. A queue is an object of the class *Queue*[*T*]:

```
┌─ Queue[T] ─────────────────────────────────────────────────────┐
│                                                                 │
│  │ max : ℕ                                                      │
│                                                                 │
│  ┌──────────────────────────┐   ┌─ INIT ──────────────────┐    │
│  │ items : seq T            │   │ items = ⟨ ⟩             │    │
│  ├──────────────────────────┤   └─────────────────────────┘    │
│  │ #items ⩽ max             │                                  │
│  └──────────────────────────┘                                  │
│                                                                 │
│  ┌─ join ───────────────────┐   ┌─ leave ─────────────────┐    │
│  │ Δ(items)                 │   │ Δ(items)                │    │
│  │ z? : T                   │   │ z! : T                  │    │
│  ├──────────────────────────┤   ├─────────────────────────┤    │
│  │ #items < max             │   │ items ≠ ⟨ ⟩            │    │
│  │ items' = items ⌢ ⟨z?⟩   │   │ z! = head items         │    │
│  └──────────────────────────┘   │ items' = tail items     │    │
│                                  └─────────────────────────┘    │
└─────────────────────────────────────────────────────────────────┘
```

This is an example of a *generic* class: the generic type T is unspecified and can be instantiated to be any actual type when a queue object is declared.

The attribute *max* is constant and denotes the maximum capacity of a queue. As the predicate part of this constant definition is 'true', it and the dividing bar are omitted, leaving the short vertical line on the left.

The attribute *items* denotes the sequence of items of T contained in the queue, with the class invariant ensuring that the length of this sequence (i.e. the number of items in the queue) does not exceed the capacity of the queue. Initially, a queue object is empty, i.e. it contains no items.

The operation *join* models the input of a new item ($z?$) that is appended to the sequence of items. This operation can occur only if the queue is not full.

The operation *leave* models the output of the head of the sequence of items ($z!$) with the tail of the sequence remaining in the queue. This operation can occur only if the queue is not empty. Notice that an alternative but semantically equivalent way of expressing the predicate of this operation would be

$$items \neq \langle \, \rangle$$

$$items = \langle z! \rangle \frown items'$$

The class *Queue* specifies queue objects that faithfully output, without loss, replication or corruption, items in the same order in which they were received. The communication channels, however, can corrupt messages, resulting in such messages not being considered further. Thus in effect, corrupted messages are lost. Moreover, it suffices to model such loss as the loss of the head of the channel at unspecified times because corrupted messages (to be 'lost') eventually become the head. This channel behaviour suggests the class *LossyQueue[T]*:

```
┌─ LossyQueue[T] ──────────────────
│ Queue[T]
│ ┌─ lose ──────────────────────
│ │ Δ(items)
│ ├──────────────────────────
│ │ items ≠ ⟨⟩
│ │ items' = tail items
│ └──────────────────────────
└──────────────────────────────
```

This inherits the class *Queue*, but in addition has the operation *lose* whereby the head of the sequence of items can be lost at any time, leaving the tail of the sequence. Notice that the head of *items* is not output when *lose* occurs; it is simply lost and cannot be recovered by the environment.

The message channel is now specified as an object of the class *MsgChan* defined by:

```
┌─ MsgChan ──────────────────────────────────────────────
│ LossyQueue[TagMsg][tm?/z?, tm!/z!]
└────────────────────────────────────────────────────────
```

That is, the message channel is a lossy queue of tagged messages (*T* is instantiated as type *TagMsg*) with the input for the *join* operation renamed *tm?* and the output for the *leave* operation renamed *tm!* (the renaming construct replaces all occurrences of *z?* by *tm?* and *z!* by *tm!*). In its fully expanded form, *MsgChan* is the class:

```
┌─ MsgChan ──────────────────────────────────────────────
│ │ max : ℕ
│
│ ┌──────────────────────────   ┌─ INIT ─────────────────
│ │ items : seq TagMsg          │ items = ⟨⟩
│ ├──────────────────────────   └────────────────────────
│ │ #items ≤ max
│ └──────────────────────────
│
│ ┌─ join ──────────────────────   ┌─ leave ─────────────────
│ │ Δ(items)                        │ Δ(items)
│ │ tm? : TagMsg                    │ tm! : TagMsg
│ ├──────────────────────────      ├──────────────────────────
│ │ #items < max                    │ items ≠ ⟨⟩
│ │ items' = items ⌢ ⟨tm?⟩          │ tm! = head items
│ └──────────────────────────      │ items' = tail items
│                                   └──────────────────────────
│
│ ┌─ lose ──────────────────────
│ │ Δ(items)
│ ├──────────────────────────
│ │ items ≠ ⟨⟩
│ │ items' = tail items
│ └──────────────────────────
└────────────────────────────────────────────────────────
```

Similarly, the acknowledgment channel is an object of the class *AckChan*:

```
 ___AckChan_____
|  LossyQueue[Tag][t?/z?, t!/z!]
|_____
```

That is, the acknowledgment channel is a lossy queue of tags (T is instantiated as type *Tag*) with the input for the *join* operation renamed $t?$ and the output for the *leave* operation renamed $t!$.

The alternating-bit protocol

The alternating-bit protocol can now be specified by the class *AltBit* which contains a transmitter object (*trans*), a receiver object (*rec*), a message channel object (*msgchan*) and an acknowledgment channel object (*ackchan*). Initially, each object is in its initial state.

```
 ___AltBit_____
|
|   _____   __INIT_____
|  |                             | |
|  | trans : Trans               | | trans.INIT
|  | rec : Rec                   | | rec.INIT
|  | msgchan : MsgChan           | | msgchan.INIT
|  | ackchan : AckChan           | | ackchan.INIT
|  |_____| |_____
|
|  transMsg ≙ trans.transMsg || msgchan.join
|
|  retrans ≙ trans.retrans || msgchan.join
|
|  accMsg ≙ msgchan.leave || rec.accMsg
|
|  rejMsg ≙ msgchan.leave || rec.rejMsg
|
|  transAck ≙ rec.transAck || ackchan.join
|
|  accAck ≙ ackchan.leave || trans.accAck
|
|  rejAck ≙ ackchan.leave || trans.rejAck
|
|  loseMsg ≙ msgchan.lose
|
|  loseAck ≙ ackchan.lose
|_____
```

With the exception of the *loseMsg* and *loseAck* operations, which are simply the promotion to the system of the *lose* operation on the message and acknowledgment channel objects respectively, each system operation involves inter-object communication. Consider, for example, the operation *transMsg* involving the operation of the same name applied to the transmitter object, performed in parallel with the operation *join* applied to the message channel object. The operation accepts a message ($m?$) from the environment, tags it, and outputs the tagged message ($tm!$). This tagged message is identified with the input ($tm?$) of the *msgchan.join* operation, i.e. the effect is that the tagged message from the transmitter is appended to the message channel. The other operations defined in the system class involve similar inter-object communication.

6.3   Complementary graphical diagrams

The alternating-bit protocol affords an opportunity to illustrate the complementary role of state diagrams, class diagrams, object diagrams and swimlane diagrams.

State diagram of the transmitter

Figure 6.3 shows a state diagram for the object *trans* : *Trans*. A state is represented by a rounded rectangular node and is characterised either by a specific assignment of values to attributes or by a set of such assignments. As states are characterised by values, a state diagram relates to an object, not a class.

The two states on the left in Figure 6.3 denote specific assignments to the attributes *current* (= $\varnothing$) and *tag* (0 or 1, which distinguish these two states). The right-hand states, however, are characterised by singleton set values of *current* containing any message tagged with the value of *tag*; again, the two states are distinguished by the value of *tag*. Clearly it would be impracticable to show individual states for each possible message value.

The assignments or sets associated with a state are characterised by a predicate. As the assignments of valid states must satisfy the class invariant, the predicate characterising a state must be at least as strong as the class invariant. This is automatically achieved by writing predicates with the understanding that they are implicitly conjoined with the class invariant.

A state transition is represented by a directed arc linking states and annotated with the name of an operation qualified by a predicate involving pre- and post-conditions. In the case of transition to a left-hand state of the diagram, the post values are unique, whereas a transition to a right-hand state must indicate the value of output *tm*! and the value of *current* in that state, i.e. the value of *current'* in terms of the operation responsible for the transition. Operations with parameters denote a family of values which imply a family of transitions.

The initial state is distinguished by the arrow from the small black circle.

Conditions are simplified in accordance with the known state context, e.g. for the *transMsg* transition from the initial state, the Object-Z specified conjunct $tm! = (tag', m?)$ is simplified to $tm! = (1, m?)$ as the value of *tag'* is 1, the value of *tag* in the new state.

State diagram of the receiver

Figure 6.4 shows the state diagram for the object *rec* : *Rec*. The two states are distinguished by the value of *exptag* (0 or 1). The diagram shows that the state is changed on acceptance of a message (when the tags match) but unchanged

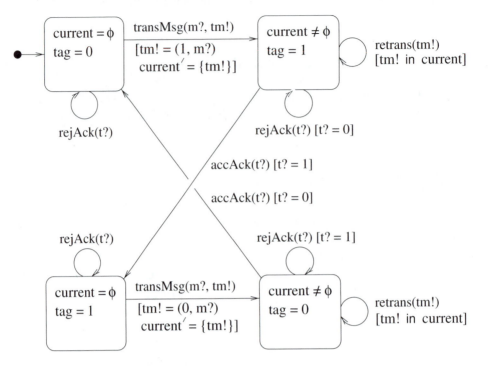

Figure 6.3: state diagram of the transmitter *trans*

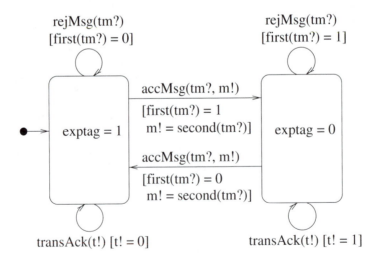

Figure 6.4: state diagram of the receiver *rec*

on rejection of a message (when the tags do not match) or on transmission of an acknowledgment.

State diagram of the message channel

Figure 6.5 shows the state diagram for the object *msgchan* : *MsgChan*. The three cases of interest for a queue are: empty; non-empty but not full; and full. The three states correspond to these three cases. The operations *leave* and *lose* differ only in that *leave* has an output whereas *lose* has not.

Class diagram of the protocol

Figure 6.6 is a class diagram of the classes which constitute the system class *AltBit*. The class node *Queue* illustrates the representation of genericity by the dotted box extension which contains the generic type or types. It is seen that the derivation *LossyQueue* retains the genericity. Instantiation of generic types by actual types is indicated by the stereotype «bind» followed by the actual type (or list of types in the case of multiple instantiation). Accordingly, Figure 6.6 shows that classes *MsgChan* and *AckChan* are derivations of *LossyQueue* instantiated with the actual types *TagMsg* and *Tag* respectively. The *MsgChan* and *AckChan* derivations also include renaming of the *z*? and *z*! parameters of *LossyQueue* operations as shown by the Object-Z renaming syntax.

Object diagram of the protocol

Figure 6.7 illustrates the nesting within the class node *AltBit* of its four constituent objects, headed by their corresponding Object-Z declared names. The figure is a convenient overview of the composition of the operations of the class *AltBit* and the flow of information via parameters. It is seen that only *transMsg* and *accMsg* communicate with the environment: this is consistent with the requirement that the protocol receives input messages and delivers them at a (remote) location. It remains to be shown that the output stream faithfully reproduces the input stream: that is the subject of Chapter 7.

Swimlane diagrams of the protocol

Figure 6.8 is a *swimlane* (or *activity*) diagram of the basic protocol cycle. The figure shows how the transmitter, receiver and channels cooperate via composition to achieve a (time) sequence of *AltBit* operations. The sequence of four *AltBit* operations shown descending down the left-hand side of the diagram is the shortest possible operational cycle of the protocol to convey one message: it has no retransmission or loss of either tagged message or acknowledgment. The diagram assumes commencement from an initialised *AltBit*, i.e. from initialised constituent objects.

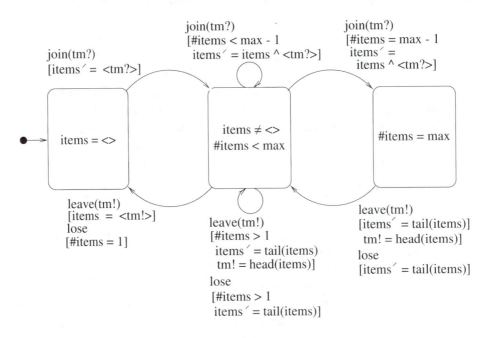

Figure 6.5: state diagram of the message channel *msgchan*

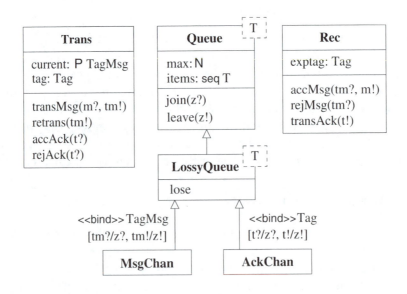

Figure 6.6: constituent classes of the class *AltBit*

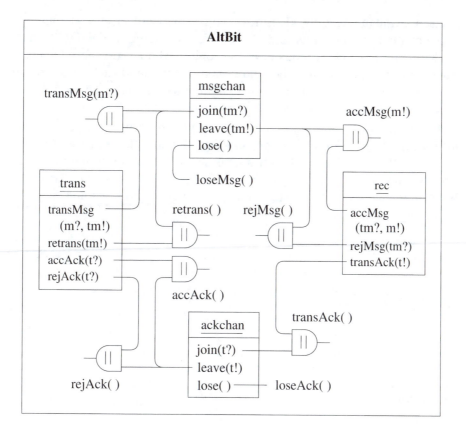

Figure 6.7: composed operations of the class *AltBit*

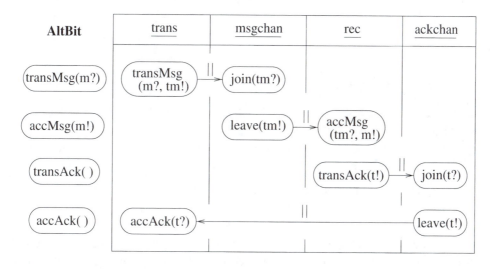

Figure 6.8: swimlane diagram of the basic protocol cycle

Each swimlane heading identifies a constituent object and the operation sequence of that object descends in the corresponding swimlane. Horizontal alignment indicates composition: the composed operations are linked, the symbol on the link indicates the kind of composition and the arrow indicates the direction of information flow (via matching parameters). The result of the composition is the operation shown in the left margin.

Figure 6.9 traces an operational sequence of the protocol which includes one retransmission of the message, a second transmission of its acknowledgment, and the rejection of the retransmissions. Again, only one message is actually conveyed by this sequence. To include the loss of the transmitted tagged message or its retransmission(s) and one or more acknowledgments would clearly extend the swimlanes considerably.

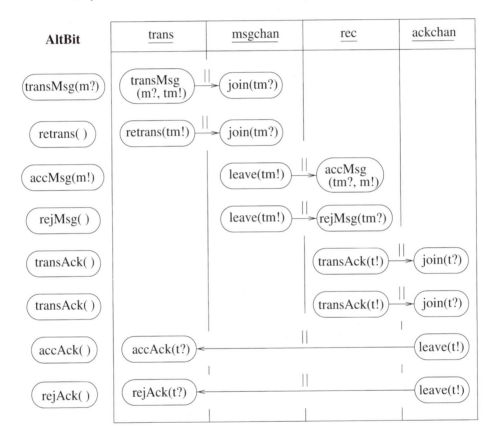

Figure 6.9: a protocol cycle including retransmission and rejection

The swimlane diagram is useful for tracing the synthesis of a particular protocol history and validating by inspection that the behaviour satisfies the intent. However, it is generally impracticable to attempt to verify the correctness of the protocol by manually tracing numerous cases: a mathematical style proof is required (see Chapter 7).

6.4   Discussion

This chapter provided an example of a specification which is claimed to achieve overall reliability despite some unreliable components. The chapter also provided an opportunity to illustrate the use of state, class, object and swimlane diagrams as complementary aids to presenting a formal specification.

In the protocol specified, the unreliability was expressible in terms of the operation *lose* associated with each of two communication channels. This operation is spurious in the sense that it can occur at any time tagged messages or acknowledgments are in transit in their respective channels and causes information to be lost. The unreliability was overcome by redundancy: the information subject to loss being copied, retained and resent until confirmation that it had been faithfully conveyed. By considering a number of traces of the protocol in operation, a degree of confidence was established in the claim that the redundancy did in fact overcome the problem. Surety, however, requires mathematical proof: this topic is the subject of Chapter 7.

Proving invariant properties 7

7.1 Introduction

A property of a system is *invariant* if it is always valid, regardless of how the system evolves. In an Object-Z specification, some invariant properties are captured explicitly by types and class invariants. But a system will generally have other invariant properties not so explicitly stated. The specification of a system can be extended to include any invariant property as a class invariant; however, as there may be many (even infinitely many) such invariant properties, it would be cumbersome (or even impossible) to attempt to include them all as class invariants.

The general strategy followed when using Object-Z to specify a class is to include in the class invariant those conditions which best clarify the functionality and intent of the class. As the class invariant holds both before and after every operation, a judicious choice of class invariant can greatly simplify the specification of operations.

Given that not all invariant properties are stated as class invariants, in this chapter we examine techniques to verify that a given property is invariant, i.e. prove from the specification that the property is always valid. In particular, we explore the role of auxiliary variables in stating properties, and the technique of structural induction for proving properties invariant.

Structural induction

To prove that a system property is invariant, it is sufficient to express the property as a predicate (called the *proposition*) and show that

- the proposition is true whenever the system is in an initial state; and

- if the proposition is true and an operation occurs, the proposition remains true.

This technique is known as proof by structural induction.

7.2   Tic tac toe revisited

To illustrate the application of structural induction, consider class *TicTacToe* in Section 5.3. We shall prove the proposition that if the game is over, either the game is drawn or there is exactly one winner. This proposition is intuitively true given the observation that the two players take turns to move, and can only move if the game is not over. Nevertheless, as intuition is subjective and can be misleading, a proof is required if we are to have confidence in the specification. Indeed as the proofs in this chapter will show, formalising intuition may require considerable care.

The first step is to define within the class *TicTacToe* the following secondary variables:

$$bposn, wposn, free : \mathbb{P}\ Posn$$
$$over, drawn : \mathbb{B}$$

where

$$bposn = board.bposn$$
$$wposn = board.wposn$$
$$free = Posn \setminus (bposn \cup wposn)$$
$$over \Leftrightarrow inLine(bposn) \vee inLine(wposn) \vee free = \varnothing$$
$$drawn \Leftrightarrow over \wedge \neg inLine(bposn) \wedge \neg inLine(wposn)$$

These secondary variables promote attributes of the underlying objects to the game level. They are required to formulate and prove the proposition.

For convenience, introduce the abbreviations

$$b == inLine(bposn) \quad \text{and} \quad w == inLine(wposn).$$

Hence the conjuncts involving *over* and *drawn* above abbreviate to:

$$over \Leftrightarrow b \vee w \vee free = \varnothing$$
$$drawn \Leftrightarrow over \wedge \neg b \wedge \neg w$$

Lemma 7.1 Within the context of the game *TicTacToe*, the proposition

$$\neg b \vee \neg w \qquad (1)$$

is invariably true. □

Proof   The proof is by structural induction.

1. Initial step.
   Initially (1) is true as $bposn = wposn = \varnothing$.

2. Induction step.
   Assume that (1) is true. If *gameResult* occurs it does not change the board positions and so (1) remains true. If *blackMove* is applicable, $\neg\ over$

is true and, from the defintion of *over*, so is ¬ *w*. If *blackMove* occurs, as *wposn* remains unchanged, ¬ *w* remains true and so (1) remains true. By symmetry, (1) remains true if *whiteMove* is applied.

Hence by structural induction (1) is invariably true. □

We can now prove the main result, i.e. if the game is over, either it is drawn or there is exactly one winner.

Proposition 7.1

$$over \Rightarrow (drawn \wedge \neg b \wedge \neg w$$
$$\vee$$
$$\neg drawn \wedge b \wedge \neg w$$
$$\vee$$
$$\neg drawn \wedge \neg b \wedge w)$$

is invariable true. □

Proof   If *over* is false, the proposition (an implication) is true. If *over* is true, the proposition reduces to its consequent (its RHS), which, by application of the distributive law, may be restated as:

$$drawn \wedge \neg b \wedge \neg w$$
$$\vee \qquad\qquad\qquad\qquad\qquad (2)$$
$$\neg drawn \wedge ((b \wedge \neg w) \vee (\neg b \wedge w))$$

In the context of *over*, the definition *drawn* ⇔ *over* ∧ ¬ *b* ∧ ¬ *w* above reduces to:

$$drawn \Leftrightarrow \neg b \wedge \neg w \qquad (3)$$

Now consider *drawn* to be also true, then by (3),

$$\neg b \wedge \neg w \qquad (4)$$

is true and therefore the first disjunct of (2) is true, and thus so is (2). The proposition then, in the context of *over* and *drawn*, is true.

It remains to prove (2) in the context of *over* and ¬ *drawn*, i.e. to prove that the following predicate is true:

$$(b \wedge \neg w) \vee (\neg b \wedge w) \qquad (5)$$

Now,

$$(5) = (b \wedge \neg w) \vee (\neg b \wedge w)$$
$$= (b \wedge \neg w) \vee (\neg b \wedge w) \vee (\neg b \wedge \neg w)$$

as (¬ *b* ∧ ¬ *w*) is false from (3) in the context of ¬ *drawn*

$$= (b \wedge \neg w) \vee (\neg b \wedge (w \vee \neg w))$$

by the associative and distributive laws

$$= (b \wedge \neg w) \vee \neg b \qquad\qquad\qquad \text{as } (w \vee \neg w) \text{ is true}$$

$$= (b \vee \neg b) \wedge (\neg w \vee \neg b) \qquad\qquad \text{by the distributive law}$$

$$= \neg w \vee \neg b \qquad\qquad\qquad \text{as } (b \vee \neg b) \text{ is true}$$

$$= true \qquad\qquad\qquad\qquad\qquad \text{by the Lemma}$$

Hence the proposition is invariably true. □

7.3   Alternating-bit protocol revisited

In the last section, secondary variables were introduced to formulate and prove a proposition to be true. Sometimes however, introducing secondary variables is insufficient and it is necessary to introduce additional, or *auxiliary*, primary variables.

To illustrate the role of auxiliary variables, we revisit the alternating-bit protocol specified in Section 6.2. It was claimed that this protocol has the property that a stream of input messages is conveyed without loss, replication or permutation. From the specification it is not obvious that this property holds — it requires proof. As we shall see, formulating the predicates to verify the correctness of the protocol requires careful analysis.

In this section we prove that the alternating-bit protocol as specified is partially correct. The correctness is partial as progress issues are not addressed, i.e. the proof does not guarantee that a stream of messages for transmission will eventually be conveyed, only that if the stream is conveyed, messages are not lost, replicated or permuted. The issue of progress is discussed further in Section 7.4.

To begin, we extend the class *AltBit* specified in Section 6.2 by adding auxiliary variables *msgsin* and *msgsout* and various secondary variables, to give the class *AuxAltBit* specified in Figure 7.1.

Variable *msgsin* denotes the sequence of messages accepted from the environment for transmission: initially this sequence is empty. The inherited operation *transMsg* is extended so that the message *m?* input from the environment is appended to *msgsin*. Variable *msgsout* denotes the sequence of messages successfully conveyed and passed back to the environment: this sequence is also initially empty. The inherited operation *accMsg* is extended so that the message *m!* output to the environment is appended to *msgsout*. Extending the state with these auxiliary variables provides the references needed to formulate the relationship between the input and output message streams.

The secondary variable *m* denotes the most recent message transmitted. (If no message has been transmitted, the value of *m* is unimportant.) The other secondary variables promote corresponding values of attributes of the underlying objects to make the values readily accessible.

AuxAltBit

> AltBit
>
> ---
> msgsin, msgsout : seq Msg
> Δ
> current : ℙ TagMsg
> tag, exptag : Tag
> msgitems : seq TagMsg
> ackitems : seq Tag
> m : Msg
>
> ---
> current = trans.current
> tag = trans.tag
> exptag = rec.exptag
> msgitems = msgchan.items
> ackitems = ackchan.items
> msgsin ≠ ⟨⟩ ⇒ m = last(msgsin)

> INIT
> msgsin = ⟨⟩
> msgsout = ⟨⟩

> transMsg
> Δ(msgsin)
> ---
> msgsin′ = msgsin ⌢ ⟨m?⟩

> accMsg
> Δ(msgsout)
> ---
> msgsout′ = msgsout ⌢ ⟨m!⟩

Figure 7.1: the class *AuxAltBit*

Next, we formalise the proposition that the sequence *msgsout* of output messages is the same as the sequence *msgsin* of input messages, except that the most recent message input might not yet have been output.

Proposition 7.2 In the context of the class *AuxAltBit*,

$$msgsin = msgsout \ \lor \ msgsin = msgsout \ ⌢ \ \langle m \rangle$$

□

Proof   The strategy of the proof is to show that the protocol evolves by cycling through three states, characterised respectively by three mutually exclusive conditions. We shall show using structural induction that the protocol is confined to these three states: as the proposition is true in each of these states, it will follow that the proposition is invariably true. The conditions characterising the states were conjectured (with some difficulty) by analysis of numerous operational sequences of the protocol; however, the proof is independent of the process of how the conditions were conjectured.

To begin, define the following three conditions:

- condition (1)

$$
\begin{aligned}
&msgsin = msgsout \;\wedge\\
&current = \varnothing \;\wedge\\
&exptag \neq tag \;\wedge\\
&\operatorname{ran} msgitems \subseteq \{(tag, m)\} \;\wedge\\
&\operatorname{ran} ackitems \subseteq \{tag\}
\end{aligned}
$$

- condition (2)

$$
\begin{aligned}
&msgsin = msgsout \frown \langle m \rangle \;\wedge\\
&current = \{(tag, m)\} \;\wedge\\
&exptag = tag \;\wedge\\
&(\exists k : \mathbb{N} \bullet \forall i : \operatorname{dom} msgitems \bullet\\
&\qquad i < k \;\Rightarrow\; first(msgitems(i)) \neq tag) \;\wedge\\
&\qquad i \geqslant k \;\Rightarrow\; msgitems(i) = (tag, m))\\
&\operatorname{ran} ackitems \subseteq \{1 - tag\}
\end{aligned}
$$

- condition (3)

$$
\begin{aligned}
&msgsin = msgsout \;\wedge\\
&current = \{(tag, m)\} \;\wedge\\
&exptag \neq tag \;\wedge\\
&\operatorname{ran} msgitems \subseteq \{(tag, m)\} \;\wedge\\
&(\exists k : \mathbb{N} \bullet \forall i : \operatorname{dom} ackitems \bullet\\
&\qquad i < k \;\Rightarrow\; ackitems(i) \neq tag\\
&\qquad i \geqslant k \;\Rightarrow\; ackitems(i) = tag)
\end{aligned}
$$

The conditions are mutually exclusive by inspection of their first two conjuncts. As the proposition is satisfied by each of these conditions, it remains to prove that

$$
\text{condition (1)} \;\vee\; \text{condition (2)} \;\vee\; \text{condition (3)}
$$

is invariably true. The proof is by structural induction.

Initial step

$$
\begin{aligned}
&msgsin = msgsout = \langle \rangle\\
&current = \varnothing\\
&1 = exptag \neq tag = 0\\
&msgitems = \langle \rangle\\
&ackitems = \langle \rangle
\end{aligned}
$$

and hence condition (1) holds.

Induction step We first observe that if any one of the three conditions is true and any of the operations *loseMsg*, *rejMsg*, *loseAck* or *rejAck* is applicable and occurs, the condition remains true as the only consequence is that the head of the message or acknowledgment channel is removed. Furthermore, if the operation *retrans* occurs, the conjunct involving *msgitems* is preserved (only conditions (2) and (3) apply and the item in *current*, viz. (tag, m), is appended to *msgitems*) and, as nothing else is affected, the condition remains true.

Similarly, if *transAck* occurs, the conjunct involving *ackitems* is preserved (in conditions (1) and (3) *tag* is appended, and in condition (2) $1 - tag$ is appended) and, as nothing else is affected, the condition remains true. Hence, to prove the induction step, we only need to consider the operations *transMsg*, *accMsg* and *accAck*. (It will be seen that these operations cause the protocol to cycle.) The proof then reduces to three cases, one for each of the conditions being true.

- Condition (1) is true. As $msgsitems = \langle \rangle$ or the tag of its tagged messages is *tag* $(\neq exptag)$, operation *accMsg* is inapplicable. Also, as *current* is empty, *accAck* is inapplicable. Hence only *transMsg* need be considered. If *transMsg* occurs,

$$msgsin' = msgsin \frown \langle m? \rangle$$
$$msgsout' = msgsout$$
$$current' = \{(tag', m?)\} = \{(tag', m')\}$$
$$tag' = 1 - tag$$
$$exptag' = exptag$$
$$msgitems' = msgitems \frown \langle (tag', m') \rangle$$
$$ackitems' = ackitems$$
$$m' = m?$$

and hence condition (2) is now true (in primed form and taking k in the quantification to be #*msgitems'*).

- Condition (2) is true. As *current* is non-empty, *transMsg* is inapplicable. Also, as ran *ackitems* $\subseteq \{1 - tag\}$, the operation *accAck* is inapplicable. Hence only *accMsg* need be considered.

The operation *accMsg* is applicable only if *msgitems* $\neq \langle \rangle$ and $k = 1$, as in this case $first(head\ msgitems) = tag = exptag$. If *accMsg* occurs,

$$msgsin' = msgsin$$
$$msgsout' = msgsout \frown \langle m! \rangle \quad (= msgsin)$$
$$current' = current$$
$$tag' = tag$$
$$exptag' = 1 - exptag$$
$$msgitems' = tail\ msgitems$$
$$ackitems' = ackitems$$
$$m! = m \ \wedge \ m' = m$$

It follows that *msgsin'* = *msgsout'* and condition (3) is now true (in primed form and taking *k* in the quantification to be any integer greater than #*ackitems'*).

- Condition (3) is true. As *current* is non-empty, *transMsg* is inapplicable. Also, *accMsg* is inapplicable as ran *msgitems* ⊆ {(*tag*, *m*)}, i.e. the tag of any item of *msgitems* is *tag*, and *exptag* ≠ *tag*. Hence only *accAck* need be considered.

The operation *accAck* is applicable only if *ackitems* ≠ ⟨⟩ and *k* = 1, as in this case *head ackitems* = *tag*. If *accAck* occurs,

$$msgsin' = msgsin$$
$$msgsout' = msgsout$$
$$current' = \varnothing$$
$$exptag' = exptag$$
$$tag' = tag$$
$$msgitems' = msgitems$$
$$ackitems' = tail\ ackitems$$
$$m' = m$$

and hence condition (1) is now true.

□

Figure 7.2 illustrates the cyclic behaviour of the alternating-bit protocol on which the above proof is based. The operations *transMsg*, *accMsg* and *accAck* which effect the cyclic transitions are interposed with operations which do not change the state. The preconditions of operations are not shown.

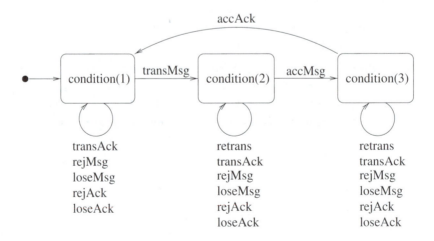

Figure 7.2: state diagram of the alternating-bit protocol

Discussion

The strategy applied here in proving partial correctness of the alternating-bit protocol can be applied in general when proving a property to be invariant. First, the system is analysed to extract its key behavioural properties. Next, auxiliary and secondary variables are introduced as required to reference quantities needed to formulate and prove a proposition. Finally, the proposition is shown to be invariant using structural induction.

The proof of correctness of the alternating-bit protocol illustrates that to formulate and prove a proposition may be complex and require a detailed analysis of the system and its behaviour. Because of this complexity and potential tedium, the issue arises as to whether the proof is correct. Although errors in a proof are possible, the discipline of formal proof greatly increases confidence in the specification. Standard inferences can be confirmed automatically by proof-checking software. As important as such an aid can be in managing the complexity of proofs, automation cannot (currently) replace the detailed system analysis upon which the formulation of suitable invariant predicates is based.

7.4   Safety and liveness

The proofs in Sections 7.2 and 7.3 are both concerned with safety issues, i.e. with proving that certain undesirable things do not happen. In Section 7.2 for example, we proved that the two tic tac toe players cannot both win the game; in Section 7.3 we proved that the alternating-bit protocol guarantees that the stream of messages received is the same as the stream transmitted, without loss, replication or permutation, except for a possible delay of one message. In other words, the proofs are to do with correctness — if the system does anything, it does it correctly.

What has not been addressed in either proof is the issue of liveness — verifying that the system makes progress. In fact as specified, liveness cannot be verified. The specification of the game of tic tac toe does not force a player to move — a player could walk away from an unfinished game and it would be without result. Similarly, the specification of the alternating-bit protocol allows the message and acknowledgment channels to lose everything, in which case no progress is made.

Although the specifications of tic tac toe and the alternating-bit protocol do not guarantee progress, in each case progress is possible. The specification of tic tac toe does not prevent a player from moving provided it is the player's turn and the game is not over. For the alternating-bit protocol, one sequence of operations which results in all messages being conveyed correctly is illustrated in the basic protocol cycle of Figure 6.8.

To guarantee progress, a specification needs to capture liveness explicitly: in the case of tic tac toe, it must be specified that valid operation sequences terminate in *gameResult*; in the case of the alternating-bit protocol, it must be specified that messages or acknowledgments repeatedly sent are eventually received. Such progress considerations are outside the scope of this book.

Polymorphic inheritance hierarchies **8**

8.1 Introduction

So far we have applied inheritance principally as a mechanism for code sharing. In this chapter we consider the wider role of inheritance in the construction of polymorphic class hierarchies that capture common structural and behavioural properties.

Commercial object-oriented programming languages, such as Java, Eiffel and C++, define polymorphism on the subclass hierarchies induced by class inheritance. The reasons for this are partly historic and partly pragmatic: the mechanism of inheritance facilitates code reuse by adaptation of an existing class, and the collection comprising the original (root) class and its subclasses is a useful basis for polymorphism, particularly if the types and signatures of the root's features are preserved in the subclasses. Polymorphism supports *dynamic binding* whereby the actual class of an instance (object) of a polymorphic type is resolved at 'run time', i.e. the specific class cannot be determined statically.

As we saw in Sections 1.9 and 1.10, Object-Z also defines a mechanism for polymorphism based on class inheritance hierarchies. A polymorphic declaration of the form $a : \downarrow A$ indicates that the value of the variable a identifies an object in one of the classes of the hierarchy consisting of A and all its subclasses. The type $\downarrow A$ is well defined if and only if the inheritance hierarchy with root class A satisfies the requirements of signature compatibility as discussed in Section 1.10, i.e. each visible feature of A is visible in every subclass, and for each operation visible in A, its communication variables in any subclass are the same as its communication variables in A. An inheritance hierarchy satisfying signature compatibility is said to be polymorphic.

In an Object-Z specification, there is no notion of run time: polymorphism facilitates type declarations that allow an object to belong to any one of a given collection of classes.

In this chapter, aspects of polymorphic inheritance hierarchies are explored further through an example based on a hierarchy of classes defining various planar geometric shapes. Particular shapes such as circles and squares are defined by inheriting and specialising more general shapes. Objects of these shape classes are then used polymorphically to construct and manipulate composite figures. This example also illustrates multiple inheritance in Object-Z.

8.2   Geometric shapes: a case study

This case study is concerned with specifying some of the various basic geometric shapes that might be found in the palette of a software drawing package: the inheritance class hierarchy to be constructed is illustrated in Figure 8.1.

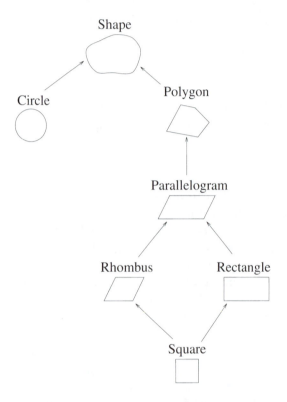

Figure 8.1: geometric shapes inheritance hierarchy

There are various ways in which the geometric shapes in this figure could be specified. One possible approach is to specify a shape in terms of its boundary, or in the case of a polygon, in terms of its vertices. Another possible approach is to define a shape by specifying the set of points it occupies in the plane. Our approach will be to specify each shape in terms of basic information sufficient for a software drawing package to construct and display the shape at a specified position in a window. For example, a circle can be specified by stipulating its radius and the position of its centre. This information would be sufficient for the drawing package to create an appropriate pixel map and display an image of the circle in a window. In this case study we will not concern ourselves with the low-level details of how such pixel maps can be created and displayed, rather our concern will be with specifying appropriate abstractions from which such displays can be constructed, and capturing within an inheritance hierarchy the logical inter-relationships between these abstractions.

Underlying concepts

The notion of a vector in the plane will be needed to define geometric shapes. Informally, a vector as defined here is an arrow starting at the origin; it can be modelled as an ordered pair of real numbers, corresponding to the end point of the vector:

$Vector == \mathbb{R} \times \mathbb{R}.$

The following declarations introduce some standard vector operators:

$|\_|$: $Vector \rightarrow \mathbb{R}$
$vecrot : \mathbb{R} \rightarrow (Vector \rightarrow Vector)$
$\_ + \_ : (Vector \times Vector) \rightarrow Vector$
$\_ \perp \_ : Vector \leftrightarrow Vector$
$\mathbf{O} : Vector$

$\mathbf{O} = (0,0)$

other details omitted

For any vector v, $|v|$ denotes the magnitude of the vector; $vecrot(\theta)$ applied to vector v rotates it anti-clockwise through angle θ. For any two vectors v and w, $v + w$ is their vector sum, and $v \perp w$ if and only if v and w are perpendicular. $\mathbf{O}$ denotes the zero vector. These vector operators are standard and their definitions can be found in any text on coordinate geometry.

A general shape

Class *Shape*, the root of the hierarchy, is specified in Figure 8.2. The primary attribute *position* denotes the position of the shape with respect to the origin. As we shall see when the subclasses of *Shape* are defined, for particular shapes *position* denotes the position of some point of interest of the shape. The secondary variable *perim* denotes the strictly positive length of the shape's perimeter. This variable is secondary as its value will be uniquely determined for a particular shape by the shape's primary attributes. No initial values are specified.

Operation *translate* translates *position* by vector v?. The intent is that the entire shape is rigidly translated by the same amount, with *position* referring to the same point of interest after translation. Operation *rotate* corresponds to a rotation of the shape by angle θ? leaving *position* unchanged. Again, the intent is that the entire shape is rigidly rotated by θ? about the same point of

```
┌─ Shape ──────────────────────────────────────────────────────────────┐
│                                                                        │
│   ┌──────────────────────────────────────────────────────────────┐    │
│   │ position : Vector                                             │    │
│   │ Δ                                                             │    │
│   │ perim : ℝ                                                     │    │
│   ├──────────────────────────────────────────────────────────────┤    │
│   │ perim > 0                                                     │    │
│   └──────────────────────────────────────────────────────────────┘    │
│                                                                        │
│   ┌─ translate ──────────────────┐   ┌─ rotate ─────────────────┐      │
│   │ Δ(position)                  │   │ θ? : ℝ                   │      │
│   │ v? : Vector                  │   └──────────────────────────┘      │
│   ├──────────────────────────────┤                                     │
│   │ position′ = position + v?    │                                     │
│   └──────────────────────────────┘                                     │
│                                                                        │
└────────────────────────────────────────────────────────────────────────┘
```

Figure 8.2: the class *Shape*

interest. For both operations, it remains for the subclasses to ensure that the intent is achieved.

The class *Shape* is like a deferred, or abstract, class in an object-oriented programming language as its role is to specify the basic features common to all shapes in the hierarchy. Abstract classes in these languages have no instances, i.e. no objects of such classes exist, as the code is usually incomplete. In contrast, in formal specification there is no need to prohibit the existence of objects of classes such as *Shape*: their semantics are well defined.

Interpreting the class *Shape* in the context of a software drawing package, the attribute *position* would be used by the package to determine where in the window to display the shape. The additional information to enable the package to construct a pixel map and display the shape is supplied in specific subclasses. In a drawing package there may well be other operations, e.g. to scale the figure: such operations are not specified here. Although an attribute *perim* would not normally be associated with shapes drawn by a software package, it is introduced into the specification to highlight certain aspects of polymorphic inheritance hierarchies.

A circle

The class *Shape* is inherited to derive classes for more specific shapes, the first example being class *Circle* in Figure 8.3. To illustrate the effect of inheritance, Figure 8.4 is the expansion of class *Circle*. *Circle* inherits *Shape* with *position* renamed to *centre*. The two primary attributes, *centre* (introduced by renaming) and *radius* (introduced by explicit declaration), are the conventional descriptors for defining a positioned circle.

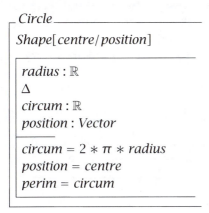

Figure 8.3: the class *Circle*

Figure 8.4: the expansion of class *Circle*

Notice that the attribute *position*, although renamed on inheritance, is reintroduced as secondary: its reintroduction ensures signature compatibility, as required for inheritance-based polymorphism.

Signature compatibility in Object-Z — defined in Section 1.10 — requires that any attribute declared in the root class must also be declared, and have the same type, in each subclass. Consequently, if an inheritance hierarchy is to be used polymorphically, an attribute *a* declared in the root class but renamed *b* in a subclass must be declared afresh in the subclass as a secondary variable, and the condition *a* = *b* inserted into the class invariant. In effect, *a* is a synonym for *b* in the subclass. Hence in this case *position* and *centre* are synonymous, as are *perim* and *circum*.

Operations *translate* and *rotate* are inherited subject to the renaming of the variable *position*. As *radius* is not in either operation's Δ-list, neither operation changes its value.

Notice that the operation *rotate* has no affect on the attributes of a circle, capturing the idea that a circle is unchanged by rotations about its centre.

A polygon

Class *Polygon* inherits *Shape* with *position* renamed to *start*, and extends (by conjunction) the operation *rotate*:

```
┌─ Polygon ──────────────────────────────────────────────
│ Shape[start / position]
│ ┌──────────────────────────────────────────────────────
│ │ edges : seq Vector
│ │ Δ
│ │ position : Vector
│ ├──────────────────────────────────────────────────────
│ │ #edges ⩾ 3
│ │ O ∉ ran edges
│ │ (∑ i : dom edges • edges(i)) = O
│ │ perim = ∑ i : dom edges • | edges(i) |
│ │ position = start
│ └──────────────────────────────────────────────────────
│
│ ┌─ rotate ──────────────────────────────────────────────
│ │ Δ(edges)
│ ├──────────────────────────────────────────────────────
│ │ edges' = edges ⨾ vecrot(θ?)
│ └──────────────────────────────────────────────────────
└────────────────────────────────────────────────────────
```

Polygon defines a shape in terms of a finite sequence *edges* of at least three non-zero vectors which sum to zero (see Figure 8.5) with attribute *perim* defined as the sum of the magnitudes of the edge vectors. Attribute *position* is reintroduced as secondary to maintain polymorphism: *position* and *start* are synonymous.

In order to understand the specification, the informal relationship between the conceptual mathematical model (the specification) and the perceptual real-world view (Figure 8.5) needs to be asserted. In this case, the understanding is that the edges of the polygon are represented by the vector sequence which commences at *start*. Effectively, the polygon is being specified in terms of its vertices, where the position of the vertices is specified relative to a distinguished vertex identified by *start*.

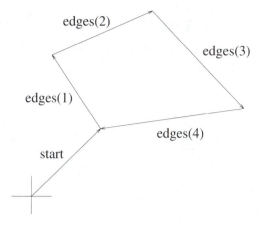

Figure 8.5: a polygon

As the operation *rotate* is inherited, the definition in *Polygon* is conjoined with that defined in *Shape*. The predicate of the operation ensures that each edge is rotated by the same given angle: the forward functional composition is logically equivalent to:

dom *edges'* = dom *edges*
$\forall\, i :$ dom *edges* • *edges'*(i) = *vecrot*$(\theta?)(edges(i))$

Thus, as *start* is unchanged, the polygon is rigidly rotated about the distinguished vertex.

Operation *translate* is inherited subject to the renaming of the variable *position*.

A parallelogram

Class *Parallelogram* inherits *Polygon* and adds the conditions that the number of edges is four and that the first and third edges sum to zero, i.e. are equal in magnitude and opposite in direction. (This condition implies that the second and fourth edges also sum to zero.)

```
┌─ Parallelogram ─────────────────
│ Polygon
│ ┌───────────────────────────────
│ │ #edges = 4
│ │ edges(1) + edges(3) = O
│ └───────────────────────────────
└─────────────────────────────────
```

The next two classes, *Rhombus* and *Rectangle*, each inherit *Parallelogram*.

A rhombus

Objects of class *Rhombus* are parallelograms which have their first and second edges of equal magnitude. (This condition implies that all four edges have equal magnitude.)

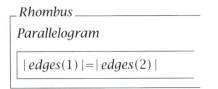

```
┌─ Rhombus ─────────────────
│ Parallelogram
│ ┌──────────────────────────
│ │ | edges(1) | = | edges(2) |
│ └──────────────────────────
└──────────────────────────────
```

A rectangle

Objects of class *Rectangle* are parallelograms with their first and second edges perpendicular. (This condition implies that all adjacent edges are perpendicular.)

```
┌─ Rectangle ───────────────
│ Parallelogram
│ ┌──────────────────────────
│ │ edges(1) ⊥ edges(2)
│ └──────────────────────────
└──────────────────────────────
```

A square

The final class in the hierarchy, *Square*, multiply inherits classes *Rhombus* and *Rectangle*, i.e. a square object has the properties of both a rhombus and a rectangle object.

```
┌─ Square ───────────────
│ Rhombus
│ Rectangle
└────────────────────────
```

Conjoining the features of the two inherited classes and simplifying the resulting predicates gives the expansion of *Square* in Figure 8.6.

Multiple inheritance, as illustrated by *Square*, conjoins the features inherited from both of the classes (see Section 1.9). In particular, identically named attributes must have identical declarations. If identically named features arise unintentionally, i.e. the variables or operations are distinct semantically, default conjunction can be avoided by renaming upon inheritance.

A composite figure

The shapes hierarchy can be used to specify a composite figure. The class shown in Figure 8.7 specifies such a figure as a set of polymorphic shapes. Secondary attribute *totalperim* is the sum of the individual perimeters of the

$start : Vector$
$edges : \text{seq } Vector$
Δ
$perim : \mathbb{R}$
$position : Vector$

$\#edges = 4$
$\mathbf{O} \notin \text{ran } edges$
$(\sum i : 1 .. 4 \bullet edges(i)) = \mathbf{O}$
$edges(1) + edges(3) = \mathbf{O}$
$|edges(1)| = |edges(2)|$
$edges(1) \perp edges(2)$
$perim = \sum i : 1 .. 4 \bullet |edges(i)|$
$position = start$

_translate_____   _rotate_____
$\Delta(start)$ $\Delta(edges)$
$v? : Vector$ $\theta? : \mathbb{R}$

$start' = start + v?$ $edges' = edges \, \begin{subarray}{c}\circ\\\circ\end{subarray} \, vecrot(\theta?)$

Figure 8.6: the expansion of class _Square_

_Figure_____

$shapes : \mathbb{P} \downarrow Shape$
Δ
$totalperim : \mathbb{R}$

$totalperim = \sum s : shapes \bullet s.perim$

$translateOne \ \widehat{=} \ [\, s? : shapes \,] \bullet s?.translate$

$rotateOne \ \widehat{=} \ [\, s? : shapes \,] \bullet s?.rotate$

$translateAll \ \widehat{=} \ \bigwedge s : shapes \bullet s.translate$

$rotateAll \ \widehat{=} \ \bigwedge s : shapes \bullet s.rotate$

Figure 8.7: the class _Figure_

constituent shapes. The shapes can be of any class in the shapes hierarchy: *s.perim* is interpreted according to the class of *s*, e.g. if *s* denotes a circle, *s.perim* has the value of *s.circum*.

Operation *translateOne* translates a nominated shape (*s?*) in *shapes*; similarly, *rotateOne* rotates a nominated shape. Operation *translateOne* applies the *translate* operation corresponding to the actual class of *s?*, e.g. if *s?* denotes a circle, *s?.centre* and therefore also *s?.position* undergo the translation. Despite the different definitions of *translate*, the operation has the same interface in all subclasses: this is necessary as *translateOne* can involve any shape. Similar considerations apply to *rotateOne*.

Operation *translateAll* is defined in terms of distributed conjunction; it translates every constituent shape in *shapes* by the same specified amount. Similarly for *rotateAll*.

8.3   Discussion

The class of an object

In the semantics of Object-Z, each object is an instance of its class and no other class. Hence an object of the class *Polygon* is not an object of the class *Rectangle*, even if it satisfies the state conditions for a rectangle. In this case, any operation defined for a rectangle but not for a general polygon cannot be applied to the object. Similarly, if an object is an instance of the class *Rectangle* it is not an object of the class *Polygon* even though it satisfies the state conditions for a polygon.

Roles of polymorphic inheritance hierarchies

When engineering software systems, polymorphic inheritance hierarchies play two distinct roles. The first is to do with class development within existing hierarchies, the second is to do with the construction of new hierarchies.

With respect to the first role, most commercial software development environments for object-oriented programming languages, such as Smalltalk, Eiffel or Java, come supplied with a comprehensive library of classes that facilitate software development through reuse based on inheritance and polymorphism. These libraries are usually divided into inheritance hierarchies corresponding to their purpose, e.g. there may be a hierarchy of collection classes for handling aggregates of objects, or a hierarchy of graphics classes for displaying objects within windows. Typically, a software engineer creates new classes that either contain instances of these library classes or extend the library hierarchies. In formal specification, this type of reuse is limited. Although Object-Z uses the standard Z library of mathematical notation for functions, relations, etc. such mathematical entities are not classes and notation reuse is not akin to inheritance or instantiation. It is possible to create specifications of collection classes that could be reused when creating new specifications involving aggregates of objects, but it is doubtful if these classes would be of such benefit to the specifier as the collection and other coded library classes are to the programmer.

With respect to the second role, however, the construction of new inheritance hierarchies is an important part of the specification of any system. Placing classes correctly into an appropriate inheritance hierarchy is a task best performed after an initial specification has been completed, as only then can the relationships between the classes be observed. Creating a suitable hierarchy usually involves modifying existing classes and creating new root classes that extract common features. Often, however, forcing classes into a polymorphic inheritance hierarchy can be counter-intuitive. An alternative approach to polymorphism is discussed in Chapter 9.

Subclass vs. subtype

The consistency of interface implied by signature compatibility does not ensure that the effect of the same-named operations in a hierarchy is uniform. As an illustration, suppose the *translate* operation had only its interface specified in the class *Shape*, with different resolutions of *translate* defined in different subclasses, e.g. circles might translate by $2 * v?$ and polygons by $v?$. This would clearly be possible even if counter-intuitive: compound figures would change their configuration on translation.

Some object-oriented implementation languages go beyond signature compatibility when defining polymorphism. Eiffel for example, imposes a form of behavioural compatibility (subtyping) on inheritance hierarchies, whereby the behaviour of a subclass is related to the behaviour of the superclass: explicitly stated pre- and post-conditions of an operation defined in a superclass are weakened or strengthened respectively in any subclass. No such restrictions are placed on polymorphic inheritance hierarchies in Object-Z. The role of signature compatibility in Object-Z is to ensure that any message that can be sent to an object of a class C, say, can also be sent to an object of any subclass of C — no other restrictions are placed on the behaviour of the object.

Class union $\mathbf{9}$

9.1 Introduction

The need arises when specifying some object-oriented systems for a form of polymorphism involving objects whose classes have little in common and therefore do not fit easily within an inheritance hierarchy. A typical example is a system which contains a set of disparate objects: often expressions involving objects in the set, regardless of their class, need to be formulated.

The class union mechanism discussed in this chapter enables such sets to be specified without the need to first create artificial inheritance hierarchies. Class unions, like polymorphic inheritance hierarchies, relax the strict typing of objects by allowing a variable to be declared as an object of some class in a given collection of classes.

9.2 Defining class union

Each object in an Object-Z specification has a unique, persistent identity that distinguishes it from every other object, regardless of class. If A is the name of a class, the identifier A denotes the set of all identities of objects of class A. In any system being specified, let $\mathbb{O}$ denote the universe of all object identities, regardless of class. For example, if $a : A$ then the value of a will be an element in A and hence in $\mathbb{O}$. Similarly, if $sa : \mathbb{P} A$, the value of sa will be a subset of A and hence a subset of $\mathbb{O}$.

If A and B are distinct classes in a system,

$$A \subseteq \mathbb{O}, \ B \subseteq \mathbb{O} \text{ and } A \cap B = \varnothing$$

Subsets of $\mathbb{O}$ can be formed by the union of sets of object identities, e.g. $A \cup B$ is a collection of object identities in $\mathbb{O}$. If we define $C == A \cup B$ then C is a *class union*; it is not itself a class — it is a set of object identities.

Given a class union such as C above, it can be used in defining other class unions; e.g. $D == C \cup E$, where E is a class or class union, defines D to be a class union. Notice, however, that every class union can be ultimately reduced to a union of underlying classes: this collection of classes is the *basis* of the class union.

9.3 Polymorphic core

Given a class union, an attribute *att* is *polymorphic with respect to the class union* if and only if every class in the basis of the union has an associated attribute *att* typed identically. Similarly, an operation *op* is polymorphic with respect to the class union if and only if:

- every class in the basis of the union has an operation *op*; and

- for each class in the basis of the union, the communication variables of operation *op* are the same, i.e. the input and output variables are identically named and typed.

The set of attributes and operations that are polymorphic with respect to a class union is the *polymorphic core* of the union. Thus, features in the core can be referenced polymorphically with respect to objects of that union type.

Polymorphism with respect to a class union is therefore similar to signature compatibility as discussed in Section 1.10 and is introduced for the same reason: it establishes a minimal condition under which a term *ob.x*, where *ob* is declared to be in a class union and feature *x* is in the polymorphic core of that union, can be interpreted regardless of the actual class of *ob*.

There are differences, however, between a class union and the classes in a polymorphic class hierarchy. In class union, there is no insistence that a feature with a name that is common to the classes in the union must be in the polymorphic core; i.e. collections are permitted where common-named attributes are not identically typed, or where common-named operations have distinct communication variables.

Furthermore, there need not be a distinguished class — in the collection — whose features form the polymorphic core of the collection, i.e. there need not exist the equivalent of the root class associated with inheritance hierarchies.

Within a specification declaring *ob* to be of class-union type, a term *ob.x* is well formed (statically valid) if *x* is a feature of at least one of the classes in the union. Furthermore, if *x* is in the polymorphic core of the union, the term *ob.x* can always be interpreted semantically, the interpretation depending on *ob*'s actual class.

However, if *x* is not in the polymorphic core, the term can be interpreted only if it appears within a *qualified* expression where *ob* is restricted to be of a class having *x* as a defined feature. This is demonstrated in the examples in the next two sections. These simple examples illustrate the use of class union to declare union types and define polymorphic operations.

9.4 Ginger Meggs: an example

Ginger Meggs, an Australian cartoon character, is a mischievous young boy whose pocket is often crammed with various bits and pieces such as marbles, string, etc. This treasure is constantly being collected and discarded. Objects can be manipulated, e.g. marbles can be polished, string can be knotted, and so on. Let *Treasure* be the class union

$$Treasure == Marble \cup String$$

where *Marble* and *String* are the following classes:

```
┌─ Marble ──────────────────────
│ ┌─────────────────────────────
│ │ diameter : ℕ
│ └─────────────────────────────
│ ┌─ polish ────────────────────
│ │ [details omitted]
│ └─────────────────────────────
└───────────────────────────────
```

```
┌─ String ──────────────────────
│ ┌─────────────────────────────
│ │ length : ℕ
│ └─────────────────────────────
│ ┌─ knot ──────────────────────
│ │ [details omitted]
│ └─────────────────────────────
└───────────────────────────────
```

Using this class union, a specification of Ginger Meggs might look like:

```
┌─ GingerMeggs ─────────────────────────────────────────
│ ┌───────────────────────────────────
│ │ pocket : ℙ Treasure
│ └───────────────────────────────────
│ ┌─ collect ───────────────────        ┌─ discard ──────────────────
│ │ Δ(pocket)                           │ Δ(pocket)
│ │ tr? : Treasure                      │ tr? : Treasure
│ ├─────────────────────                ├────────────────────
│ │ tr? ∉ pocket                        │ tr? ∈ pocket
│ │ pocket' = pocket ∪ {tr?}            │ pocket' = pocket \ {tr?}
│ └─────────────────────                └────────────────────
│
│ polishMarble ≙ [ tr? : pocket | tr? ∈ Marble ] • tr?.polish
│
│ knotString ≙ [ tr? : pocket | tr? ∈ String ] • tr?.knot
└───────────────────────────────────────────────────────
```

The attribute *pocket* is a set of class-union type: each element of *pocket* is a reference to an object of either the *Marble* or *String* class.

The operations *collect* and *discard* can accept any treasure, but the operations *polishMarble* and *knotString* can only accept treasures of the appropriate class. The terms *tr?.polish* and *tr?.knot* are qualified as they appear within expressions where the class of *tr?* is restricted to ensure that the terms can be interpreted. Qualification is needed as the operations *polish* and *knot* are not in the polymorphic core of the class union *Treasure*. In fact, the polymorphic core of *Treasure* is empty.

As specified, Ginger Meggs can only have marbles and string in his pocket. To enable worms and other treasure to be collected, the type of *pocket* would need to be extended, e.g. by redefining

Treasure == *Marble* ∪ *String* ∪ *Worm*,

where class *Worm* contains specific operations for worms (the precise nature of which is left to the reader's imagination).

If *Treasure* is so extended, the operations *collect* and *discard* as previously specified can be interpreted with respect to the extended *Treasure*. However, qualified worm operations of the form

[*tr?* : *pocket* | *tr?* ∈ *Worm*] • *tr?*. · · ·

would need to be added to the class to enable Ginger Meggs (technically, an object of class *GingerMeggs*) to perform an operation on a nominated worm in his pocket.

In general, a class-union type can be extended without affecting existing specifications using that type provided the extended type has the same polymorphic core as the original class-union type, as then unqualified terms of the form *ob.x* where *x* is a feature in the polymorphic core can still be interpreted.

Defining *Treasure* as a class union when specifying Ginger Meggs is appropriate as there seems to be no a-priori inheritance class structure that would include classes as distinct as *Marble*, *String* and *Worm*. Certainly any such inheritance hierarchy would not be polymorphic as defined in Section 1.10.

9.5   A communications channel: an example

One kind of polymorphism supported by essentially all programming languages is function and operator overloading. In procedural languages the assignment operator is polymorphic: it supports the assignment of the value of a boolean expression to a boolean variable, the value of an integer expression to an integer variable, etc. The following simple (and somewhat unrealistic) example is based on this idea.

Classes *Nat* and *Bool* are defined in Figure 9.1. The behaviour of objects of these classes is completely different: the interface and functionality of even the common-named operations *update* and *val* are different. However, consider the use of the class union

NatBool == *Nat* ∪ *Bool*

in the definition of the class *Channel* in Figure 9.1.

The attributes *sender* and *receiver* are declared to be references to objects in either the *Nat* or *Bool* classes. The class invariant, however, places upon the values of these attributes the restriction that they be in the same class.

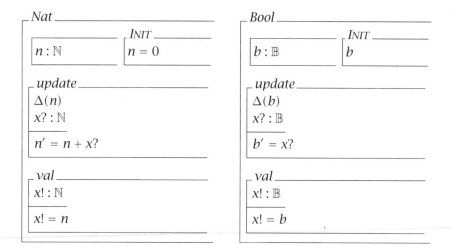

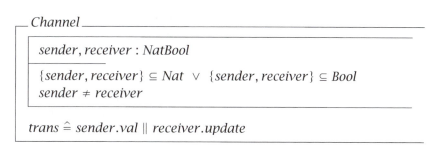

Figure 9.1: classes *Nat*, *Bool* and *Channel*

The polymorphic core of *NatBool* is empty, for although operations *update* and *val* occur in both *Nat* and *Bool*, the communication variables of these operations differ between the classes. Despite this, the operation *trans* can still be interpreted polymorphically: the class invariant ensures *sender* and *receiver* are in the same class and therefore the output (*x!*) from the sender will have the same type as the input (*x?*) to the receiver.

9.6   A telephone system: a case study

This case study develops a specification of a greatly simplified telephone system consisting of a collection of phones that each conform to the core operations of making and breaking connections, but which can exhibit quite different functionality outside this core. The system consists of two types of phones: plain phones which can be involved in only one connection at a time, and call-waiting phones which can be involved in two connections simultaneously. The specification given here uses class union to declare phone objects that can be either of the two types of phone. This approach is compared and contrasted with the traditional approach using polymorphic inheritance hierarchies.

Informal description

- A phone system consists of a collection of plain and call-waiting phones. The term 'phone' refers to either a plain or call-waiting phone.

- A plain phone can be connected to at most one other phone at any particular time, i.e. when connected, a plain phone cannot become involved in any other connection.

- A call-waiting phone, on the other hand, can be connected to one or two other phones at any particular time. However, if (and only if) it is connected to two phones, one of these connections is 'on hold' while the other is 'current'. Connection does not imply 'conversation': conversation between two phones is implied when the phones are connected to each other and neither has the other on hold. When a call-waiting phone has only one connection, it can accept a new connection: the new connection becomes the current connection, while the original connection is placed on hold. A call-waiting phone with one of its connections on hold may 'swap' its connections, placing the current connection on hold and making the on-hold connection current.

- A connection between two phones can be broken. The disconnection can only be instigated by a phone for which the connection is current, i.e. a call-waiting phone cannot disconnect a call it has on hold.

As a simplification, the detailed phases such as the ringing and answering of phones are not modelled: it is assumed that connection occurs immediately a call is successful.

The intention of the specification is to model the dynamic relationships between connections that can occur within a phone system consisting of both plain and call-waiting phones. The specification given here captures an abstract perceptual view of the phone system: it is not a specification of the implementation of the system.

A class union of phones

It is necessary to declare object references which may refer to objects (phones) of either class *PlainPhone* or *CallWaitingPhone*. Hence define the class union:

> *Phone* == *PlainPhone* ∪ *CallWaitingPhone*.

A plain phone

A plain phone is defined as an object of the class *PlainPhone*:

_PlainPhone_____

  _____ _INIT_____

  $current : \mathbb{P}\ Phone$ $current = \varnothing$

  _____

  $\#current \leqslant 1$
  $self \notin current$

  _requestConnection_____ _acceptConnection_____
  $\Delta(current)$ $\Delta(current)$
  $to? : Phone$ $from? : Phone$

  $current = \varnothing$ $current = \varnothing$
  $current' = \{to?\}$ $current' = \{from?\}$

  _disconnect_____
  $\Delta(current)$

  $current \neq \varnothing$
  $current' = \varnothing$

Attribute *current* is a set which is at most singleton: if empty, the plain phone is not connected, otherwise it contains the identity of the phone to which it is connected. The occurrence of *Phone* in the declaration of *current* may appear recursive as the definition of *Phone* includes *PlainPhone*. However, as a type, *Phone* is a set of object identities: *current* simply models the fact that a plain phone may reference another phone. The conjunct *self* $\notin$ *current* ensures that a plain phone is never connected to itself.

Operation *requestConnection* models an idle plain phone sending a connection request: the identity of the phone being called (*to?*) is placed in *current*. The communication variable is an input as it represents information that needs to be supplied by the environment before the operation can proceed.

Operation *acceptConnection* models an idle plain phone accepting a connection request: the identity of the calling phone (*from?*) is recorded in *current*.

Operation *disconnect* models a connected plain phone terminating its connection.

A call-waiting phone

The class *CallWaitingPhone* is specified in Figure 9.2. Like a plain phone, attribute *current* is a set which is at most singleton; if empty the call-waiting phone has no connections, otherwise it contains the identity of the connected phone which, in the case of two connections, is not on hold. The attribute *onhold* is also a set which is at most singleton; it is either empty or it contains the identity of the connected phone on hold. Notice that the invariant ensures that if the set *onhold* is non-empty, the set *current* is also non-empty, i.e. it

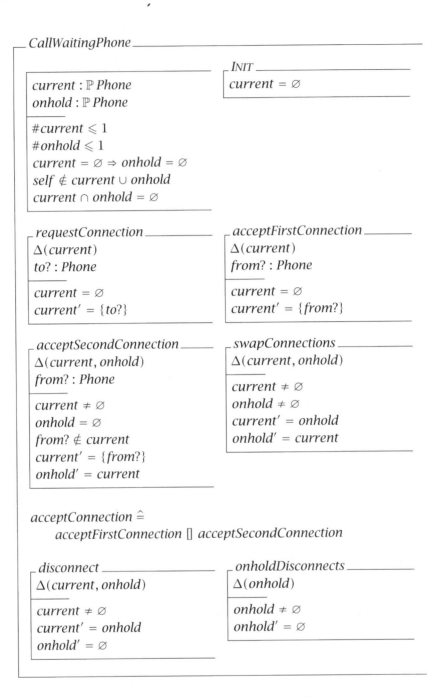

Figure 9.2: the class *CallWaitingPhone*

is not possible for a call-waiting phone to have a connection on hold if that is its only connection. Furthermore, the phone on hold is distinct from the current phone and neither can be *self*, i.e. a call-waiting phone, like a plain phone, cannot be connected to itself.

Operation *requestConnection* is similar to the same-named operation for a plain phone. Operation *acceptFirstConnection* models a call-waiting phone with no connections accepting a connection (the connection becomes the current connection). Operation *acceptSecondConnection* models a call-waiting phone with one connection accepting a new connection (the new connection becomes the current connection and the prior connection is put on hold). The *acceptConnection* operation is a choice between *acceptFirstConnection* and *acceptSecondConnection*. If a further connection is possible, exactly one of these two operations is applicable.

Operation *swapConnections* models a call-waiting phone with two connections swapping the connection on hold with the current connection, i.e. the connection previously on hold becomes the current connection and vice versa.

Operation *disconnect* removes the current connection. If there is a connection on hold it becomes the current connection; if not, the call-waiting phone becomes idle, i.e. has no connections.

Operation *onholdDisconnects* models the effect of its on-hold connection being disconnected by the held phone. The current connection is unaffected.

The phone system

The class *PhoneSystem* specifies a phone system as an aggregation of phones undergoing their various connections:

$$
\begin{array}{l}
\hline
\textit{PhoneSystem} \\
\hline
\begin{array}{l}
\textit{phones} : \mathbb{P}\ \textit{Phone}
\end{array}
\quad
\begin{array}{l}
\textit{INIT} \\
\hline
\forall\, p : \textit{phones} \bullet p.\textit{INIT}
\end{array} \\[4pt]
\hline
\textit{connect} \;\widehat{=}\; [\,\textit{from?}, \textit{to?} : \textit{phones}\,] \bullet \\
\qquad \textit{from?.requestConnection} \wedge \textit{to?.acceptConnection} \\[4pt]
\textit{swapConnections} \;\widehat{=}\; [\,p? : \textit{phones} \mid p? \in \textit{CallWaitingPhone}\,] \bullet \\
\qquad p?.\textit{swapConnections} \\[4pt]
\textit{disconnect} \;\widehat{=}\; [\,\textit{from?}, \textit{to} : \textit{phones} \mid \textit{to} \in \textit{from?.current}\,] \bullet \\
\qquad \textit{from?.disconnect} \\
\qquad \wedge \\
\qquad ([\,\textit{from?} \in \textit{to.current}\,] \wedge \textit{to.disconnect} \\
\qquad \;[\!] \\
\qquad [\,\textit{to} \in \textit{CallWaitingPhone}\,] \bullet \\
\qquad\qquad [\,\textit{from?} \in \textit{to.onhold}\,] \wedge \textit{to.onholdDisconnects}) \\
\hline
\end{array}
$$

Attribute *phones* is declared polymorphically to denote the set of all plain and call-waiting phones in the system. The polymorphic core of the class union *Phone* comprises the attribute *current* and the operations *requestConnection*, *acceptConnection* and *disconnect*.

Operation *connect* establishes the connection between the phones identified by *from?* and *to?*, regardless of their class, because the constituent operations *requestConnection* and *acceptConnection* are in *Phone*'s polymorphic core. The operation *connect* involves the phone *from?* requesting connection to the phone *to?* which is able to accept the connection. Communication variables *to?* and *from?* serve the dual role of identifying the phones to be connected at the system level and of supplying the information to record the connection in the individual phones.

Operation *swapConnections* is restricted to a call-waiting phone, so the identified phone (*p?*) is qualified to ensure this. The operation is the promotion of the same-named operation defined in the class *CallWaitingPhone*.

Operation *disconnect* captures the situation where the phone *from?* instigates the disconnection of its current connection. The identification of the currently connected phone (*to*) does not need to be an input from the environment as it can be deduced from the condition *to* ∈ *from?.current*. The operation disconnects the phones identified by *from?* and *to* regardless of their class because the consituent operation *disconnect* is in the polymorphic core. The choice construct and qualification [*to* ∈ *CallWaitingPhone*] ensure that *onholdDisconnects* is relevant only in the case when *to* is a call-waiting phone with *from?* on hold.

Discussion

Consider specifying the phone system without using class union. One approach would be to define *CallWaitingPhone* by inheriting *PlainPhone*, adding *onhold*, the extra state invariants and the two operations *swapConnections* and *onholdDisconnects*, and redefining the operation *acceptConnection*. The redefinition would be effected by renaming the inherited operation to something arbitrary (and not placing this renamed operation in the visibility list) and defining *acceptConnections* afresh in the subclass. The class union *Phone* could then be replaced by ↓*PlainPhone*.

Another approach would be to define *PlainPhone* by inheriting the class *CallWaitingPhone* and adding the invariant *onhold* = ∅, i.e. a plain phone can be considered to be a call-waiting phone that is permitted only one connection. Such an artificial hierarchy would have operations such as *swapConnections* being inapplicable only because the preconditions could never be satisfied.

A third approach would be to define an abstract *PHONE* superclass with both *PlainPhone* and *CallWaitingPhone* as subclasses. The skeleton of operations common to the subclasses would be lifted to the superclass, with the detail being left to the subclasses.

Although each of these approaches via a polymorphic inheritance hierarchy could work, they are best conceived only in hindsight, and each results in a rather artificial inheritance hierarchy. An implementation may well take one of these approaches as object-oriented programming languages are traditionally designed to facilitate polymorphic inheritance structures. Class union, on the other hand, offers a more direct and less artificial approach, and is particularly suitable for formal specification when the architectural design of the system is still evolving.

9.7 A mass transit railway: a case study

A mass transit railway system consists of a network of stations. To travel on the network, a passenger inserts a ticket into a station's entrance barrier and, provided the ticket is valid for entry, access to the network is given. The ticket is returned to the passenger after passing through the barrier. When the destination station is reached, the passenger inserts the same ticket into the station's exit barrier and this time, provided the ticket is valid for the trip just completed, exit is permitted. Again, after passing through the barrier the ticket is returned to the passenger.

Passengers can purchase several types of ticket: single-trip tickets, which are valid for one trip only on the day of purchase, multi-trip tickets, which are valid for any number of trips until the value of the ticket is exhausted, and season tickets, which are valid for any number of trips within a specified number of days.

The main purpose of this case study is to capture the functionality of the different ticket types. The approach taken is to specify ticket functionality from the point of view of a passenger, i.e. as perceived by an observer of the railway system. In order to do this, however, it is necessary to conceptualise and abstract various other objects in the system, such as the stations, a database to record the fare structure, and a clock to keep track of the days. In the specification, class union is used to define ticket types. As the various ticket types have quite different functionality and interfaces, placing them within a polymorphic inheritance hierarchy would be difficult: the class union mechanism, however, is ideal in this situation.

Informal description

- The mass transit railway network consists of a set of stations. For simplicity, it will be assumed this set is fixed, i.e. stations are neither added to nor removed from the network.

- The fare for a trip depends only upon the stations where the passenger joins and leaves the network, i.e. the actual route taken by the passenger when in the network is irrelevant. The fare structure can be updated from time to time.

- Three types of tickets can be purchased.

    Single-trip tickets permit only a single trip, and only on the day the ticket is purchased. The ticket has a value in the range $1 to $10, and the passenger is permitted to leave the network if and only if the fare for the trip just completed does not exceed the ticket's value.

    Multi-trip tickets are valid for any number of trips provided the current value of the ticket remains greater than zero. A ticket's initial value is either $50 or $100. Each time the passenger leaves the network the value of the ticket is reduced by the fare for the trip just completed.

If this fare exceeds the value remaining on the ticket, the passenger is still permitted to leave the network and the value of the ticket is set to zero. A multi-trip ticket expires after two years even if it has some remaining value.

Season tickets are valid either for a week, a month or a year. Within that period no restrictions whatsoever are placed upon the trips that can be undertaken.

- As tickets are expensive to produce, they can be reissued, i.e. tickets can have their expiry date and value reset. (The type of a ticket cannot be changed.)

Although tickets are issued to passengers, the essential interaction is between tickets and stations; thus passengers are not modelled.

A station

A station is modelled as an object of class *Station*: it has no attributes and only one operation, *supplyId*, which outputs the identity of the station to the environment.

```
┌─ Station ─────────────────────

│  ┌─ supplyId ──────────────────
│  │  station! : Station
│  ├──────────────────────────
│  │  station! = self
│  └──────────────────────────

└──────────────────────────────
```

A station's identity is supplied when a ticket is inserted into either its entrance or exit barrier. On entrance, the identity of the station is stored on the ticket so that on exit, the identity of the exit station can be combined with the identity of the entry station enabling the trip to be recorded for statistical purposes, and the fare to be calculated for single- and multi-trip tickets.

The central database of fares

Information about the network's fare structure is stored in a central database, as specified by the class *FareDataBase* in Figure 9.3. The attribute *fare* is a partial function denoting the cost in dollars of trips on the network: given any two stations s and f in the network, $fare(s, f)$ will be the cost (modelled as a natural number) of taking a trip from s to f. In practice, it may well be the case that $fare(s, f) = fare(f, s)$, i.e. the fare structure is symmetric, with the direction of travel not influencing the fare charged. Also, it could be expected that $fare(s, s) = 0$ for any station s, i.e. no cost is incurred if a passenger leaves the network at the point entered. However, as there is no reason to insist such properties hold, they are not stated as class invariants.

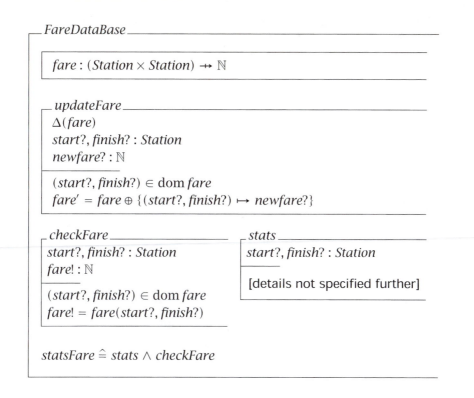

Figure 9.3: the class *FareDataBase*

The *INIT* schema has been omitted from this class, indicating that when a network first operates, no restrictions are placed on the possible fare structure.

Operation *updateFare* enables the fare structure to be modified: a new fare (*newfare?*) for the trip from station *start?* to station *finish?* can be inserted into the database.

Operation *checkFare* looks up the database and outputs the cost of a trip (*fare!*) from station *start?* to station *finish?*.

Operation *stats* is only partially specified. Its purpose is to enable information about a trip to be recorded by the database for statistical purposes: a description of the statistics collected is not relevant at this level of abstraction. As we shall see, for single- and multi-trip tickets the fare also must be calculated, so the operation *statsFare* conjoining *stats* and *checkFare* is required. However, for season tickets, only statistics need be collected, so only the operation *stats* is required on exit.

Features common to tickets

To specify the various ticket objects in the system, first the class *BaseTicket* (see Figure 9.4) capturing the features common to each type of ticket is defined, then specific ticket types are specified as subclasses. The attributes *value* and

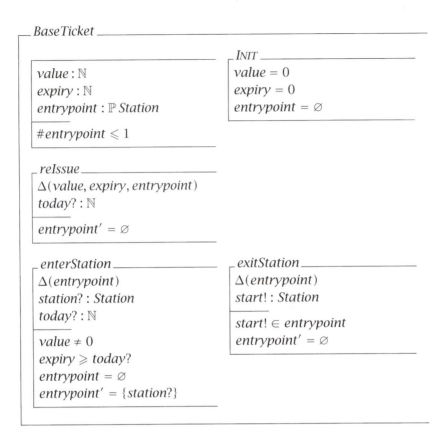

Figure 9.4: the class *BaseTicket*

expiry denote the current value and expiry date of the ticket respectively. To simplify the specification, dates will be modelled as natural numbers (see the class *Clock* below).

The attribute *entrypoint* is a set that is either empty or contains the identity of one station. If the set is empty, the ticket is inactive, i.e. it is not being used for a trip. If the set is not empty, the ticket is actively being used for a trip, in which case *entrypoint* contains the identity of the station where the ticket gained access to the network.

Initially, both *value* and *expiry* are zero and the ticket is inactive, i.e. the set *entrypoint* is empty.

The operation *reIssue* enables a ticket to be reissued (or even issued for the first time). The input (*today?*), denoting the date when the operation occurs, and the complete Δ-list are given, but the precise way attributes change will be specified when the subclasses denoting specific ticket types are defined. However, in all cases the ticket will be inactive (i.e. *entrypoint'* = ∅) after reissue. As specified here, a ticket can be reissued at any time, although normally a passenger would only present a ticket for reissuing when its current value has reached zero or when it has expired.

The operation *enterStation* models what happens when a ticket is inserted into a station's entrance barrier and given access to the network. To succeed, the ticket must have a non-zero value, have not yet expired (i.e. *expiry* ⩾ *today?*) and be inactive. The identity of the entrance station (*station?*) is stored on the ticket.

At the destination, the ticket is inserted into the exit barrier and permission to leave is granted only if the ticket is active (i.e. has an entry-point station's identity recorded in the set *entrypoint*). The ticket outputs the entry-point station (*start!*) and becomes inactive.

A single-trip ticket

$$\begin{array}{|l}
\hline
\_SingleTripTicket_____ \\
BaseTicket \\
\hline
SingleValue == 1 .. 10 \\
\hline
\begin{array}{|l}
\_reIssue\_\_\_\_ \\
\hline
value' \in SingleValue \\
expiry' = today? \\
\hline
\end{array}
\quad
\begin{array}{|l}
\_exitStation\_\_\_\_ \\
\Delta(value) \\
fare? : \mathbb{N} \\
\hline
fare? \leqslant value \\
value' = 0 \\
\hline
\end{array} \\
\hline
\end{array}$$

When reissued, a single-trip ticket is given a particular value in the range $1 to $10 as specified by the local type *SingleValue*. The expiry date is set to be the day of purchase, ensuring that the ticket is valid for entry to the network only on that day.

When leaving the network, the ticket is valid if and only if it has been activated (this condition is inherited) and the cost of the trip just completed does not exceed the ticket's purchased value. The value of the ticket is set to zero, ensuring that the ticket cannot be used again without being reissued.

A multi-trip ticket

$$\begin{array}{|l}
\hline
\_MultiTripTicket_____ \\
BaseTicket \\
\hline
MultiValue == \{50, 100\} \\
\hline
\begin{array}{|l}
\_reIssue\_\_\_\_ \\
\hline
value' \in MultiValue \\
expiry' - today? = 730 \\
\hline
\end{array}
\quad
\begin{array}{|l}
\_exitStation\_\_\_\_ \\
\Delta(value) \\
fare? : \mathbb{N} \\
\hline
value' = \\
\quad max\{0, value - fare?\} \\
\hline
\end{array} \\
\hline
\end{array}$$

When reissued, a multi-trip ticket is given a value of either $50 or $100 as specified by the local type *MultiValue*. The expiry date is set to be two years (730 days) from the date of purchase.

When leaving the network, the value of the ticket is reduced by the cost of the trip or set to zero, as specified by the predicate

$$value' = max\{0, value - fare?\}.$$

The inherited operation *enterStation* ensures that a ticket must have non-zero value to be granted access, but this value may be less than the cost of the trip to be undertaken; however, the operation *exitStation* will still succeed and the ticket's value will be set to zero (so that it cannot be used again unless reissued). Hence, when using a multi-trip ticket, if it is valid for entry it will be valid for exit.

A season ticket

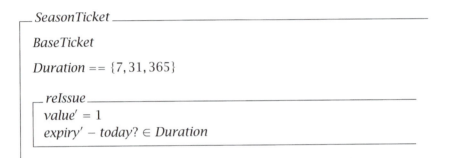

When reissued, a season ticket is given a nominal value of 1: this value is sufficient to gain entry and remains unchanged throughout the life of the ticket. The expiry date is set so that the ticket is valid for a week (7 days), a month (31 days) or a year (365 days), as specified by the local type *Duration*.

Class union of tickets

In order to specify declarations involving all ticket types, define the class unions

   TripTicket == *SingleTripTicket* ∪ *MultiTripTicket*

and

   Ticket == *TripTicket* ∪ *SeasonTicket*.

Both unions are required as we need to distinguish between single- or multi-trip tickets where the fare for each trip must be calculated, and season tickets where the fare for a trip is not relevant.

The clock

So as to maintain the date, the system has a clock that can output the current date (operation *supplyDate*) and increment the date at the beginning of each day (operation *newDay*).

```
┌─ Clock ──────────────────────────────────────────────────────────┐
│ ┌─────────────────────────────┐  ┌─ INIT ─────────────────────┐   │
│ │ date : ℕ                    │  │ date = 1                   │   │
│ └─────────────────────────────┘  └────────────────────────────┘   │
│ ┌─ supplyDate ────────────────┐  ┌─ newDay ───────────────────┐   │
│ │ today! : ℕ                  │  │ Δ(date)                    │   │
│ ├─────────────────────────────┤  ├────────────────────────────┤   │
│ │ today! = date               │  │ date′ = date + 1           │   │
│ └─────────────────────────────┘  └────────────────────────────┘   │
└───────────────────────────────────────────────────────────────────┘
```

The date is modelled as a natural number starting at 1, i.e. the attribute *date* in effect records the number of days the system has been in existence.

The mass transit railway

The mass transit railway specified in Figure 9.5 consists of a set of stations, a set of tickets, a database to record the fare structure, and a clock.

The attribute *tickets* is defined as a set of objects of any of the classes in the class union *Ticket*. Using this class union ensures that each ticket in the set is either a season ticket, a multi-trip ticket or a single-trip ticket, capturing the understanding that the class *BaseTicket* was introduced only as a common ancestor (i.e. *BaseTicket* is in effect a deferred class; no objects of this class exist in the system). In any case, a declaration *tickets* : $\mathbb{P} \downarrow BaseTicket$ would not be valid because the hierarchy is not polymorphic (see Section 1.10) as the interface of the operation *exitStation* varies between subclasses.

The class invariant

$$\text{dom } database.fare = stations \times stations$$

ensures that the partial function *fare* of the object *database* records the cost of a trip between two stations if and only if those stations are in the network. This implies that it is possible to enter or leave at any station in *stations*.

The operations *reIssueTicket* and *startTrip* are both polymorphic in that the class of the selected ticket object (*t?*) is not uniquely specified. Hence the effect of these operations will depend upon the actual class of *t?*. The resulting flow of information for these operations is graphically illustrated in Figure 9.6.

The operation *reIssueTicket* has the clock sending the current date (*today!*) to ticket *t?* which is reissued.

The operation *startTrip* models at the system level the effect of inserting a valid ticket (*t?*) into the entrance barrier of a station (*s?*).

The operation *tripTicketFinishTrip* models the effect of inserting a multi-trip or single-trip ticket (*t?*) into the exit barrier of a station (*s?*). The resulting

$\underline{\quad MassTransitRailway}\underline{\qquad\qquad\qquad\qquad\qquad\qquad\qquad}$

$\begin{array}{ll}
stations : \mathbb{P}\ Station \\
tickets : \mathbb{P}\ Ticket \\
database : FareDataBase \\
clock : Clock
\end{array}$
$\qquad\begin{array}{l}
\underline{INIT}\underline{\qquad\qquad\qquad} \\
\forall\ t : tickets \bullet t.INIT \\
clock.INIT
\end{array}$

$dom\ database.fare =$
      $stations \times stations$

$reIssueTicket \;\widehat{=}\; clock.supplyDate \parallel (\,[\,t? : tickets\,]\, \bullet t?.reIssue)$

$startTrip \;\widehat{=}\; clock.supplyDate \wedge (\,[\,s? : stations\,]\, \bullet s?.supplyId)$
        $\parallel$
        $(\,[\,t? : tickets\,]\, \bullet t?.enterStation)$

$finishStation \;\widehat{=}\; [\,s? : stations\,]\, \bullet s?.supplyId[\,finish!\,/\,station!\,]$

$tripTicketFinishTrip \;\widehat{=}$
    $finishStation \wedge$
          $(\,[\,t? : tickets \mid t? \in TripTicket\,]\, \bullet t?.exitStation)$
    $\parallel$
    $database.statsFare$

$seasonTicketFinishTrip \;\widehat{=}$
    $finishStation \wedge$
          $(\,[\,t? : tickets \mid t? \in SeasonTicket\,]\, \bullet t?.exitStation)$
    $\parallel$
    $database.stats$

$updateFare \;\widehat{=}\; database.updateFare$

$newDay \;\widehat{=}\; clock.newDay$

Figure 9.5: the class *MassTransitRailway*

flow of information for this operation is illustrated graphically in Figure 9.7. The parallel operator is used to model the bidirectional communication between the ticket and exit station on the one hand and the database on the other. By the semantics of $\parallel$, all inter-object communication is hidden.

The operation *seasonTicketFinishTrip* specifies what happens when a season ticket (*t?*) is inserted into the exit barrier of a station (*s?*). This operation is the promotion of the operation *exitStation* defined originally in the class *BaseTicket*, i.e. provided the ticket has been activated earlier at some entrance barrier, the operation will succeed, exit will be granted and the ticket will become inactive.

Finally, the operations *updateFare* and *newDay* promote the operations of the same names defined on the objects *database* and *clock* respectively.

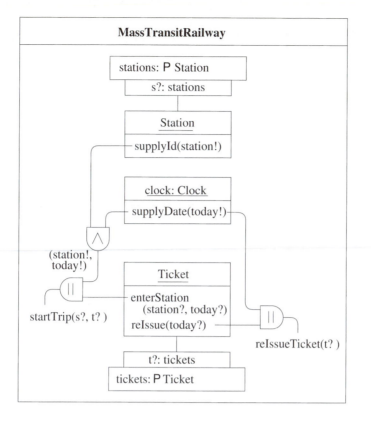

Figure 9.6: the *reIssueTicket* and *startTrip* operations

Figure 9.8 is a class diagram for the mass transit railway: it illustrates the class union, inheritance and aggregation relationships between the classes. The solid diamond arrow is UML's composition operator — it indicates that the stations, tickets, database and clock are unique to the particular mass transit railway system. This notation is equivalent to graphical nesting as used in Figures 9.6 and 9.7.

The '1' adjacent to the *Clock* class indicates that the railway has one such clock. Similarly, it has one associated database. The asterisk adjacent to the *Station* class indicates that a railway has many such stations. Similarly it has many associated tickets. Input/output parameters are not shown.

Discussion

The use of a central database to record the network's fare structure raises issues to do with the distribution of information (see the magnetic key system case study in Section 3.2). As a mass transit railway network is in all probability spread over a large area, having to check fares centrally could create communication problems. An alternative would be for each station to store locally the cost of each trip terminating at that station. In this case, exit from

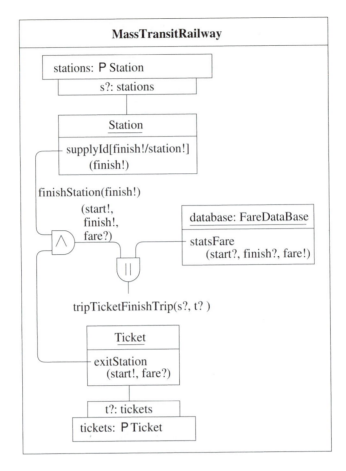

Figure 9.7: the *tripTicketFinishTrip* operation

the station could be enabled even if the rest of the network went down, which may have security and other advantages. In this specification, the main issue was the functionality and behaviour of the various ticket types. Whether information about the fare structure is distributed or centralised does not affect that functionality.

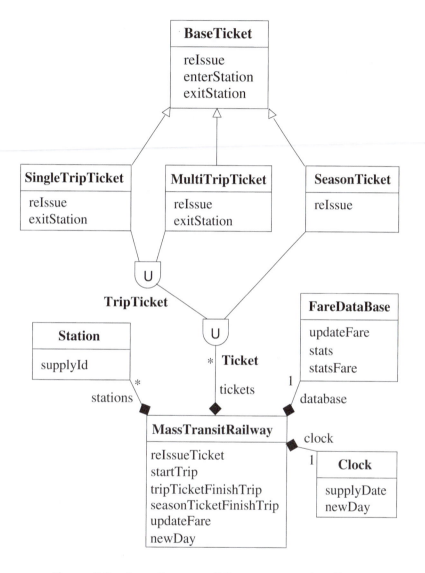

Figure 9.8: class diagram of the mass transit railway

Object containment **10**

10.1 Introduction

A situation common to virtually all object-oriented systems is that some objects reference other objects so as to facilitate the sending and receiving of messages. In general, the association between objects determined by the object references will result in a complex structure whose design and specification is a crucial part of a system's development.

Consider for example a banking system consisting of account, customer and branch objects. In such a system, customers will reference the accounts they own in order to deposit, withdraw, etc. Similarly, branches will reference the accounts of their customers in order to maintain records of transactions, authorise access, add bank charges, and so on.

Although the structure of the object references in this system is complex, it illustrates a commonly occurring pattern: if each account is held at a unique branch, the accounts held at one branch will be distinct from the accounts held at any other branch. This association between branches and their accounts is an example of object containment. A branch is said to *contain* the accounts held at that branch. The basic property of object containment is that an object cannot be contained by two distinct objects at the same time. When formally specifying a system, specifying which objects are contained within other objects gives valuable information about the object reference structure.

Notice that object containment does not imply exclusive control, e.g. an account may be contained by a branch but can also be referenced and hence operated by the customer owning the account. The customer's ability to reference the account does not imply that the customer contains the account. Object containment is achieved by specific declaration, not by access ability. If a bank permits an account to be jointly owned, each joint owner would have the common reference to the account, but these references could not be 'contained' by the owners because the basic property of object containment would not hold: the accounts of distinct owners would not be distinct.

As another example, consider a system consisting of car and wheel objects. Each car will have attributes that reference its wheels. As wheels are not shared between cars, distinct car objects will reference distinct wheel objects and may therefore contain their wheels. In addition to the wheel references, a car object may reference those people who have permission to drive it. As a person may have permission to drive several cars, references in cars to their approved drivers could not be contained. In general an object 'has a' set of references to other objects, some of which may be 'contained'.

Object containment is sometimes an important property of recursive structures. For example, consider the situation of Russian dolls. Each doll is either solid or hollow, and each hollow doll contains another doll that is itself either solid or hollow. A fundamental property of this set of recursively embedded dolls is that no doll directly or indirectly contains itself.

The notion of object containment suggested by these examples can be captured in Object-Z by class invariants. In this chapter we look at some examples of this and introduce extensions to the Object-Z language so as to enable object reference structures arising from containment to be specified succinctly.

10.2   A file system: an example

To illustrate how notions of object containment can be captured in Object-Z, consider a shared computer system consisting of files and users. A file is an object of the class *File*:

$$
\begin{array}{|l|}
\hline
\text{\_\_} \textit{File} \text{_____} \\
\hline
\begin{array}{|l|}
\hline
\textit{contents} : \text{seq } \textit{Char} \\
\hline
\end{array}
\quad
\begin{array}{|l|}
\hline
\textit{modify} \text{_____} \\
\hline
\text{[details omitted]} \\
\hline
\end{array} \\
\hline
\end{array}
$$

Attribute *contents* is a sequence of characters (suppose *Char* is a given type) which can be altered by the unspecified operation *modify*.

A user is an object of the class *User*:

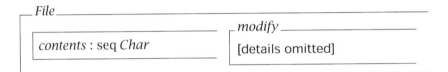

The attribute *owned* denotes the set of files owned by a user. Other users can, however, be granted access to these files. The attribute *accessible* denotes the set of all files accessible to the user: it comprises all files owned by the user together with those owned by others to which access has been granted.

The operation *modify* corresponds to a user selecting and modifying any accessible file, with the distributed choice operator indicating that, at least from the perspective of an observer, the user's choice of file is made non-deterministically.

In practice, the class *User* would also contain operations so that a user can grant another user access to a file in the set *owned*, or be granted access to a file owned by another user, and so on. Such details are not specified here.

A file server has an associated set of users as specified by the class *Server*:

Server

$users : \mathbb{P} \, User$

$\forall \, u_1, u_2 : users \bullet u_1 \neq u_2 \Rightarrow u_1.owned \cap u_2.owned = \varnothing$

$modify \mathrel{\widehat{=}} [\,] \, u : users \bullet u.modify$

The class invariant captures the condition that users contain the files they own, i.e. the files owned by distinct users are distinct.

A computer installation consists of a set of servers as specified by the class *Installation*:

Installation

$servers : \mathbb{P} \, Server$

$\forall \, s_1, s_2 : servers \bullet s_1 \neq s_2 \Rightarrow$
$\quad s_1.users \cap s_2.users = \varnothing \, \wedge$
$\quad \quad \forall \, u_1 : s_1.users; \; u_2 : s_2.users \bullet u_1.owned \cap u_2.owned = \varnothing$
$\forall \, s_1 : servers \bullet \forall \, u_1 : s_1.users \bullet \forall \, f : u_1.accessible \bullet$
$\quad \exists \, s_2 : servers \bullet \exists \, u_2 : s_2.users \bullet f \in u_2.owned$

$modify \mathrel{\widehat{=}} [\,] \, s : servers \bullet s.modify$

The containment notion that users at distinct file servers are distinct is captured by the class invariant

$$\forall \, s_1, s_2 : servers \bullet s_1 \neq s_2 \Rightarrow s_1.users \cap s_2.users = \varnothing.$$

However, this does not capture all the object containment structure in this class. From the invariant of the class *Server*, distinct users at any one file server own distinct files, but this by itself does not imply that the files of users at distinct file servers are distinct. This condition needs to be stated explicitly by the invariant

$$\forall \, s_1, s_2 : servers \bullet s_1 \neq s_2 \Rightarrow$$
$$\forall \, u_1 : s_1.users; \; u_2 : s_2.users \bullet u_1.owned \cap u_2.owned = \varnothing.$$

The final conjunct of the class invariant, i.e.

$$\forall s_1 : servers \bullet \forall u_1 : s_1.users \bullet \forall f : u_1.accessible \bullet$$
$$\exists s_2 : servers \bullet \exists u_2 : s_2.users \bullet f \in u_2.owned,$$

captures the condition that any file to which a user has access must be owned by some user at the installation.

To go one step further, suppose there is a network of computer installations as specified by the class *Network*:

Network

installations : $\mathbb{P}$ *Installation*

$\forall i_1, i_2 : installations \bullet i_1 \neq i_2 \Rightarrow$
$\quad i_1.servers \cap i_2.servers = \emptyset \wedge$
$\quad\quad \forall s_1 : i_1.servers;\ s_2 : i_2.servers \bullet$
$\quad\quad\quad s_1.users \cap s_2.users = \emptyset \wedge$
$\quad\quad\quad\quad \forall u_1 : s_1.users;\ u_2 : s_2.users \bullet$
$\quad\quad\quad\quad\quad u_1.owned \cap u_2.owned = \emptyset$

modify $\widehat{=}$ $[\!]$ $i : installations \bullet i.modify$

In this case the class invariant first captures the containment notion that servers at distinct installations are distinct. As before, however, the containment structures captured at lower levels need to be extended to this level: the class invariant explicitly states that users at servers at distinct installations are distinct, and that the files owned by users at distinct installations are distinct. (The specification assumes that users at one installation cannot access files at other installations.)

Discussion

In this example, the properties of object containment were specified in Object-Z by writing explicit class invariants. As a consequence, the resulting invariants can be complex, particularly as object containment is often a significant aspect of a system's design. Furthermore, containment invariants at one level need to be extended when aggregates are formed (e.g. the invariant in *Server* capturing the containment of files by their owners needed to be extended explicitly in *Installation*, and this in turn needed to be extended explicitly in *Network*).

In the next section, extensions to Object-Z are introduced to simplify the specification of containment.

10.3   Notation for object containment

Let $\mathbb{O}$ denote the universe of all possible object identities in a system, as defined in Chapter 9. Suppose each class has the implicit secondary variable declaration *contained* : $\mathbb{P}\mathbb{O}$. Two mechanisms will be described for specifying the value of *contained*; the first by specific invariants, the second by annotation within declarations. Informally, if *ob* is any object in the system, *ob.contained* denotes the set of object identities accessible by *ob* which are by definition contained by *ob*, with the global containment constraint that no object can be contained by two different objects at the same time. Furthermore, an object cannot contain itself directly or indirectly (this notion is formulated precisely below).

As an illustration, for the class *User* defined in the last section, *contained* would be specified as equal to *owned* and thus, from the implicit global containment constraint, files owned by distinct users would be distinct without the need for the explicit invariants. Object identities in *accessible* would not be in *contained*, unless they are also in *owned*. In the class *Server*, *contained* would be defined as the set *users*, capturing the notion that users in distinct servers are distinct, while in the class *Installation*, *contained* would be defined as the set *servers*, capturing the notion that servers in distinct installations are distinct. Thus, nomination of containment eliminates the need for complex invariants to specify it.

The following predicates capture formally the properties of containment.

1. No object is contained by two distinct objects.

$$\forall \, ob_1, ob_2 : \mathbb{O} \bullet$$
$$ob_1 \neq ob_2 \;\Rightarrow\; ob_1.contained \cap ob_2.contained = \varnothing$$

2. No object directly or indirectly contains itself.

$$\nexists s : \mathrm{seq}\,\mathbb{O} \bullet$$
$$\#s > 1$$
$$\forall \, i : 1 \mathinner{\ldotp\ldotp} \#s{-}1 \bullet s(i+1) \in s(i).contained$$
$$s(1) = s(\#s)$$

i.e. there is no chain $s_1, s_2, \ldots$ of objects where s_1 contains s_2, s_2 contains s_3, and so on, and where the chain eventually comes back to s_1. That is, the partial order of containment defined between objects is acyclic.

In any system, these two predicates are implicit global invariants. For example, the file system introduced in the last section can now be respecified. The class *File* is as before, but the other classes become:

┌─ *User* ──
│
│ *owned* : $\mathbb{P}$ *File*
│ *accessible* : $\mathbb{P}$ *File*
│ ───
│ *contained* = *owned*
│ *owned* $\subseteq$ *accessible*
│ ───
│ *modify* $\mathbin{\hat{=}}$ $[\,]$ f : *accessible* $\bullet$ f.*modify*
│
└──

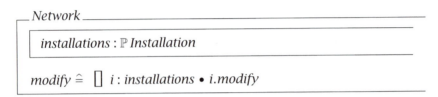

Server _____

$users : \mathbb{P}\ User$

$contained = users$

$modify \mathrel{\widehat{=}} \;[\,]\; u : users \bullet u.modify$

Installation _____

$servers : \mathbb{P}\ Server$

$contained = servers$
$\forall s_1 : servers \bullet \forall u_1 : s_1.users \bullet \forall f : u_1.accessible \bullet$
$\quad \exists s_2 : servers \bullet \exists u_2 : s_2.users \bullet f \in u_2.owned$

$modify \mathrel{\widehat{=}} \;[\,]\; s : servers \bullet s.modify$

Network _____

$installations : \mathbb{P}\ Installation$

$modify \mathrel{\widehat{=}} \;[\,]\; i : installations \bullet i.modify$

The class invariants capturing the containment structure and stated explicitly before are now omitted as they follow directly from the global properties of the implicit secondary variable *contained*. As a consequence, the specification has become much more succinct.

If *contained* is not explicitly defined within the state predicate, it is assumed to be the empty set. In all previous case studies, *contained* was not mentioned; consequently, any required containment properties were captured explicitly.

Notice that specifying *contained* to be non-empty within a class places conditions upon any system into which objects of that class are placed. For example, the predicate *contained = owned* in *User* results in the condition that no file can be owned by two users in the one system.

Looking at the class *Network*, it would seem reasonable to equate *contained* with *installations*, capturing the intuitive notion that an installation can be part of only one network. However, as specified there are no aggregates of network objects, so specifying containment is unnecessary. In general, it is only meaningful to give a value to *contained* if the possibility exists that objects of that class will become components of an enclosing system.

A notational simplification

If an attribute always identifies a directly contained object or set of such objects, this can be indicated when the attribute is declared by appending a subscript '$_©$' to the appropriate type. This removes the necessity to write an explicit predicate involving the implicit secondary variable *contained*. For example, adopting this syntactic convention in the specification of the file system, the classes *File* and *Network* are unchanged, but the other three classes become:

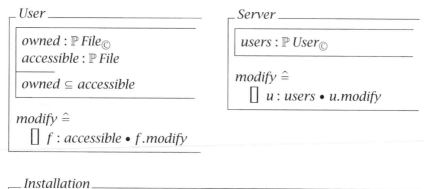

The subscript '$_©$' is appended to the type of the attribute rather than the attribute itself because the attribute may identify a complex data structure rather than the identity of an object that can be referenced. For example, the declaration

$$owned : \mathbb{P}\ File_©$$

in the *User* class declares *owned* to be a set, not an object reference. From its type, *owned* is a set of identities of objects of class *File* that can be referenced by a user object; the $_©$ implies these references are to contained objects. Type declarations involving $_©$ can be converted into corresponding declarations without $_©$ by stating explicit predicates involving *contained*; for instance, if A, B, C, D, E and F are arbitrary classes, the class declaration on the left in Figure 10.1 is a syntactic shorthand for the class declaration on the right.

Notice that a syntactic simplification using $_©$ cannot always be applied, e.g. suppose A is some class and Y is a class defined by:

Y

$sa : \mathbb{P}\ A$

$contained \subseteq sa$

[other features omitted]

$$
\begin{array}{|l}
\hline
X \underline{\hspace{4cm}} \\
\hline
as : \mathbb{P}\, A_{\copyright} \\
bl : \mathrm{seq}\, B_{\copyright} \\
cf : \mathbb{N} \nrightarrow C_{\copyright} \\
d_1, d_2 : D_{\copyright} \\
e : E \\
fs : \mathbb{P}\, F \\
\hline
\text{[other features omitted]} \\
\hline
\end{array}
\qquad
\begin{array}{|l}
\hline
X \underline{\hspace{4cm}} \\
\hline
as : \mathbb{P}\, A \\
bl : \mathrm{seq}\, B \\
cf : \mathbb{N} \nrightarrow C \\
d_1, d_2 : D \\
e : E \\
fs : \mathbb{P}\, F \\
\hline
contained = \\
\quad as \cup (\mathrm{ran}\, bl) \\
\qquad \cup (\mathrm{ran}\, cf) \cup \{d_1, d_2\} \\
\hline
\text{[other features omitted]} \\
\hline
\end{array}
$$

Figure 10.1: relating $\copyright$ to the attribute *contained*

Then the declaration $sa : \mathbb{P}\, A_{\copyright}$ would not now be a correct simplification because it would imply that *contained* = *sa*. The situation here, however, is unlikely to arise when modelling real systems. In Object-Z *contained* is a reserved word.

Discussion

The use of specific notation for object containment enables commonly occurring aspects of the global object reference structure to be succinctly captured at the local object level. More generally, it is common practice to associate conditions about the global environment with the local objects themselves. For example, the command *Keep Out of Reach of Children* is printed on the label of a medicine bottle but really constrains the environments into which the bottle can be placed. The advantage of associating global conditions with local objects is that, as this section has illustrated, system invariants can be greatly simplified, and the need to restate the conditions for each possible environment is eliminated.

10.4   Object containment in recursive structures

Recursively defined acyclic structures such as trees have the property that any node in the structure is linked to a set of nodes each determining a distinct substructure having no nodes in common. In terms of the ideas discussed in this chapter, a node 'contains' the nodes to which it is linked. This section illustrates the specification of such structures using Object-Z. First, a set of recursively embedded Russian dolls is specified in terms of the static contain-

ment relationship between the dolls. Then a sorted binary tree is specified
in terms of the tree's construction via operations defined recursively over the
structure.

Russian dolls: an example

A set of Russian dolls consists of hollow dolls recursively embedded one inside
the other, with the innermost doll being solid (see Figure 10.2).

Figure 10.2: Russian dolls

Consider first an Object-Z specification that does not use the special notation for object containment. To begin, let *Doll* be the class union

$$Doll == SolidDoll \ \cup \ HollowDoll$$

where *SolidDoll* and *HollowDoll* are the classes:

```
┌─ SolidDoll ────────────────
│  ┌─────────────────────────
│  │ inside : ℙ Doll
│  ├─────────────────────────
│  │ inside = ∅
│  └─────────────────────────
└────────────────────────────
```

```
┌─ HollowDoll ────────────────
│  ┌──────────────────────────
│  │ next : Doll
│  │ inside : ℙ Doll
│  ├──────────────────────────
│  │ inside =
│  │    {next} ∪ next.inside
│  │ self ∉ inside
│  └──────────────────────────
└─────────────────────────────
```

The attribute *next* identifies the next doll directly embedded within a hollow doll: as *next* has type *Doll*, the next doll can be either solid or hollow.

Because a hollow doll can embed a hollow doll and so on, it is necessary
to ensure that a hollow doll does not embed (directly or indirectly) itself. To
specify this, the attribute *inside* is included. Attribute *inside* denotes the set
of all dolls directly or indirectly embedded. This set will be empty for a solid

doll, as it embeds no dolls. For a hollow doll, however, *inside* will comprise *next* and all dolls inside *next*. As *inside* has type $\mathbb{P}\,Doll$, its members can be solid or hollow dolls. The predicate *self* $\notin$ *inside* ensures non-circularity.

As we are interested only in specifying the embedding relationship between the dolls, neither of these classes has operations defined.

A set of dolls can now be specified by the class

```
┌─ RussianDolls ───────────────
│ ┌──────────────────────────
│ │ outermost : Doll
│ │
│ └──────────────────────────
└──────────────────────────────
```

where the attribute *outermost* identifies the largest doll. The set of dolls is then captured recursively from the definition of the class union *Doll*.

Consider now this same specification, but using the notation for object containment. The class union *Doll* and the class *RussianDolls* are unchanged, but the other two classes become:

```
┌─ SolidDoll ──────────────        ┌─ HollowDoll ───────────────
│ ┌──────────────────────         │ ┌──────────────────────────
│ │                               │ │ next : Doll◎
│ │                               │ │
│ └──────────────────────         │ └──────────────────────────
└──────────────────────────        └──────────────────────────────
```

The class invariants stated explicitly before can now be deleted as they follow from the global properties implied by object containment. At this level of abstraction, *SolidDoll* becomes a featureless class: its role is simply to end the recursive embedding.

A sorted binary tree: an example

In this section, a specification of a sorted binary tree is constructed from two types of nodes: value nodes and null nodes. Value nodes (objects of class *ValNode*) each have a natural number value (*val*), and reference a left node (*lnode*) and a right node (*rnode*). If the *val* of a value node is *n*, say, then if *lnode* is a value node, *lnode* and every value node directly or indirectly referenced by *lnode* has *val* < *n*, while if *rnode* is a value node, *rnode* and every value node directly or indirectly referenced by *rnode* has *val* ⩾ *n*.

Null nodes (objects of the class *NullNode*) are featureless. An empty tree is represented by a null node, and each leaf of a non-empty tree is a value node with *lnode* and *rnode* referencing null nodes. A null node is conceptually different from the null pointer of programming languages. A null node object is a genuine object: its presence acts as a boundary to the recursion.

To ensure that the structure is a tree, starting at any node the collection of nodes rooted at the node's *lnode* (including *lnode*) must be distinct from the collection rooted at the node's *rnode*, and neither collection may contain the start node. The specification given here captures this requirement explicitly by the containment notation.

To begin, let *Node* be defined as the class union

$$Node == NullNode \cup ValNode$$

where *NullNode* is the class

```
┌─ NullNode ──────────────────
│ ┌──────────────────────────┐
│ └──────────────────────────┘
└─────────────────────────────
```

and *ValNode* is the following class:

```
┌─ ValNode ──────────────────────────────────────────────
│ ↾(insert)
│
│ ┌──────────────────────────┐   ┌─ INIT ──────────────────
│ │ val : ℕ                  │   │ lnode ∈ NullNode
│ │ lnode, rnode : Node_©     │   │ rnode ∈ NullNode
│ │ ─────────────────────    │   └─────────────────────────
│ │ lnode ≠ rnode            │
│ └──────────────────────────┘
│
│ ┌─ less ───────────────────┐   ┌─ grEq ──────────────────
│ │ val? : ℕ                 │   │ val? : ℕ
│ │ ───────────              │   │ ───────────
│ │ val? < val               │   │ val? ⩾ val
│ └──────────────────────────┘   └─────────────────────────
│
│ ┌─ leftNullToVal ──────────┐   ┌─ rightNullToVal ────────
│ │ Δ(lnode)                 │   │ Δ(rnode)
│ │ val? : ℕ                 │   │ val? : ℕ
│ │ ───────────              │   │ ───────────
│ │ lnode ∈ NullNode         │   │ rnode ∈ NullNode
│ │ lnode′ ∈ ValNode         │   │ rnode′ ∈ ValNode
│ │ lnode′.val = val?        │   │ rnode′.val = val?
│ │ lnode′.INIT              │   │ rnode′.INIT
│ └──────────────────────────┘   └─────────────────────────
│
│   insert ≙ less ∧ (leftNullToVal
│                        []
│                    [ lnode ∉ NullNode ] ∧ lnode.insert)
│            []
│        grEq ∧ (rightNullToVal
│                    []
│                [ rnode ∉ NullNode ] ∧ rnode.insert)
└─────────────────────────────────────────────────────────
```

The left and right referenced nodes can each be either a value node or a null node; in any case they are distinct objects (*lnode* ≠ *rnode*). Initially, they are both null nodes.

The operation *less* (respectively *grEq*) tests if a given input value (*val?*) is less than (respectively greater than or equal to) the attribute *val*.

When *lnode* references a null node, the operation *leftNullToVal* takes an input value (*val?*) and replaces the null node by a value node with value *val?* and referencing null left and right nodes (i.e. *lnode'.INIT*). Operation *rightNullToVal* is defined similarly.

Operation *insert* is defined recursively over the structure. If the input (*val?*) is less than the value of the node (operation *less*) either a null left node is replaced by a new value node (operation *leftNullToVal*), or a non-null left node (*lnode* ∉ *NullNode*) undergoes its insert operation (*lnode.insert*). On the other hand, if the input value is greater than or equal to the value of the node (operation *grEq*) the equivalent happens to the right node. The preconditions for each of the choices made within the operation *insert* cover each case and are disjoint; thus precisely one course of action will be chosen when *insert* is applied to a value node object. Notice that *insert* is the only visible operation: the others are auxiliary.

With the class union *Node* specified, a sorted binary tree can now be defined as an object of the class *SortedBinaryTree*:

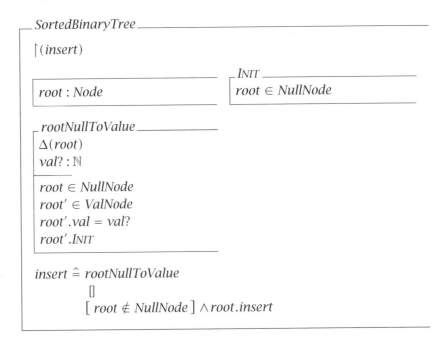

In this class the attribute *root* identifies the first node of the tree, initially a null node.

Operation *rootNullToValue* adds the first input value (*val?*) to the tree: the initial null root node is replaced by a value node with value *val?* and null left and right attached nodes (i.e. *root'.INIT*).

Operation *insert* either replaces a null root node (*rootNullToValue*), or applies the insert operation recursively to a non-null root node (*root.insert*). Other sorted binary tree operations (e.g. deleting a node) are not modelled.

10.5   A retail chain: a case study

This case study models stock control within a retail chain of supermarkets, and illustrates the conciseness of object containment to specify the uniqueness of object references. The study also illustrates the progressive promotion of operations through a number of levels.

Informal description

- A retail chain comprises a number of supermarkets and a central ware-house which stores bulk quantities of items for restocking the supermarkets.

- Each item for sale by the chain has an associated bar-code identifier.

- Each supermarket has its own database where the brief description, the selling price and the number in stock for each item are maintained.

- A supermarket can change the description or selling price of any item independently of other supermarkets in the chain.

- A supermarket's database adjusts the number of each item held whenever the supermarket sells an item or receives fresh stock.

- A supermarket's individual checkouts scan each item sold and display its description and unit cost by access to the database using the item's code. In effect, the checkout acts as a communications channel between the database and the customer. Each checkout also accumulates the cost of purchases so far by the current customer and displays that total on request. There is also provision to clear the total cost and the display in readiness for the next customer.

In practice, but not modelled in this case study, there would also be provision within each supermarket for accumulating the total sales in a given period for each checkout and for gathering other statistical information. This would be specified by providing a checkout record in the database for each checkout and updating it when events of interest occur.

In a fully centralised system, a checkout record would also accumulate the costs of the associated current customer's purchases.

A supermarket checkout

A checkout is modelled as having a bar-code scanner, a display and a tally unit for accumulating a customer's costs. Let the given sets

$[Code, Char]$

denote the set of bar codes and the character set for displays respectively: the natures of these sets are not important at this level of abstraction.

Define the following two types to model text and monetary values respectively.

$$String == seq\ Char$$

$$Cents == \mathbb{N}$$

A checkout's scanner is modelled by the class *Scanner*:

```
┌─ Scanner ──────────────────────
│  ┌─ scan ──────────────────────
│  │ code?, code! : Code
│  ├──────────────────────────────
│  │ code! = code?
│  └──────────────────────────────
└────────────────────────────────
```

The class consists of just the operation *scan* which models the reading of the bar code (*code?*) by the checkout operator and the transmission of the code (*code!*). It will be seen later that the database receives the code and returns the item's description and price for display and cost accumulation.

A checkout's display is modelled by the class *Display*:

```
┌─ Display ────────────────────────────────────────────
│
│  ┌──────────────────────────────────────────────────
│  │ string : String
│  │ cents : Cents
│  └──────────────────────────────────────────────────
│
│  ┌─ clear ───────────────      ┌─ update ─────────────
│  │ Δ(string, cents)            │ Δ(string, cents)
│  ├───────────────────          │ string? : String
│  │ string' = ⟨⟩                │ cents? : Cents
│  │ cents' = 0                  ├──────────────────────
│  └───────────────────          │ string' = string?
│                                 │ cents' = cents?
│                                 └──────────────────────
└────────────────────────────────────────────────────────
```

The display has two fields, one for text, the other for monetary values. The class has only two operations: one clears both display fields and the other updates them to given values.

A checkout's tally unit is modelled by the class *Tally* in Figure 10.3. The operation *clear* models the clearing of the total in readiness for the next customer. Operations *inc* and *getTotal* model the incrementing and outputting of the total so far respectively.

A checkout scans item codes, transmits codes to the database, displays the accessed description and cost of individual items, and is responsible for accumulating the costs of the current customer's purchases.

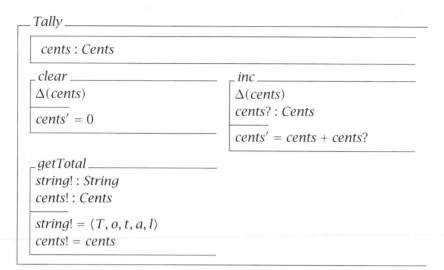

Figure 10.3: the class *Tally*

A checkout is an object of class *Checkout*:

Checkout

scanner : *Scanner*©
display : *Display*©
tally : *Tally*©

$newCust \mathrel{\widehat{=}} display.clear \land tally.clear$

$sellItem \mathrel{\widehat{=}} scanner.scan \land display.update \land tally.inc$

$displayCustTotal \mathrel{\widehat{=}} tally.getTotal \parallel display.update$

Attributes *scanner*, *display* and *tally* reference the checkout's scanner, display and tally unit respectively. The subscripts '©' indicate that the referenced components are contained, capturing the requirement that distinct checkouts have distinct components.

Operation *newCust* clears the new customer's associated display and total. Operation *sellItem* models the purchase of an item at the checkout: it combines scanning, displaying the item's description and cost and increasing the total so far. As previously implied, this will require cooperation with the database.

Operation *displayCustTotal* is a provision to display the customer's total cost so far together with the text message '*Total*'. The operation would also be used to provide the total cost at the end of service for the current customer: in that case, the checkout's next operation would be *newCust*. In this study, the actual handling of money between the customer and the checkout operator is not modelled.

An item record

Information about a particular item in a supermarket is retained in that supermarket's database by an item record — an object of the class *ItemRec*:

ItemRec

description : *String*
sellprice : *Cents*
held : $\mathbb{N}$

---

newDescription
$\Delta(description)$
string? : *String*

description' = *string?*

newSellPrice
$\Delta(sellprice)$
cents? : *Cents*

sellprice' = *cents?*

---

descSellPrice
string! : *String*
cents! : *Cents*

string! = *description*
cents! = *sellprice*

clearStock
$\Delta(held)$

held' = 0

---

restock
$\Delta(held)$
num? : $\mathbb{N}$

held' = *held* + *num?*

decStock
$\Delta(held)$

held > 0
held' = *held* − 1

---

sellItem $\widehat{=}$ *descSellPrice* $\wedge$ *decStock*

Attributes *description*, *sellprice* and *held* denote the description, selling
price and number in stock of the item respectively (for a particular supermarket). No initial values are specified for these attributes.

Operations *newDescription* and *newSellPrice* change the description and
selling price of the item respectively and *descSellPrice* outputs the item's description and selling price.

Operation *clearStock* resets the number held to zero. The item can be restocked (operation *restock*) with the result that a given number of units (*num?*)
is added to the stock.

Operation *decStock* decrements by one the number of units of the item
held, provided the supermarket has at least one unit of the item in stock.

Selling an item (operation *sellItem*) conjoins *descSellPrice* and *decStock*.

A database of item records

A supermarket's database as specified by the class *Database* consists of a collection of item records accessed by item code:

$$
\begin{array}{l}
\rule{5cm}{0.4pt}\,Database \rule{5cm}{0.4pt} \\[2pt]
\quad \boxed{itemRec : Code \rightarrowtail ItemRec_{©}} \\[6pt]
\quad newDescription \mathrel{\widehat{=}} [\, code? : \mathrm{dom}\ itemRec \,] \bullet \\
\qquad itemRec(code?).newDescription \\[4pt]
\quad newSellPrice \mathrel{\widehat{=}} [\, code? : \mathrm{dom}\ itemRec \,] \bullet \\
\qquad itemRec(code?).newSellPrice \\[4pt]
\quad clearStock \mathrel{\widehat{=}} [\, code? : \mathrm{dom}\ itemRec \,] \bullet \\
\qquad itemRec(code?).clearStock \\[4pt]
\quad restock \mathrel{\widehat{=}} [\, code? : \mathrm{dom}\ itemRec \,] \bullet itemRec(code?).restock \\[4pt]
\quad sellItem \mathrel{\widehat{=}} [\, code? : \mathrm{dom}\ itemRec \,] \bullet itemRec(code?).sellItem
\end{array}
$$

The partial one-one function *itemRec* records the items to be stocked by the supermarket. The domain of *itemRec* denotes the set of item codes of inventory items. If attribute *held* in the record of an inventory item is zero, the supermarket currently has no units of that item in stock. Thus, there is a clear distinction between items which are intended to be stocked (inventory items) but are currently out of stock and items which are not on the inventory. As *itemRec* is a one-one function, distinct codes associate with distinct item records.

The subscript '$©$' attached to *ItemRec* in the declaration of *itemRec* indicates that the item records in the range of *itemRec* are contained, capturing the requirement that distinct databases have distinct item record objects, i.e. in this model, item records are maintained independently by each supermarket, not shared between databases.

The schema

$$[\, code? : \mathrm{dom}\ itemRec \,]$$

which occurs in the definition of all of the operations, provides a common context: it identifies one of the item codes known to the database. In this context, the expression *itemRec*(*code?*) identifies the corresponding item record. Operations *newDescription*, *newSellPrice*, *clearStock*, *restock* and *sellItem* therefore promote the same-named operations defined on the identified item record.

No initial value for *itemRec* is specified. In practice, there would be provision for adding and removing items to and from the supermarket's inventory, i.e. for adding and removing item codes and their corresponding records to and from the supermarket's database — such details are not modelled here.

A supermarket

A supermarket consists of a collection of checkouts and a database, as specified by the class *Supermarket*:

Supermarket ─────────────────────────────

> *checkouts* : $\mathbb{P}$ *Checkout*©
> *database* : *Database*©

> *newDescription* $\hat{=}$ *database.newDescription*
>
> *newSellPrice* $\hat{=}$ *database.newSellPrice*
>
> *clearStock* $\hat{=}$ *database.clearStock*
>
> *restock* $\hat{=}$ *database.restock*
>
> *newCust* $\hat{=}$ [*cko?* : *checkouts*] • *cko?.newCust*
>
> *sellItem* $\hat{=}$
>   [*cko?* : *checkouts*] • *cko?.sellItem* ‖ *database.sellItem*
>
> *displayCustTotal* $\hat{=}$
>   [*cko?* : *checkouts*] • *cko?.displayCustTotal*

The checkout objects constituting the set *checkouts* are contained as is the attribute *database*, indicating that in this model of the retail chain, distinct supermarkets have distinct checkouts and distinct databases.

Operations *newDescription*, *newSellPrice*, *clearStock* and *restock* promote the same-named operations defined on the database to the supermarket level. Similarly, operations *newCust* and *displayCustTotal* promote the same-named operations defined on the selected checkout (*cko?*).

Operation *sellItem* models the selected checkout accepting an item's code (*code?*) from the environment and passing it to the database to access the item record which provides the item's description and selling price for display. The bi-directional communication between the checkout and database is hidden.

A warehouse

Supermarkets are restocked from a central warehouse specified by the class *Warehouse* in Figure 10.4. The function *stock* indicates the number held in the warehouse of each item (as identified by that item's code). The domain of *stock* denotes the set of codes of all items in the warehouse's inventory. If the image of an item code in the domain is zero, the warehouse has no units of that item currently in stock. Thus, as in *Database*, there is a clear distinction between inventory items which are currently out of stock and items which are not in the inventory.

Operation *clear* resets the number of units of a given item (*code?*) to zero; operation *supply* models a given number (*num?*) of a given item (*code?*) being

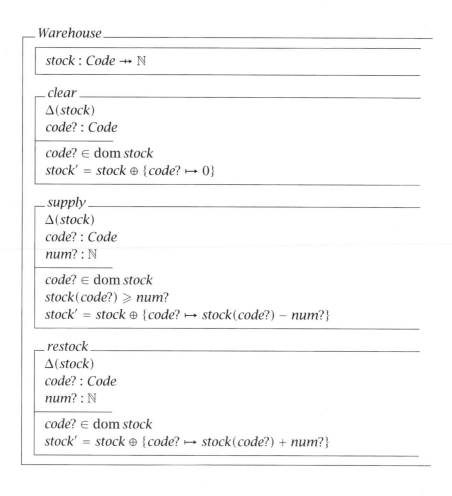

Figure 10.4: the class *Warehouse*

removed from the warehouse (e.g. to restock a supermarket); operation *restock* models the restocking of the warehouse by a given number (*num?*) of a given item (*code?*). The model does not provide for adding or deleting items to the warehouse's inventory of items (dom *stock*).

The retail chain

A retail chain consists of a collection of supermarkets and a warehouse, as specified by the class *RetailChain* in Figure 10.5. The supermarket objects in the set *supermarkets* and the object *warehouse* are contained, indicating that if this model were to be further extended, distinct retail chains would contain distinct supermarket and warehouse objects.

All operations except *restockSupermarket* are straightforward promotions and *restockSupermarket* combines the warehouse's *supply* operation with the selected supermarket's *restock* operation.

RetailChain

$supermarkets : \mathbb{P}\ Supermarket_{©}$
$warehouse : Warehouse_{©}$

$newDescription \mathrel{\hat{=}}$
    $[\ sm? : supermarkets\ ] \bullet sm?.newDescription$

$newSellPrice \mathrel{\hat{=}} [\ sm? : supermarkets\ ] \bullet sm?.newSellPrice$

$clearStock \mathrel{\hat{=}} [\ sm? : supermarkets\ ] \bullet sm?.clearStock$

$newCust \mathrel{\hat{=}} [\ sm? : supermarkets\ ] \bullet sm?.newCust$

$sellItem \mathrel{\hat{=}} [\ sm? : supermarkets\ ] \bullet sm?.sellItem$

$displayCustTotal \mathrel{\hat{=}}$
    $[\ sm? : supermarkets\ ] \bullet sm?.displayCustTotal$

$clearWarehouse \mathrel{\hat{=}} warehouse.clear$

$restockWarehouse \mathrel{\hat{=}} warehouse.restock$

$restockSupermarket \mathrel{\hat{=}}$
    $warehouse.supply \wedge ([\ sm? : supermarkets\ ] \bullet sm?.restock)$

Figure 10.5: the class _RetailChain_

Discussion

A retail chain has aggregations of supermarkets, checkouts, databases, item records, scanners, tally units and displays. Some aggregations are the direct consequence of the set constructor ($\mathbb{P}$), e.g. the use of $\mathbb{P}$ within the declaration $checkouts : \mathbb{P}\ Checkout_{©}$ in class _Supermarket_. As sets contain distinct elements, checkout objects in _checkouts_ have distinct object identities, i.e. there are no aliases (i.e. no replicated object identities) within the one set of checkouts of an individual supermarket.

However, there is the larger aggregation of checkouts arising from the multiplicity of supermarkets and it is essential that checkouts in different supermarkets be distinct, i.e. that there be no aliases with respect to checkouts across supermarkets. This requirement is ensured by containment, i.e. the presence of $_{©}$ in the declaration of _checkouts_. Similarly, the declaration $supermarkets : \mathbb{P}\ Supermarket_{©}$ in class _RetailChain_ ensures that supermarkets within a retail chain and across chains are distinct by the properties of $\mathbb{P}$ and $_{©}$ respectively.

The declarations in class _Checkout_ do not include set construction — scanner, display and tally unit multiplicity arises from checkout multiplicity, and containment ensures the uniqueness of these components across checkouts, whether or not the checkouts are in the same supermarket.

Without the notion of — and notation for — containment, the specification would have required numerous additional predicates to ensure, for example, that displays were unique within and across supermarkets. To specify display uniqueness across supermarkets, a denotation for the set of display object identifiers within individual supermarkets would be needed. These denotations would then be applied in class *RetailChain* where supermarkets can be related.

The role of the bar code in this case study is interesting, not only because of the very visible use of bar-code scanners in practice. The specification ensures that item records in the databases of different supermarkets are distinct. However, different databases may need to accommodate the same product item. This is resolved by the global declaration and access of bar codes and the fact that item records in different databases can relate to the same bar code, i.e. item bar codes are shared, not item records.

It could be argued that the bar-code inventories of supermarkets should be subsets of the bar-code inventory of the warehouse. This could be imposed in class *RetailChain* by inclusion of the class invariant

$$\forall\, s : supermarkets \bullet$$
$$\mathrm{dom}(s.database.itemRec) \subseteq \mathrm{dom}(warehouse.stock)$$

However, as supermarkets would wish to sell residual stocks of items which have been removed from the chain's current inventory, the invariant has not been included in the specification.

This case study also illustrates the use of abstraction in specification. For example, in practice, a checkout would supply its identity with the item's code to the supermarket's database so that the database could subsequently return the required information to the checkout in question. This detail is avoided in class *Supermarket*: operation *sellItem* uses parameter *cko?* to identify the checkout, and the parallel operator effects the bi-directional interchange.

This study also shows the extent of specification text needed to promote operations through several levels. For example, operation *newDescription* in class *RetailChain* promotes the selected supermarket's *newDescription* operation; this operation in *Supermarket* promotes in turn the *newDescription* operation of the supermarket's database; and this operation in *Database* in turn promotes the selected item's *newDescription* operation.

Computational systems 11

11.1 Introduction

Many systems have components that are constructed specifically to facilitate numerical or logical computations. A way of approaching computations within an object-oriented system is to associate expressions with specific objects, where each expression can be evaluated to give a value within some given domain. An expression may contain variables: hence its value can change as the system evolves. Furthermore, an expression can be defined in terms of other (sub) expressions, leading to a tree-like structure.

In this chapter, the Object-Z notation is used to effectively give a denotational semantics of expressions. Traditionally when defining denotational semantics, the abstract syntax, static semantics and dynamic semantics of expressions are defined separately using distinct formal structures. In the approach adopted here, however, an object-oriented specification of expressions is constructed where each expression is modelled as an object, with the result that both the abstract syntax and semantics of an expression is encapsulated within the one class. Furthermore, the polymorphic nature of expressions and values is modelled by class union, while the tree structure of expressions is captured by object containment. This is illustrated through the specification of a spreadsheet.

11.2 A spreadsheet: a case study

Spreadsheets are among the most widely used computer packages, emulating and extending the traditional ledger by allowing rows and columns of information to be systematically organised and processed.

Informal description

- A spreadsheet consists of a set of cells. In practice the cells are arranged in a rectangular array, but as this geometry is irrelevant to the computational aspects of concern in this case study, it will not be modelled.

- Associated with each cell is an expression which is either text, a number, a reference to a cell, or a compound numeric expression.

- An expression is a compound numeric expression if it is constructed by application of the numeric operators, i.e. negation, addition, subtraction, multiplication and division.

- Each expression evaluates to text, a number, or erroneous.

- The value of a text or number expression is that text or number.

- The value of a reference to a cell is the value of the expression associated with that cell.

- The value of a compound numeric expression follows conventional mathematical procedures.

- An expression evaluates to erroneous if and only if

  - it is a compound numeric expression that on evaluation involves division by zero;
  - it is a compound numeric expression with a sub-expression which does not evaluate to a number;
  - it is defined cyclically by referring directly or indirectly to the cell with which it is associated;
  - it is a reference to a cell whose expression evaluates to erroneous.

- Each cell displays the value of its associated expression. The detailed conversion of an expression's value to its display format is not modelled. That is, for the purpose of this case study, the focus is on cells, expressions and their values.

To illustrate the way expressions are associated with cells and evaluated, consider the spreadsheet in Figure 11.1 consisting of cells $c_1, c_2, \ldots, c_{12}$. For the purpose of illustration, text expressions are distinguished from other expressions by being placed within quotation marks. Displays are typical of how they would appear in reality.

cell	c_1	c_2	c_3	c_4	c_5	c_6
expression	'ok'	'c_1'	c_1	$c_1 + 2$	2	$c_5 + c_6$
display	ok	c_1	ok	**err**	2	**err**

cell	c_7	c_8	c_9	c_{10}	c_{11}	c_{12}
expression	$c_5 - 2$	c_5 / c_7	c_{10}	c_9	c_{11}	c_9
display	0	**err**	**err**	**err**	**err**	**err**

Figure 11.1: a spreadsheet

Expression values

To model the polymorphic nature of an expression's value, let *Value* be defined by the class union:

$$Value == Text \cup Num \cup Error$$

where *Text*, *Num* and *Error* are the classes:

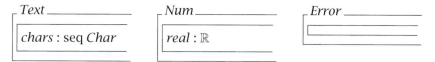

    A value which is textual or numeric is modelled as an object of class *Text* or *Num* respectively, whereas the value of an erroneous expression is modelled as an object of class *Error*.

A cell

The class *Cell* specifies cell objects. The attribute *exp* denotes a cell's associated expression object (the class union *Exp* is defined later), while the secondary variable *value* denotes the value of the associated expression, the basis for the cell's display. The secondary variable *refs* denotes the set of cells which are referenced directly or indirectly by the cell's expression: it is used to detect circular cell references as will be elaborated later.

Cell

$exp : Exp_{©}$
Δ
$value : Value$
$refs : \mathbb{P}\, Cell$

$refs = exp.refs$
$self \notin refs \Rightarrow value = exp.value$
$self \in refs \Rightarrow value \in Error$

INIT

$exp \in TextExp$
$value.chars = \langle\, \rangle$

newExp

$\Delta(exp)$
$exp? : Exp$

$exp' = exp?$

    Cells (technically) contain their associated expressions as indicated by the decoration © in the declaration of *exp*, i.e. distinct cell objects contain distinct expression objects. Notice that the syntactic form of expressions associated with distinct cells may well be identical, e.g. the expressions associated with cells c_{10} and c_{12} in Figure 11.1 are both references to cell c_9, but nevertheless the expressions are modelled as distinct objects. This allows an expression object associated with a cell to be changed without affecting the expression objects associated with other cells.

The invariant of the *Cell* class indicates that a cell's value is the value of its associated expression, except that if the cell directly or indirectly references itself, the value is erroneous. For example, the value of cell c_6 in Figure 11.1 is erroneous because its *refs* set $\{c_5, c_6\}$ contains itself. Similarly, cell c_{10} directly references c_9, but as cell c_9 references c_{10}, the set *refs* for c_{10} is $\{c_9, c_{10}\}$ and so the value of c_{10} is erroneous. Similarly for c_9. (Expression attributes *value* and *refs* are defined within the expression classes below.)

The cell's attributes *value* and *refs* are secondary because their values depend upon those of the associated expression. For example, suppose that the expression associated with cell c_9 in Figure 11.1 is changed from a reference to c_{10} to the expression $3+c_7$. Then the value of c_9 would become an object of class *Num* with real attribute 3, while the set *refs* for c_9 would become $\{c_5, c_7\}$. At the same time, although the expressions associated with cells c_{10} and c_{12} (i.e. references to c_9) do not change syntactically, their values become 3 and their *refs* become $\{c_5, c_7, c_9\}$.

Initially, a cell has an associated text expression that corresponds to the empty string. (The class *TextExp* is defined below; the value of an object of the class *TextExp* is an object of the class *Text*.) It will be seen that the *refs* attribute of a text expression is empty so that initially $self \notin refs$ applies. The operation *newExp* models the replacement of the cell's expression by a new expression from the environment.

An expression

An expression is an object of one of the classes *TextExp*, *NumExp*, *RefExp*, *NegExp*, *DivExp*, *AddExp*, *SubtExp* or *MultExp*, as defined by the class union:

$$Exp == TextExp \cup NumExp \cup RefExp \cup NegExp \cup$$
$$DivExp \cup AddExp \cup SubtExp \cup MultExp$$

The eight constituent classes are derived by inheritance from the root class *BaseExp* as shown in Figure 11.2. Referring to the figure, the classes on the left constitute the class union *Exp*, while those on the right are auxiliary: they contain common features and simply facilitate derivation through inheritance.

Class *BaseExp* has two secondary variables, *value* and *refs*, that are common to all expressions: specific details of the secondary variables are elaborated in the subclasses later.

```
┌─ BaseExp ──────────────────────
│
│  Δ
│  value : Value
│  refs : ℙ Cell
│
└────────────────────────────────
```

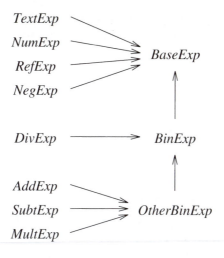

Figure 11.2: the inheritance hierarchy of expression classes

The class *TextExp* inherits *BaseExp* and adds the attribute *text* identifying an object of class *Text*. As no restrictions are placed upon *text*, any sequence of characters can form a text expression.

$$
\begin{array}{|l}
\hline
\text{\textit{TextExp}} \rule[-2pt]{0pt}{2pt} \\
\hline
\text{\textit{BaseExp}} \\
\hline
\quad \text{\textit{text} : \textit{Text}} \\
\hline
\quad \textit{value} = \textit{text} \\
\quad \textit{refs} = \varnothing \\
\hline
\end{array}
$$

The value of a text expression is the object *text* itself (in practice, the associated cell will display the underlying sequence of characters, e.g. cells c_1 and c_2 in Figure 11.1). No cells are referenced by text expressions.

The class *NumExp* specifies expressions that correspond to an explicit real number. The class is constructed similarly to *TextExp*, with attribute *num* identifying an object of class *Num* and indicating that any real number can form a numerical expression.

$$
\begin{array}{|l}
\hline
\text{\textit{NumExp}} \rule[-2pt]{0pt}{2pt} \\
\hline
\text{\textit{BaseExp}} \\
\hline
\quad \text{\textit{num} : \textit{Num}} \\
\hline
\quad \textit{value} = \textit{num} \\
\quad \textit{refs} = \varnothing \\
\hline
\end{array}
$$

The class *RefExp* specifies expressions that consist simply of a reference to some cell in the spreadsheet. It inherits *BaseExp* and adds the attribute *cell* denoting the cell referenced.

```
┌─ RefExp ──────────────────────
│ BaseExp
│ ┌──────────────────────────
│ │ cell : Cell
│ ├──────────────────────────
│ │ value = cell.value
│ │ refs = {cell} ∪ cell.refs
```

The *value* attribute of a reference expression is the same as that of the referenced *cell*. The total set *refs* of cells directly or indirectly referenced by a reference expression is obtained by adding the direct reference *cell* to the set which *cell* already references directly or indirectly. If a *RefExp* is associated with a cell, the cell's value and therefore its display, is that of the referenced cell (e.g. cells c_3 and c_{12} in Figure 11.1).

An interesting special case arises when a cell references itself (e.g. cell c_{11} in Figure 11.1). In this case, the predicate *self* ∈ *refs* ⇒ *value* ∈ *Error* in class *Cell* determines that the value of the cell is erroneous, and hence, as the expression takes its referenced cell's value, it too is erroneous.

The remaining expression classes model compound expressions, i.e. expressions that are defined recursively in terms of sub-expressions.

Class *NegExp* specifies a numeric negation expression that has as value the negative of that of its sub-expression. This class inherits *BaseExp* and adds the attribute *exp* denoting the sub-expression. The sub-expression *exp*, like all sub-expressions declared in classes specifying compound expressions, is contained. This ensures that sub-expressions of an expression form an acyclic structure; i.e. an expression cannot contain itself as a sub-expression.

```
┌─ NegExp ──────────────────────────────
│ BaseExp
│ ┌──────────────────────────────────
│ │ exp : Exp©
│ ├──────────────────────────────────
│ │ exp.value ∉ Num  ⇒  value ∈ Error
│ │ exp.value ∈ Num  ⇒  value ∈ Num ∧
│ │                        value.real = −exp.value.real
│ │ refs = exp.refs
```

If the value of the sub-expression is not in *Num*, i.e. from the definition of class union *Value*, is in *Text* or *Error*, the value of the numeric negation expression is erroneous. This captures the requirement that the error message is displayed if a cell's expression attempts to take the negative of text or an erroneous expression. If the value of the sub-expression is in *Num*, so also is *value*, and the latter's *real* attribute is the negative of that of the sub-expression's value. The set of cells referenced by a numeric negation expression is just the set referenced by the sub-expression.

The remaining compound expression classes all model binary numeric expressions. The class *BinExp* specifies the structure common to each binary expression; it inherits *BaseExp* and adds the attributes exp_1 and exp_2 denoting the sub-expressions which are combined.

```
┌─ BinExp ─────────────────────────
│ BaseExp
│ ┌────────────────────────────────
│ │ exp₁, exp₂ : Exp©
│ ├────────────────────────────────
│ │ exp₁ ≠ exp₂
│ │ value ∈ Num ∪ Error
│ │ refs =
│ │    exp₁.refs ∪ exp₂.refs
│ └────────────────────────────────
```

The condition $exp_1 \neq exp_2$ ensures that the two sub-expressions are distinct objects. Notice that exp_1 and exp_2 may be syntactically the same, e.g. in the expression $3 * c_5 + 3 * c_5$, both exp_1 and exp_2 are $3 * c_5$, but nevertheless they are modelled as distinct objects. This ensures that the structure of sub-expressions is not only acyclic, but in fact forms a tree; thus, one sub-expression can be altered without affecting any other sub-expression which may by coincidence have the same syntactic structure.

The invariant of the class *BinExp* states that the value of evaluating any binary expression is either numeric or erroneous (i.e. it cannot be text). The set of cells referenced by the expression is the union of the sets of cells referenced by its sub-expressions.

The class *DivExp* inherits *BinExp*; it models the binary division of the two inherited sub-expressions exp_1 and exp_2.

```
┌─ DivExp ─────────────────────────────────────────
│ BinExp
│ ┌──────────────────────────────────────────────
│ │ value ∈ Num  ⇔  exp₁.value ∈ Num ∧
│ │                  exp₂.value ∈ Num ∧
│ │                  exp₂.value.real ≠ 0
│ │ value ∈ Num ⇒
│ │    value.real = exp₁.value.real / exp₂.value.real
│ └──────────────────────────────────────────────
```

The value of a division binary expression is a real number if and only if both sub-expressions evaluate to real numbers and the value of the divisor is not zero. In this case, the value is of class *Num* with real attribute equal to the quotient. If the value is not in *Num*, it must be in *Error* since, from the definition of *BinExp*, the value of all binary expressions must be numeric or erroneous.

The remaining binary expression classes, *AddExp*, *SubtExp* and *MultExp*, each inherit the class *OtherBinExp*.

OtherBinExp

BinExp

$value \in Num \Leftrightarrow$
  $exp_1.value \in Num \land$
  $exp_2.value \in Num$

OtherBinExp inherits *BinExp* and adds to the inherited invariant the condition that the values of these remaining expressions are numeric if and only if the values of both of their sub-expressions are numeric, i.e. unlike division, the operations of addition, subtraction and multiplication can be performed on any real numbers.

The class *AddExp* models binary addition expressions.

AddExp

OtherBinExp

$value \in Num \Rightarrow$
  $value.real = exp_1.value.real + exp_2.value.real$

The *real* attribute of the value of an addition binary expression is the sum of the real attributes of the values of exp_1 and exp_2. As in *DivExp*, if the resultant value is not in *Num*, it must be in *Error* since the value of all binary expressions and therefore all 'other binary expressions' must be numeric or erroneous.

The classes *SubtExp* and *MultExp*, corresponding to binary subtraction and multiplication respectively, are similar to *AddExp*.

SubtExp

OtherBinExp

$value \in Num \Rightarrow$
  $value.real = exp_1.value.real - exp_2.value.real$

MultExp

OtherBinExp

$value \in Num \Rightarrow$
  $value.real = exp_1.value.real * exp_2.value.real$

The spreadsheet

A spreadsheet can now be defined as an object of the class *Spreadsheet*:

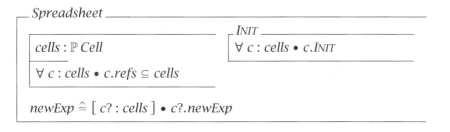

A spreadsheet consists of a set of cells, as modelled by the attribute *cells*. Initially each cell is in its initial state (i.e. displaying the empty string). A new expression can be associated with any cell, but subject to the class invariant that the set of cells directly or indirectly referenced by the expression is a subset of *cells*.

Discussion

Modelling expressions as objects enables both the abstract syntax and semantics to be captured within the one class construct. Consider, for example, addition binary expressions modelled as objects of the class *AddExp*. The declaration of the sub-expressions exp_1 and exp_2 captures abstractly the syntactic idea that an addition binary expression involves the combination of two sub-expressions. The class invariant then captures the semantic evaluation of an addition binary expression by defining it recursively as the addition of the values of the two sub-expressions.

The use of object containment when declaring sub-expressions ensures that no expression contains itself as a sub-expression. Without the notion of object containment such a property would need to be captured by additional invariants in each class.

Notice that the expression classes have no operations: operations for modifying expressions could have been defined, but that goes beyond the level of abstraction modelled here. Rather, changing a cell's associated expression is modelled by whole replacement of its expression.

The reader familiar with the Z free-type construct may have noticed that using the class union *Value* to denote the various possible values obtained when expressions are evaluated illustrates how class union can be used in contexts that traditionally would have been modelled using the free-type construct. To be specific, using free types, *Value* would have been defined by

$$Value ::= text\langle\!\langle seq\ Char \rangle\!\rangle \mid num\langle\!\langle \mathbb{R} \rangle\!\rangle \mid error.$$

However, this definition would have resulted in more complex predicates when defining the expression classes, e.g. the predicate in the class *AddExp* would become

$$value \in \operatorname{ran} num \Rightarrow$$
$$value = num(num^{\sim}(exp_1.value) + num^{\sim}(exp_2.value))$$

where $\sim$ denotes function inverse. The use of class union as a substitution for free types avoids this and generally simplifies the specification.

The definition of *Exp* as a class union effectively groups all of the 'leaf' classes of the expression inheritance hierarchy. An alternative would have been to name the root expression class *Exp*, not *BaseExp*, and replace all sub-expression class types by $\downarrow Exp$. However, this would have admitted the auxiliary classes, *Exp*, *BinExp* and *OtherBinExp*, which are abstract, to be cell expressions or sub-expressions.

Functional abstraction 12

12.1 Introduction

The art of specification is abstraction, i.e. capturing essential functionality, thereby avoiding the distraction of inessential detail and maximising the scope for implementation.

This chapter specifies the essential functionality of a virtual memory which gives the illusion that a fast, relatively small, primary memory has the capacity of a large secondary memory. At the highest level of abstraction, the virtual memory is precisely the illusion, i.e. one large memory. The specification presented here is at the next lower level of abstraction: it focuses on the movement of whole pages between the two memories without concern for distractions such as the word detail of pages, the bit detail of words, the nature of the processor or the commands which request pages.

The chapter also provides further examples of genericity, non-determinism and recursion, applies the nice properties of one-one functions, defines the '∥' version of the parallel operator, and achieves a concise description of the virtual memory by careful design of its constituent objects and their intercommunication.

12.2 A virtual memory: a case study

Informal description

- A virtual memory comprises a fast-access, limited-capacity primary memory, a slow-access, large-capacity secondary memory, a processor and a page map. The map records which pages of secondary memory currently occupy primary memory and which of those pages have been modified (written to) by the processor since occupying primary memory.

- The functionality of interest is independent of the details within a page such as the number of words per page, the field structure of words or the bit detail of fields.

- The primary memory is sectioned into page-sized slots called *frames* that are contiguously numbered from zero to the maximum frame number.

- The secondary memory (conceptually *the* memory from the processor's perspective) is sectioned into pages of equal size which are contiguously numbered from zero to the maximum page number.

- Initially the content of primary memory is unspecified and the page map is empty, recording that no page of secondary memory has been copied into a primary memory frame.

- The processor can only access a page for reading or writing if it is in primary memory, i.e. occupies a frame. If framed, the frame number of the requested page is found from the associations maintained in the page map.

- If a new page is requested, i.e. the page is not framed, a copy of the page is taken from secondary memory and placed in a frame and the selected frame number is associated with the page number by inserting the pair in the page map.

- When a new page is requested there are three distinct cases: their preconditions and responses are as follows.

  - One or more frames are vacant: one is selected non-deterministically to receive the incoming page.
  - All frames are occupied but at least one resident page is unmodified: one of the frames holding an unmodified page is selected non-deterministically and its page is displaced by the new page.
  - All frames are occupied and all of their pages are modified: a frame is selected non-deterministically, its page is copied to its home position in secondary memory and the new page is copied from secondary memory to the vacated frame (this is called *page swapping*).

- The processor in effect sees a large, fast primary memory with occasional delays while secondary memory is accessed.

- A modified page is only copied to secondary memory when its containing frame is selected to contain a new page. However, there must be provision to save all modified pages currently in primary memory from time to time.

The memories

Let the given type

  [*Page*]

denote the set of all pages, and declare the maximum frame number of the primary memory and the maximum page number of the secondary memory to be respectively:

  $maxframenr, maxpagenr : \mathbb{N}$

Define the sets of frame and page numbers to be:

$FrameNr == 0..maxframenr$

$PageNr == 0..maxpagenr$

The following class *Memory* is generic: it is used to derive the primary and secondary memories. *Memory* has a generic type *Index*, each value of which references a page as indicated by the total function *page*.

Memory[Index]

$page : Index \rightarrow Page$

---
sendPage

$index? : Index$

$page! : Page$

$page! = page(index?)$

receivePage

$\Delta(page)$

$index? : Index$

$page? : Page$

$page' = page \oplus$
$\quad \{index? \mapsto page?\}$

Operation *sendPage* outputs the page at a given index position; *receivePage* overwrites the page at a given index position by a given page.

Class *PriMemory*, modelling primary memory, is derived by inheritance from *Memory* with the generic type instantiated to *FrameNr* and all occurrences of *index?* renamed to *framenr?*.

PriMemory

$\upharpoonright(sendPage, receivePage, swapPage)$

$Memory[FrameNr][framenr?/index?]$

$swapPage \triangleq sendPage[oldpage!/page!] \land receivePage$

Operation *swapPage* replaces the page (*oldpage!*) at a given frame number (*framenr?*) with a new page (*page?*). Using conjunction to define this operation ensures that the sent and received pages occupy the same numbered frame.

Class *SecMemory*, modelling secondary memory, is also derived by inheritance from *Memory*. The generic type is instantiated to *PageNr* and all occurrences of *index?* are renamed to *pagenr?*.

SecMemory

$\upharpoonright(sendPage, receivePage, swapPage)$

$Memory[PageNr][pagenr?/index?]$

$swapPage \triangleq sendPage$
$\qquad\qquad \land$
$\qquad\qquad receivePage[oldpagenr?/pagenr?, oldpage?/page?]$

Operation *swapPage* models the receipt at location *oldpagenr?* of the page displaced from primary memory (*oldpage?*) and the sending of the requested page (*page!*) from location *pagenr?*. Note that in the renaming within the *receivePage* component of *swapPage*, *oldpagenr?* renames *pagenr?*, not *index?*, because *index?* is renamed throughout *SecMemory* to *pagenr?* by inheritance.

The processor

The processor is modelled as an object of class *Processor*.

```
┌─ Processor ────────────────────────────────────────────────
│  ⌈(requestPage)
│
│  ┌─ requestPage ──────────────────────────────────────────
│  │  pagenr! : PageNr
│  │  modify! : 𝔹
│  │  framenr? : FrameNr
│  └────────────────────────────────────────────────────────
└───────────────────────────────────────────────────────────
```

Operation *requestPage* nominates the number of the page to be accessed (*pagenr!*) and indicates whether or not the page will be modified (*modify!*). (In reality, the processor accesses a word with either a write command which potentially modifies the word or a read-only command — the 'whole' virtual memory address is partitioned into a page number and a word location within the page. This study ignores such word detail as the main concern of a virtual memory is page control.)

As will be seen later, the response to *requestPage* is the number of the frame (*framenr?*) which holds or will hold the requested page. (In reality, the processor then accesses the requested word in primary memory using the address consisting of *framenr?* and the word location within the page.) In Object-Z (as in Z), all operations and their compositions are atomic. Thus in *requestPage*, the request (*pagenr!* and *modify!*) and response (*framenr?*) are modelled as occurring simultaneously. It will be seen that *requestPage* will be composed with map operations at the system level to provide *framenr?*.

The page map

The role of the page map is to record

- page-location information, i.e. which pages are currently in which frames;

- page-modification information, i.e. the modification status of each framed page.

A page request may require both kinds of information to be updated. It is possible, and desirable, to specify separately the updating of each kind of information and to subsequently combine the two update specifications. Class

LocationUpdate (Figure 12.1) specifies the updating of page-location information, class *ModificationUpdate* specifies the updating of page-modification information, and class *PageMap* combines the two kinds of updates. Operations of these classes do not specify the transfer of pages: their design anticipates cooperation with the memory and processor objects where page transfer is specified. We now consider each class in detail.

Consider class *LocationUpdate*. Attribute *map* records the page-location information, i.e. the association between occupied frame numbers and resident page numbers. This association is one-one because an occupied frame holds exactly one page and at most one copy of a page is framed at any given time. A nice property of a one-one association is that its inverse is also one-one. Thus, the association can be modelled as a one-one function from page numbers to frame numbers or vice versa. As an occupancy enquiry starts with a page number, it is intuitive to model the association from page numbers to frame numbers.

However, overall the operations were found to be more conveniently specified by declaring *map* to be expressed from frame numbers to page numbers. Thus, the domain of *map* is the set of frame numbers of occupied frames and its range is the set of page numbers of framed pages. When all frames are occupied (dom *map* = *FrameNr*), *map* becomes total. Initially, *map* is empty.

Attribute *mods* is the set of page numbers of framed pages which are modified; it is referred to in specifying two operations but is unchanged within this class.

It is often the case in specification that an operation has a basic form which is then enhanced to provide full functionality. The convention is to subscript the basic operation with zero, say op_0, to signify that the operation will be enhanced to *op*. Operation $knownPage_0$ models the case of the requested page being already framed (*pagenr?* $\in$ ran *map*): it outputs the frame number (*framenr!*) using the inverse of *map*. (It will be seen in the class *PageMap* that $knownPage_0$ is enhanced to *knownPage* by also updating the requested page's modification status.)

Operation $newPage_0$ represents the case of the requested page not being framed (*pagenr?* $\notin$ ran *map*) and either there is an unoccupied frame or all frames are occupied but at least one resident page is unmodified. These situations require a new page to be copied from secondary memory; however, there is no need to first copy a modified page from primary memory to its home location in secondary memory before displacing it, i.e. there is no page swapping.

If a free frame exists (dom *map* $\subset$ *FrameNr*), the new page is placed in any one of these (*framenr!* $\notin$ dom *map*). If on the other hand all frames are occupied (dom *map* = *FrameNr*), the new page displaces an unmodified page (*map*(*framenr!*) $\notin$ *mods*). Depending on the subcase, the map subsequently includes the new page number by extension using union or by displacement using overwrite.

Operation $swapPage_0$ covers the remaining case: i.e. the requested page not being framed and all frames being occupied by modified pages (*mods* =

```
┌─ LocationUpdate ────────────────────────────────────────────────
│
│  ┌──────────────────────────────┐  ┌─ INIT ────────────────────
│  │ map : FrameNr ⤖ PageNr       │  │ map = ∅
│  │ mods : ℙ PageNr              │  └──────────────────────────
│  └──────────────────────────────┘
│
│  ┌─ knownPage₀ ──────────────────────────────────────────────
│  │ pagenr? : PageNr
│  │ framenr! : FrameNr
│  ├──────────────────────────────────────────────────────────
│  │ pagenr? ∈ ran map
│  │ framenr! = map~(pagenr?)
│  └──────────────────────────────────────────────────────────
│
│  ┌─ newPage₀ ────────────────────────────────────────────────
│  │ Δ(map)
│  │ pagenr? : PageNr
│  │ framenr! : FrameNr
│  ├──────────────────────────────────────────────────────────
│  │ pagenr? ∉ ran map
│  │ dom map ⊂ FrameNr ⇒
│  │    framenr! ∉ dom map ∧
│  │    map' = map ∪ {framenr! ↦ pagenr?}
│  │ dom map = FrameNr ⇒
│  │    map(framenr!) ∉ mods ∧
│  │    map' = map ⊕ {framenr! ↦ pagenr?}
│  └──────────────────────────────────────────────────────────
│
│  ┌─ swapPage₀ ───────────────────────────────────────────────
│  │ Δ(map)
│  │ pagenr?, oldpagenr! : PageNr
│  │ framenr! : FrameNr
│  ├──────────────────────────────────────────────────────────
│  │ pagenr? ∉ ran map
│  │ dom map = FrameNr
│  │ mods = ran map
│  │ oldpagenr! = map(framenr!)
│  │ map' = map ⊕ {framenr! ↦ pagenr?}
│  └──────────────────────────────────────────────────────────
│
│  ┌─ saveModPage₀ ────────────────────────────────────────────
│  │ framenr! : FrameNr
│  │ pagenr! : PageNr
│  ├──────────────────────────────────────────────────────────
│  │ (framenr!, pagenr!) ∈ (map ▷ mods)
│  └──────────────────────────────────────────────────────────
│
└──────────────────────────────────────────────────────────────
```

Figure 12.1: the class *LocationUpdate*

ran *map*). As will be seen, space is made for the requested page by copying the page from any frame *framenr*! in *FrameNr* back to its home location (*oldpagenr*!). It will also be seen that the requested page is copied from secondary memory to the vacated frame.

Examination of the preconditions of the above three operations shows that they partition the state space, i.e. exactly one is applicable in any state satisfying the class definition.

Operation *saveModPage*$_0$ identifies a frame-number, page-number pair in *map* corresponding to some framed page which has been modified: it is applied when saving modified pages. The operation does not change the state.

The class *ModificationUpdate* specifies the updating of page-modification information:

$$\boxed{\begin{array}{l} \underline{\textit{ModificationUpdate}} \\[4pt] \boxed{\begin{array}{l} mods : \mathbb{P}\; PageNr \end{array}} \\[4pt] \boxed{\begin{array}{l} \underline{\textit{condAddMod}} \\ \Delta(mods) \\ pagenr? : PageNr \\ modify? : \mathbb{B} \\ \hline modify? \;\Rightarrow\; mods' = mods \cup \{pagenr?\} \\ \neg\, modify? \;\Rightarrow\; mods' = mods \end{array}} \\[4pt] \boxed{\begin{array}{l} \underline{\textit{remMod}} \\ \Delta(mods) \\ pagenr? : PageNr \\ \hline mods' = mods \setminus \{pagenr?\} \end{array}} \\[4pt] \boxed{\begin{array}{l} \underline{\textit{noMods}} \\ mods = \varnothing \end{array}} \\[4pt] swapMod \;\widehat{=}\; remMod[\,oldpagenr?\,/\,pagenr?\,] \;{}^{\circ}_{9}\; condAddMod \end{array}}$$

The declaration of attribute *mods* in this class is identical to its declaration in class *LocationUpdate* and with the same meaning. (That the two appearances denote the same quantity is captured later by multiple inheritance in *PageMap*.)

Operations *condAddMod* and *remMod* update the modification status of framed pages. Operation *condAddMod* adds the requested page number to set *mods* if modification is notified (*modified?* is true): as we shall see, it is applied whenever a page is requested.

Operation *remMod* removes the number of a displaced page (*pagenr?*) from *mods*. The operation, with *pagenr?* renamed to *oldpagenr?*, is applied in the case of page swapping to remove the reference to the displaced page (*oldpagenr?*) . It is also applied whenever a modified page is copied to its home location in secondary memory. Both *condAddMod* and *remMod* are always applicable.

Operation *noMods* is simply a predicate indicating that no framed page is modified.

Operation *swapMod* is sequential: it removes the old page number from the set of modified pages and conditionally adds the new page number. It is always applicable as its components are always applicable.

The class *PageMap* combines the page-location and page-modification update specifications by multiple inheritance:

PageMap

$\restriction(\textit{INIT}, \textit{knownPage}, \textit{newPage}, \textit{swapPage}, \textit{saveModPage}, \textit{noMods})$

LocationUpdate
ModificationUpdate

$\textit{mods} \subseteq \text{ran } \textit{map}$

$\textit{knownPage} \mathrel{\hat{=}} \textit{knownPage}_0 \wedge \textit{condAddMod}$

$\textit{newPage} \mathrel{\hat{=}} \textit{newPage}_0 \wedge \textit{condAddMod}$

$\textit{swapPage} \mathrel{\hat{=}} \textit{swapPage}_0 \mathbin{\|_!} \textit{swapMod}$

$\textit{saveModPage} \mathrel{\hat{=}} \textit{saveModPage}_0 \mathbin{\|_!} \textit{remMod}$

The class invariant imposes the constraint that the set of page numbers of modified pages can be at most the range of *map*. As *PageMap* inherits *LocationUpdate*'s initial predicate, namely *map* = ∅, it follows that *mods* is also initially empty.

Operations, *knownPage*, *newPage* and *swapPage*, are the enhanced versions of their zero-subscripted counterparts: they maintain both the location and modification information for the three principal cases detailed above. From the previous observations on the preconditions of the constituents of the enhanced operations, the preconditions of the enhanced operations partition the state space, i.e. exactly one is applicable in any state satisfying the class signature and invariant.

Operation *swapPage* uses the operator '$\|_!$' which is a variation of the parallel operator '$\|$': the difference is that $\|_!$ does not hide the output of a matching input/output communication pair. Thus, *oldpagenr*! is not hidden in its communication with matching *oldpagenr*? — as will be seen, it is required by the secondary memory when receiving a displaced modified page.

Operation *saveModPage* enhances *saveModPage*$_0$ by also removing the selected page number *pagenr*! from *mods*. By using the $\|_!$ operator, *pagenr*! is not hidden and therefore the output of *saveModPage* comprises both *framenr*! and *pagenr*!. As will be seen later, this provides the address information for the primary and secondary memories respectively to send and receive the modified page.

The virtual memory

Class *VirtualMemory* assembles the memories, processor and page map:

┌─ *VirtualMemory* ──────────────────────────────────────
│ ⌈(*INIT*, *request*, *saveAllModPages*)
│ ┌──
│ │ *pri* : *PriMemory*
│ │ *sec* : *SecMemory*
│ │ *proc* : *Processor*
│ │ *pagemap* : *PageMap*
│ └──
│
│ ┌─ *INIT* ───
│ │ *pagemap.INIT*
│ └──
│
│ *request* ≙
│   *proc.requestPage*
│   ∥
│   (*pagemap.knownPage*
│   ▯
│   *pagemap.newPage* ∥₁ *pri.receivePage* ∥ *sec.sendPage*
│   ▯
│   *pagemap.swapPage* ∥₁ *pri.swapPage* ∥ *sec.swapPage*)
│ *saveModPage* ≙
│   *pagemap.saveModPage* ∥ *pri.sendPage* ∥ *sec.receivePage*
│ *saveAllModPages* ≙
│   (*saveModPage* ⨟ *saveAllModPages*)
│   ▯
│   *pagemap.noMods*
└──

Operation *request* is the parallel composition of a processor request with one of three alternatives. The formal specification text defining *request* is complemented by Figure 12.2. As the processor's operation *requestPage* is always applicable, and the preconditions of the three page map operations partition the state space, and the preconditions of the memory operations are always applicable, operation *request* is always applicable. The ∥₁ operator is associative but ∥ is not. Constructs with chains of ∥ or chains of mixed ∥₁ and ∥ are associated left to right (i.e. left associatively). The ∥₁ operator is needed where shown in the specification of *request* to retain (not to hide) *framenr!* for communication with the processor. In the third alternative of the choice construct, using ∥₁ also retains *oldpagenr!* but it is subsequently hidden by that alternative's ∥ operation as it matches *oldpagenr?* of *sec.swapPage*.

Note that the resultant communication interfaces of the three alternatives of the choice construct are identical — (*pagenr?*, *modify?*, *framenr!*) — which co-matches that of the processor exactly. Furthermore, as the processor's

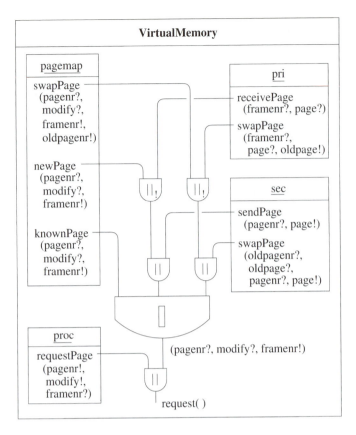

Figure 12.2: the *request* operation of *VirtualMemory*

requestPage is composed with the choice construct using ‖ which hides communicating variables, *VirtualMemory*'s operation *request* has no resultant communication variables.

Operation *saveModPage* models the saving of one modified page from primary memory to secondary memory with the guidance of the page map which outputs the required primary and secondary memory addresses.

Operation *saveAllModPages* progressively saves modified pages until all are saved (i.e. the page map's *noMods* operation becomes applicable). Its definition is recursive: it is equivalent to a sequence of *saveModPage* operations of length equal to the number of modified pages terminated by operation *noMods*. As *saveModPage* reduces the page map's *mods* but not its *map*, operation *saveAllModPages* leaves the page map's *map* unchanged.

Operation *saveModPage* leaves primary memory unchanged as *sendPage* is read-only: thus, operation *saveAllModPages* also leaves the primary memory unchanged. Immediately after saving all modified pages then, the pages in primary memory agree with the pages in secondary memory (the modified pages were just copied from primary memory), i.e. there is no need to reinitialise the page map.

Discussion

An alternative to specifying page-by-page iteration to save all modified pages is to specify an en-bloc saving. This may be achieved as follows.

1. The page map sends to primary memory the submap $map \rhd mods$ (i.e. the set of frame number, page number pairs where the page numbers are those of modified pages). Suppose this submap is output as $modmap!$.

2. The primary memory receives $modmap!$ as $modmap?$, inverts it (result type $PageNr \rightarrowtail FrameNr$) and functionally composes this inverse with attribute $page$ (of type $FrameNr \twoheadrightarrow Page$) to give a function whose type is $PageNr \twoheadrightarrow Page$. This function is expressed as $(modmap?)^{\sim} \, {}_{9}^{\circ} \, page$ and denotes the secondary memory locations which need updating and their corresponding modified pages. Suppose the function is sent to secondary memory as $modpage!$.

3. The secondary memory receives $modpage!$ as $modpage?$ and overwrites attribute $page$ with it ($page' = page \oplus modpage?$) thereby achieving the en-bloc saving.

Due to the power of functional operators and the ability to use functional types for communication variables, the en-bloc specification is more concise than the recursive version. Also, the en-bloc specification is more abstract: in reality, saving is iteratively page-by-page, in fact word-by-word. The en-bloc specification prescribes precisely the essential functionality of saving all modified pages — the essence of specification.

The *VirtualMemory* class specification (as with other classes which include composed operations) does not show explicitly the communication variables of composed operations. Rather, the communication variables need to be deduced from the component operations. As seen above, diagrams such as Figure 12.2 can complement and assist in this regard.

Semantic issues of Object-Z **13**

13.1 Introduction

This book focuses on the notation, scope and practical application of Object-Z with the meaning of constructs presented informally and illustrated by example. However, in defining a language, questions arise about the precise form which constructs may take and, for each valid form, the precise meaning. Such questions are answered by means of a formal (i.e. a rigorous mathematical) description of the language. Formal descriptions are often extensive and complex; nevertheless, without a formal description finer points of interpretation cannot be resolved and misunderstandings arise which may have serious implications in practice.

The need for a formal description of a formal specification language such as Object-Z is essential as formal specification is the basis for validation with respect to requirements and for verification with respect to implementation.

Formal descriptions of languages typically commence with an *abstract syntax*, i.e. a set of rules for forming language constructs from their essential components. An abstract syntax, in contrast to a *concrete* syntax, abstracts away detail such as the actual symbol set of keywords and operators; also, it is free from the concern of precedence of operators — this is resolved on parsing with respect to a concrete syntax. Collectively, the abstract syntax enables an abstraction of the highest-level concrete language constructs (whole specifications in the case of Object-Z) to be constructed from the primitives of the language (integers, attributes, etc.).

The meaning of language constructs is conveyed by *semantics*. A *denotational* semantics typically proceeds from abstract syntax through a *static* semantics to a *dynamic* semantics. The role of static semantics is to eliminate a range of language constructs which conform to the abstract syntax but nevertheless cannot be given a semantic interpretation. The word 'static' implies that such elimination is based on considerations such as type consistency, agreement in number of actual and formal parameters, and other aspects which do not depend on the values of dynamic quantities such as variables. Tools which check for conformity to syntax and static semantics are commonly called *type checkers*. A dynamic semantics maps valid language constructs (i.e. those with correct syntax and static semantics) to the values which they *denote* in pre-scribed semantic domains.

An *axiomatic* semantics is a theory of the language comprising axioms and rules of inference which assert facts and provide a deductive basis for reasoning respectively. An axiomatic semantics is particularly useful to prove conjectured properties about systems implied by their formal specifications. An axiomatic semantics is required when using a computer-aided proof assistant to discharge proof obligations which arise within a rigorous development methodology, e.g. an obligation to show that the result of a refinement step satisfies the specification.

A denotational semantics and an axiomatic semantics, if purporting to describe formally the same language, are related. The relationship is expressed by saying that the denotational semantics is a *model* of the axiomatic semantics, while the existence of such a model establishes that the axiomatic semantics is *sound*, i.e. that it cannot prove contradictory properties. The topic of axiomatic semantics is not discussed further in this book.

The semantics of object orientation is complex as the issues of classes, object identity, inheritance and polymorphism must be addressed. As Object-Z is so oriented, its formal description is also complex and considerable research has been invested exploring various approaches and expressing its semantics.

Inclusion of a complete semantics for Object-Z is beyond the scope of this book. The remainder of this chapter introduces the following selection of denotational semantic issues:

- object identity;

- composed operations for conjunctive, parallel, sequential and choice composition not involving operation application, with an informal introduction to the formal semantics for each kind of composition;

- inheritance.

An understanding of the Z schema calculus is assumed. Appendix C presents the concrete syntax of Object-Z.

13.2   Semantics of object identity

The ability to identify and reference objects uniquely, as illustrated in previous chapters, is an essential aspect of object orientation. The semantics of object identity in Object-Z extends the type system of Z to include *ObjectType*, the set of object types, as shown in Figure 13.1.

ObjectType is a subset of *Type*: it is constructed from *ClassName*, the set of class names, by the total one-one function *objectT*, i.e. each class name maps to a distinct object type. The function *carrier*, also one-one, maps each type to a distinct set of values permitted for that type; thus it maps each object

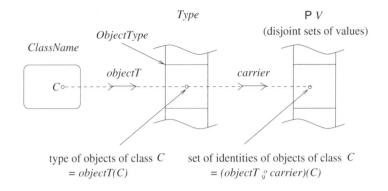

Figure 13.1: functions and sets defining object identity

type to a distinct set of object identities. In summary, distinct classes map to distinct object types which map to disjoint sets of object identities.

For a given specification, types of interest are constructed iteratively from the specification's given types and object types using the notions of power set, Cartesian product, and so on. Thus, object types may appear in the declaration of sets, relations, functions, etc. To accommodate genericity and renaming in classes, *ClassName* in the above description needs to be widened to *ClassDes* (the set of all class designators). The details are omitted.

There is no a priori understanding that declared variables of the same object type refer to distinct objects or that distinct sets of identities of objects of the one class are disjoint. This freedom permits the introduction of object identity aliases but also imposes obligations with regard to alias control, i.e. specifications must be specific about the intended equality or otherwise of object identities.

As seen in Chapter 10, the notion of object containment considerably reduces the amount of explicit specification text required to ensure that certain object identities are distinct or that certain sets of object identities are disjoint.

13.3   Informal semantics of composed operations

This section introduces the semantics of operations and their composition informally using examples. Section 13.4 formalises the general case of composing operations within a class.

Consider the specification of the rather contrived class *CountStack* in Figure 13.2. Within this specification, local operation *push* denotes the pair:

$$
(\quad
\begin{array}{|l}
\hline
\Delta State \\
n? : \mathbb{N} \\
\hline
items' = \langle n? \rangle \frown items \\
\hline
\end{array}
\quad , \; \{items\} \;)
$$

The first component of the pair, called the schema component, is a schema

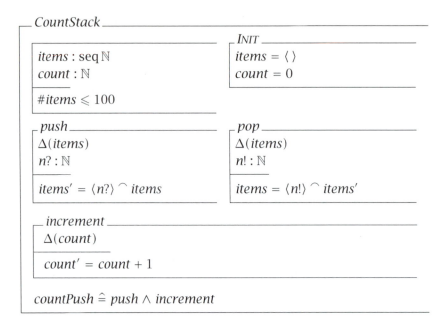

$$
\begin{array}{l}
\textit{CountStack} \\
\hline
\textit{items} : \text{seq} \, \mathbb{N} \qquad\qquad \textit{INIT} \\
\textit{count} : \mathbb{N} \qquad\qquad\qquad \textit{items} = \langle\,\rangle \\
\qquad\qquad\qquad\qquad\qquad\; \textit{count} = 0 \\
\#\textit{items} \leqslant 100 \\
\\
\textit{push} \qquad\qquad\qquad\qquad \textit{pop} \\
\Delta(\textit{items}) \qquad\qquad\qquad \Delta(\textit{items}) \\
n? : \mathbb{N} \qquad\qquad\qquad\qquad n! : \mathbb{N} \\
\textit{items}' = \langle n?\rangle \frown \textit{items} \quad \textit{items} = \langle n!\rangle \frown \textit{items}' \\
\\
\textit{increment} \\
\Delta(\textit{count}) \\
\textit{count}' = \textit{count} + 1 \\
\\
\textit{countPush} \ \widehat{=}\ \textit{push} \wedge \textit{increment}
\end{array}
$$

Figure 13.2: the class *CountStack*

formed from *push* by replacing its Δ-list by $\Delta State$ which is the schema conjunction *State* $\wedge$ *State'*, where *State* and *State'* are the unprimed and primed versions respectively of *CountStack*'s state schema.

The second component, called the δ-set, is the set of attributes corresponding to *push*'s Δ-list. Inclusion of $\Delta State$ in the schema component of the denotation provides the basis for defining state transitions which respect the class invariant.

The attributes are constrained by their types and the class invariant and, in this case, *items* is further constrained by the predicate of the schema component, i.e. the predicate of *push*. The denotation is said to be 'open' with respect to *count*. Open attributes are distinguished by not belonging to the δ-set component of the denotation.

The operation *cs.push*, where *cs* identifies an object of class *CountStack*, is a remote operation: its denotation is formed from the above denotation of *push* by

1. conjoining *count'* = *count* to the predicate of the schema component as *count* is not in the δ-set component,

2. adding *count* to the δ-set component, and

3. qualifying *items* and *count* by *cs* to *cs.items* and *cs.count* respectively throughout the denotation.

Parts 1 and 2 above 'close' the denotation, and part 3 'qualifies' the closed denotation with respect to the particular object. Input and output variables remain unqualified — they model the communication interface of the operation.

Delaying the closure of open attributes until an operation is referenced remotely facilitates the composition of operations within the class. For example, the intent of operation *countPush* to satisfy both *push* and *increment* would not be satisfied if *push* imposed the constraint $count' = count$ or if *increment* imposed $items' = items$.

The denotational semantics of a composed operation, such as *countPush*, is expressed in terms of the denotations of its constituent operations, the expression depending on the kind of composition as outlined below. The discussion below refers to compositions of operations within the one class. The semantics of compositions which involve remote operations is not considered further in this book.

Conjunctive composition

For operations op_1 and op_2 with denotations (σ_1, δ_1) and (σ_2, δ_2) respectively, their conjunction $op_1 \wedge op_2$ (see Section 1.6) has denotation

$$(\sigma_1 \wedge \sigma_2,\ \delta_1 \cup \delta_2)$$

Thus, *countPush* denotes

$$\left(\quad \begin{array}{|l}
\Delta State \\
n? : \mathbb{N} \\
\hline
items' = \langle n? \rangle \frown items \\
count' = count + 1
\end{array} \quad,\ \{items, count\}\ \right)$$

It is noted that the conjunction symbol $\wedge$ is overloaded: in $op_1 \wedge op_2$ it indicates operation conjunction in Object-Z, whereas in $\sigma_1 \wedge \sigma_2$ it indicates schema conjunction as defined in the semantics of Z.

Input and output variables of op_1 and op_2 become input and output variables of their associated schemas σ_1 and σ_2. These variables are subject to merging in conjoining σ_1 and σ_2 in the same way as other schema variables, i.e. identically named variables are considered to be semantically identical. For example, if *increment* also had an input $n? : \mathbb{N}$, it would be merged with $n?$ of *push*. If σ_1 and σ_2 each had an input $x?$ and an output $x!$, the $x?$'s would be merged and the $x!$'s would be merged, but $x?$ would not be identified with $x!$ — with conjunction there is no notion of an output of one schema being an input to the other, i.e. there is no inter-operation communication between complementary input/output pairs.

Parallel composition

Parallel composition is similar to conjunction except that an input variable of one operation and an output variable of the other which have identical base names are equated, i.e. there is inter-operation communication between this complementary pair . For example, if σ_1 has an output of $x!$ and σ_2 has an input $x?$, they form a complementary pair and are equated. Similarly, if σ_2 has an output of $y!$ and σ_1 has an input $y?$, they too are equated. Inter-operation communication in parallel composition may therefore be bi-directional (unlike piping in Z which is left-to-right only). There are two versions of parallel composition: the $\|$ version (see Section 1.7) hides complementary inputs and outputs (i.e. communication is fully internalised), whereas the $\|_!$ version (see Section 12.2) hides only the inputs of complementary pairs (i.e. communication is only partially internalised as the outputs remain exposed). The need for two versions is justified on the basis of numerous case studies.

The $\|$ version

In defining the semantics of $\|$, it is necessary to systematically rename the input and output variables of each complementary pair to a single replacement name which is distinct both from other replacement names and from all names in scope. For example, suppose σ_1 has an output $x!$ and σ_2 has an input $x?$ and suppose these variables are each replaced by a new variable c. The resultant denotation of $op_1 \| op_2$ for this example is

$$((\sigma_1[c/x!] \wedge \sigma_2[c/x?]) \setminus (c),\ \delta_1 \cup \delta_2)$$

Renaming $x!$ and $x?$ to c effects the communication, and hiding c internalises the communication. The need to introduce c is seen as follows. Suppose that instead of introducing c, it was proposed to rename the $x?$ of σ_2 to $x!$ to effect the linkage with the $x!$ of σ_1, and hide $x!$. This would fail in the case where σ_2 also has an output $x!$ as it too would be linked and hidden. A similar problem arises with a proposal to rename the $x!$ of σ_1 to $x?$ and hide $x?$ as σ_1 may also have an input $x?$.

The $\|_!$ version

The introduction of new variables to replace complementary input/output variables is not necessary in this version of parallel. Returning to the example where σ_1 has $x!$ and σ_2 has both $x?$ and $x!$, suppose that $x?$ is renamed to $x!$. This effects the desired linkage, hides the linked input and leaves the linked output exposed. The exposed $x!$ is merged with σ_2's $x!$ as required (residual inputs/outputs, after inter-operation communication is effected, are subject to conjunction semantics).

The resultant denotation of $op_1 \|_! op_2$ for this example is

$$(\sigma_1 \wedge \sigma_2[x!/x?],\ \delta_1 \cup \delta_2)$$

Sequential composition

The definition of the sequential composition $op_1 \mathbin{\mathring{\,}_9} op_2$ (see Section 1.9) of operations op_1 and op_2 requires the introduction of an intermediate state: the transitions prescribed by σ_1 are sequentially composed with the transitions prescribed by σ_2 via the intermediate state. In cases where δ_1 and δ_2 differ, attributes in the difference set $\delta_2 \setminus \delta_1$ are closed in conjunction with the transitions of σ_1 and, similarly, attributes $\delta_1 \setminus \delta_2$ are closed in conjunction with the transitions of σ_2. Without such closure, the values of attributes in the two difference sets, i.e. those in the union of δ_1 and δ_2 but not their intersection, become non-deterministic. Sequential composition comprises all linking transitions in the manner of forward relational composition.

Sequential composition also effects left-to-right, internalised communication. This is defined by identifying each output of σ_1 which complements an input of σ_2, replacing the two variables with a new single variable and subsequently hiding it.

Returning to the example where σ_1 has an output $x!$, σ_2 has a complementary input $x?$ and c is the replacement variable, the resultant denotation of $op_1 \mathbin{\mathring{\,}_9} op_2$ for this example is

$$((close(\sigma_1[c/x!], \delta_2 \setminus \delta_1) \mathbin{\mathring{\,}_9} close(\sigma_2[c/x?], \delta_1 \setminus \delta_2)) \setminus (c), \; \delta_1 \cup \delta_2)$$

where $close(\sigma, atts)$ returns the given schema σ with additional conjuncts of the form $att' = att$ for each att in $atts$.

The symbol '$\mathbin{\mathring{\,}_9}$' denotes Z sequential composition: it is overloaded as it also denotes Object-Z sequential composition.

Sequential composition in Object-Z and in Z, despite its definition in terms of an intermediate state, is atomic, i.e. overall the resultant operation is denoted by the pair comprising the resultant schema and δ-set. Sequential composition is 'angelic' in the sense that the resultant schema comprises just linkages which connect — there is no implication of commitment to a linkage of the first operation which does not connect to a linkage of the second, i.e. no implication of blocking in the intermediate state. The model is therefore akin to relational composition, in contrast to a sequence of two computer language imperatives where the first proceeds without consideration of the second.

Choice composition

A requirement for choice composition is that the component operations have identical input/output names and types, i.e. the operations have identical input/output interfaces. Transitions from a given state for a particular input are the union of the corresponding transitions of the component operations. Thus, for the conditions under consideration, if both operations have transformations, they form a collection of possible transitions; if only one operation has transitions, that operation determines the outcome; and if neither operation has a transition, the composition is inapplicable.

Where δ_1 and δ_2 differ, attributes in the difference set $\delta_2 \setminus \delta_1$ are closed in conjunction with the transitions of σ_1 and, similarly, attributes $\delta_1 \setminus \delta_2$ are closed in conjunction with the transitions of σ_2. This extends the definition of transitions arising from one operation to ensure that attributes which are in the overall composition but not in that operation's Δ-list do not change.

The resultant denotation of $op_1 \; [] \; op_2$ is

$$(\; close(\sigma_1, \; \delta_2 \setminus \delta_1) \; \vee \; close(\sigma_2, \; \delta_1 \setminus \delta_2), \; \; \delta_1 \cup \delta_2 \;)$$

where '$\vee$' is the Z schema disjunction operator.

13.4   Formal semantics of composed operations

So far, the semantics of composed operations, particularly with respect to inter-operation communication, has been presented by example. This section defines the denotations for composed operations not involving operation application. The following preliminaries assist the definitions.

Preliminary definitions

Functions *i_vars* and *o_vars* return the set of names of the input and output variables respectively of a given schema. The names include the ? and ! suffixes.

Function *comp* returns the complement of a given input or output name, thus, $comp(x?) = x!$ and vice versa.

Renaming is denoted by a pair of equal-length sequences of names. For example

$$S[ns_1 / ns_2]$$

denotes the replacement in schema S of each name in the sequence of names ns_2 by the corresponding name in the same length sequence ns_1. Names in ns_2 must be distinct, i.e. $\#ns_2 = \#\text{ran } ns_2$, and replacement is simultaneous.

Relation *setseq* relates a set of names to sequences of those names without replication, i.e. $x \; \underline{setseq} \; y \Leftrightarrow (\text{ran } y = x \wedge \#y = \#\text{ran } y)$. This relation is used to construct a sequence of names in arbitrary order from a set of names so as to facilitate their subsequent renaming.

Function *close* takes a schema σ and a set of attributes *atts* and returns the schema

$$\sigma \wedge A$$

where A is the schema with declaration part comprising declarations of the form $att, att' : T$ for each att in $atts$, T being the type of att, and predicate part comprising conjuncts of the form $att' = att$ for each att in $atts$. Function *close* is used to extend an operation schema to include additional attributes and ensure that they do not change.

Sequential schema composition in Z is defined as follows:

$$R \mathbin{{}^\circ_9} S \mathrel{\hat=} (R[v''/v'] \wedge S[v''/v]) \setminus (\operatorname{ran} v'')$$

where v is a sequence of arbitrary order formed from the unprimed state variables common to schemas R and S, and v' and v'' are namewise decorated versions of v.

Function *sig* returns the signature of a given schema, i.e. returns the partial function which maps the names of the schema's variables to their declared types.

Symbol $\mathcal{M}$ indicates 'the denotation of' in the following:

$$\textbf{let } \mathcal{M}(op_1) \equiv (\sigma_1, \delta_1)$$
$$\mathcal{M}(op_2) \equiv (\sigma_2, \delta_2)$$
$$\mathcal{M}(op_1 \odot op_2) \equiv (\sigma, \delta)$$

where $\odot \in \{\wedge, \|, \|_!, \mathbin{{}^\circ_9}, \,[]\,\}$.

Components σ and δ are now defined for the five composition operators.

Conjunctive composition

$$\sigma \mathrel{\hat=} \sigma_1 \wedge \sigma_2$$
$$\delta \mathrel{\hat=} \delta_1 \cup \delta_2$$

From the semantics of Z schema conjunction and set union, conjunctive composition is commutative and associative.

Parallel composition (|| version)

let $co\_set_1 == o\_vars(\sigma_1) \cap comp(\!| \, i\_vars(\sigma_2) \, |\!)$
   (the set of output names of σ_1 which complement input names of σ_2)
let $co\_set_2 == o\_vars(\sigma_2) \cap comp(\!| \, i\_vars(\sigma_1) \, |\!)$
   (the set of output names of σ_2 which complement input names of σ_1)
let $cio\_set_1 == co\_set_1 \cup comp(\!| \, co\_set_2 \, |\!)$
   (the set of input/output names of σ_1 which complement input/output
   names of σ_2)
let cio_seq_1 be a sequence such that cio_set_1 *setseq* cio_seq_1
let $cio\_seq_2 == cio\_seq_1 \mathbin{{}^\circ_9} comp$
   (the namewise complement of cio_seq_1: $\mathbin{{}^\circ_9}$ denotes forward functional
   composition)
let new_seq be a sequence of distinct names not otherwise in scope such that
   $\#new\_seq = \#cio\_seq_1$

$$\sigma \mathrel{\hat=} (\sigma_1[new\_seq/cio\_seq_1] \wedge \sigma_2[new\_seq/cio\_seq_2]) \setminus \operatorname{ran} new\_seq$$
$$\delta \mathrel{\hat=} \delta_1 \cup \delta_2$$

Parallel composition, || version, is commutative but non-associative because of hiding (without explicit parentheses, left association is implied).

Parallel composition ($\|_!$ version)

let co_set_1 and co_set_2 be defined as above
let co_seq_1 be a sequence such that $co\_set_1 \ \underline{setseq} \ co\_seq_1$
let $ci\_seq_2 == co\_seq_1 \ _9^\circ \ comp$
             (the namewise complement of co_seq_1)
let co_seq_2 be a sequence such that $co\_set_2 \ \underline{setseq} \ co\_seq_2$
let $ci\_seq_1 == co\_seq_2 \ _9^\circ \ comp$

$$\sigma \mathrel{\widehat{=}} \sigma_1[co\_seq_2/ci\_seq_1] \wedge \sigma_2[co\_seq_1/ci\_seq_2]$$
$$\delta \mathrel{\widehat{=}} \delta_1 \cup \delta_2$$

Parallel composition, $\|_!$ version, is commutative and associative.

Sequential composition

let co_set_1, co_seq_1 and ci_seq_2 be as defined under $\|_!$
let new_seq be a sequence of distinct names not otherwise in scope such that
$\#new\_seq = \#co\_seq_1$

$$\sigma \mathrel{\widehat{=}} (close(\sigma_1[new\_seq/co\_seq_1], \ \delta_2 \setminus \delta_1) \ _9^\circ$$
$$close(\sigma_2[new\_seq/ci\_seq_2], \ \delta_1 \setminus \delta_2)) \setminus (\mathrm{ran}\ new\_seq)$$
$$\delta \mathrel{\widehat{=}} \delta_1 \cup \delta_2$$

Sequential composition is non-commutative and non-associative (without explicit parentheses, left association is implied).

Choice composition

$$\sigma \mathrel{\widehat{=}} close(\sigma_1, \ \delta_2 \setminus \delta_1) \ \vee \ close(\sigma_2, \ \delta_1 \setminus \delta_2)$$
$$\delta \mathrel{\widehat{=}} \delta_1 \cup \delta_2$$

The following equality ensures that the input/output interfaces of op_1 and op_2 are identical

$$(i\_vars(\sigma_1) \cup o\_vars(\sigma_1)) \lhd sig(\sigma_1) =$$
$$(i\_vars(\sigma_2) \cup o\_vars(\sigma_2)) \lhd sig(\sigma_2)$$

Choice composition is commutative and associative.

Conjunctive and parallel composition involve schema conjunction, sequential composition involves schema sequential composition, and choice composition involves schema disjunction.

13.5 Semantics of inheritance

Throughout the following subsections, class C inherits classes A and B.

Constant and type definitions

Let the constant and type definitions of A and B be $defs_A$ and $defs_B$ respectively and let the constant and type definitions introduced locally in C be $local\_defs_C$.

The constant and type definitions inherited by C, denoted inh_defs_C, are collectively $defs_A$ and $defs_B$. The totality of constant and type definitions of C, denoted $defs_C$, is collectively inh_defs_C and $local\_defs_C$.

Defined quantities with the same name must have identical definitions. It is noted that $defs_A$ and $defs_B$ may include inherited definitions.

State schema

Let the states of A and B be denoted by schemas $state_A$ and $state_B$ respectively and let the state schema-text introduced locally in C be $local\_state_C$. The inherited state schema of C, denoted inh_state_C, and the resultant state schema of C, denoted $state_C$, are defined as follows.

$$inh\_state_C \; \hat{=} \; state_A \wedge state_B$$
$$state_C \; \hat{=} \; inh\_state_C \bullet local\_state_C$$

The definition of $state_C$ is expressed as an environment enrichment instead of a conjunction because $local\_state_C$ may reference quantities declared in inh_state_C, i.e. technically $local\_state_C$ by itself need not satisfy the schema requirement that all references refer to defined constants or types in scope or variables declared in the schema.

Names common to $state_A$ and $state_B$ may be intentional (e.g. A and B may have a common ancestor) or coincidental. If intentional, merging as defined is appropriate; if coincidental, however, the clash must be resolved by renaming. It is noted that $state_A$ and $state_B$ may include inherited components.

Initial state schema

Let the initial state schemas of A and B be $init_A$ and $init_B$ respectively and let the initial predicate introduced locally in C be $local\_init_C$. The inherited initial schema of C, denoted inh_init_C, and the resultant initial schema of C, denoted $init_C$, are defined as follows:

$$inh\_init_C \; \hat{=} \; init_A \wedge init_B$$
$$init_C \; \hat{=} \; (inh\_init_C \wedge state_C) \bullet local\_init_C$$

Inclusion of $state_C$ in $init_C$ ensures that the initial schema includes the resultant (inherited plus local) state schema, i.e. initial states are a subset of the resultant valid states. Again, $init_A$ and $init_B$ may include inherited components.

Operations

Suppose A has an operation named *op* with denotation in A of $(\sigma\_op_A, \delta\_op_A)$. In C, this denotation is modified to reflect interpretation in $state_C$ rather than $state_A$ by conjoining σ_op_A with $\Delta state_C$. If B also has an operation named *op* with denotation in B of $(\sigma\_op_B, \delta\_op_B)$, C inherits an operation named *op* with denotation in C of

$$(\sigma\_op_A \wedge \sigma\_op_B \wedge \Delta state_C, \; \delta\_op_A \cup \delta\_op_B)$$

Let this be expressed as $(inh\_\sigma\_op_C, \; inh\_\delta\_op_C)$.

If the occurrence of the common name *op* in A and B is coincidental, multiple inheritance is eliminated by renaming.

If C also includes specification text for an operation named *op*, let its local denotation (i.e. ignoring the inherited denotation of *op* but including $\Delta state_C$ in the schema component) be

$$(local\_\sigma\_op_C, \; local\_\delta\_op_C)$$

Then the resultant operation *op* in C is denoted by

$$(inh\_\sigma\_op_C \wedge local\_\sigma\_op_C, \; inh\_\delta\_op_C \cup local\_\delta\_op_C)$$

Again, coincidental same-name occurrences are eliminated by renaming. In summary, same-named operations are merged by conjoining their schemas, after modification to reflect the state of the inheriting class, and uniting their δ-sets.

Discussion

There is an important consequence of basing the denotation of an inherited operation on its *denotation* in the inherited class, rather than on its *defining text* in that class. The following simple example illustrates the distinction.

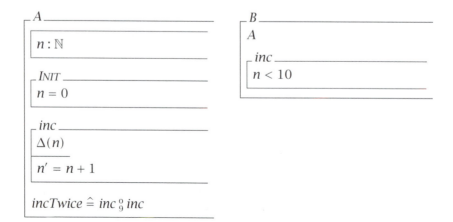

Class B inherits class A and modifies the inherited operation inc by conjunction with the local inc definition in B which strengthens inc's precondition. The denotation of $incTwice$ in B is based on its denotation in A, i.e. on the denotation of inc in A, not on the denotation of inc in B. Thus, attribute n of an object of class B can be incremented in steps of 2 indefinitely by application of $incTwice$. In contrast, had the semantics been such that the defining text of $incTwice$ were inherited, application of $incTwice$ to an object of class B would be limited.

The distinction is one of early semantic interpretation (in the inherited class) versus late semantic interpretation (in the inheriting class).

Advocates for early interpretation argue that the actual definition text is merely a means (usually not unique) to the end, i.e. to define the denotation of the operation. On the other hand, advocates for late interpretation would argue that the dependence of $incTwice$ on inc as expressed in A is important and should persist on redefinition of inc in B.

An important advantage of early interpretation is that certain properties derivable from the inherited class persist in the inheriting class and this effects reuse of work performed on the inherited class. In addition, refinements of an inherited class are potentially reusable in the refinement of the inheriting class.

There is an obligation, however, to show which properties or refinements of an inherited class persist in the context of the inheriting class. For example, reachability of states in general is not inherited as new operations introduced in the inheriting class may enable inherited attributes to reach further states.

Late interpretation denies any semantic notion of inheritance whereas early interpretation affords a basis for relating the denotations of the inherited and inheriting classes.

Early interpretation was adopted for Object-Z because of the importance of potential reuse of properties and refinements and a semantic notion of inheritance.

Returning to the above example, $incTwice$ in B can be explicitly specified in terms of inc in B, if that is required, as follows.

$$
\begin{array}{|l}
\hline
B \\
\hline
A[\,oldIncTwice/incTwice\,] \\
\\
\quad \begin{array}{|l} \hline inc \\ \hline n < 10 \\ \hline \end{array} \\
\\
incTwice \mathrel{\widehat{=}} inc \mathbin{\substack{\circ \\ 9}} inc \\
\hline
\end{array}
$$

Renaming the inherited $incTwice$ to $oldIncTwice$ avoids it being conjoined with the $incTwice$ reintroduced in B.

Developing denotational and axiomatic semantics for an object-oriented specification language, such as Object-Z, requires all aspects of classes, object identity, inheritance and polymorphism to be addressed: it is a task of considerable magnitude.

Background notation A

A.1 Introduction

This appendix defines and illustrates with simple examples the notation used throughout the book for the fundamental mathematical concepts of predicates, sets, relations, functions and sequences. Readers familiar with the Z toolkit will find nothing new here. Readers who are unfamiliar with Z but familiar with the basic concepts of finite mathematics will notice that the notation varies slightly from that in common mathematical use. Readers who are unsure of their background in finite mathematics are advised to read this appendix carefully and, if necessary, consult an introductory textbook on Z (see Appendix D).

A glossary of notation is given in Appendix B.

A.2 Predicate calculus

A predicate is some statement that evaluates to *true* or *false*. For instance,

- today is Tuesday
- 13 is a factor of 29
- $x + y = 9$
- given any natural number, there is a natural number that is larger

are each predicates whose truth value can be deduced from the context within which the predicate appears. For example, in any context that includes the natural numbers, the second predicate above always evaluates to *false*, while the fourth always evaluates to *true*. The truth value of the first predicate, however, depends on whether or not the statement is made on a Tuesday, while the truth value of the third predicate depends on the values of x and y (e.g. if $x = 3$ and $y = 6$ it evaluates to *true*; if $x = 3$ and $y = 7$ it evaluates to *false*).

An important question arises: given the context, how can the truth value of a predicate be determined, e.g. how can we be sure that the fourth predicate above evaluates to *true*? The understanding is that underlying any system there is a set of axioms and inference rules enabling the truth value of each predicate that appears in the system to be evaluated. Throughout this book the intuitive and commonly understood properties of mathematical entities such as numbers and sets will be assumed; no attempt will be made to justify statements about such entities by appealing to fundamental axioms, even although it is understood that such a rigorous axiomatic development could (perhaps with difficulty) be carried out if demanded.

Predicate operators

There are various operators for modifying and combining predicates. Suppose P and Q are predicates; then:

negation

$\neg P$ (not P)

is a predicate that is *true* if and only if P is *false*, e.g.

$\neg (11 < 3)$ is *true*
$\neg (2 + 2 = 4)$ is *false*

conjunction

$P \wedge Q$ (P and Q)

is a predicate that is *true* if and only if both P and Q are *true*, e.g.

$(11 > 3) \wedge (2 + 2 = 4)$ is *true*
$(11 < 3) \wedge (2 + 2 = 4)$ is *false*
$(11 < 3) \wedge (2 + 2 = 5)$ is *false*

disjunction

$P \vee Q$ (P or Q)

is *true* if and only if P is *true*, Q is *true*, or both are *true*, e.g.

$(11 > 3) \vee (2 + 2 = 4)$ is *true*
$(11 < 3) \vee (2 + 2 = 4)$ is *true*
$(11 < 3) \vee (2 + 2 = 5)$ is *false*

implication

$P \Rightarrow Q$ (P implies Q)

is a predicate that is *true* if and only if P is *false* or Q is *true*, e.g.

$(11 > 3) \Rightarrow (2 + 2 = 4)$ is *true*
$(11 < 3) \Rightarrow (2 + 2 = 4)$ is *true*
$(11 > 3) \Rightarrow (2 + 2 = 5)$ is *false*
$(11 < 3) \Rightarrow (2 + 2 = 5)$ is *true*

equivalence

$$P \Leftrightarrow Q \quad (P \text{ if and only if } Q)$$

is *true* if and only if P and Q are both *true* or both *false*: e.g.

$$(11 > 3) \Leftrightarrow (2 + 2 = 4) \quad \text{is } true$$
$$(11 < 3) \Leftrightarrow (2 + 2 = 4) \quad \text{is } false$$
$$(11 < 3) \Leftrightarrow (2 + 2 = 5) \quad \text{is } true$$

The above definitions are summarized in Figure A.1, where T denotes *true* and F denotes *false*.

P	$\neg P$
T	F
F	T

negation

P	Q	$P \wedge Q$
T	T	T
F	T	F
T	F	F
F	F	F

conjunction

P	Q	$P \vee Q$
T	T	T
F	T	T
T	F	T
F	F	F

disjunction

P	Q	$P \Rightarrow Q$
T	T	T
F	T	T
T	F	F
F	F	T

implication

P	Q	$P \Leftrightarrow Q$
T	T	T
F	T	F
T	F	F
F	F	T

equivalence

Figure A.1: predicate operators

Universal quantification

Consider the predicate 'given any two distinct natural numbers, one is larger than the other'. This can be expressed formally as

$$\forall x : \mathbb{N}; \ y : \mathbb{N} \bullet x \neq y \ \Rightarrow \ (x > y \ \vee \ y > x)$$

where '$\forall$' is the universal quantifier (read as 'for all'). Such predicates are called *universally quantified expressions* or *universal quantifications* and have the following syntactic structure.

- Following the quantifier is a list of declarations separated by semi-colons. In this case there are two declarations

$$x : \mathbb{N} \quad \text{and} \quad y : \mathbb{N}$$

introducing variables x and y and declaring them to be of type $\mathbb{N}$, where $\mathbb{N}$ denotes the set of natural numbers $\{0, 1, 2, \ldots\}$. This indicates that the value of both x and y will be some natural number. As x and y are of the same type in this case, the declaration could have been syntactically simplified to $x, y : \mathbb{N}$.

- The delimiter '•' immediately follows the list of declarations to indicate that the declarations are completed.

- Following this delimiter is the 'body' of the quantification; it is a predicate and involves the declared variables and possibly global variables. In this case the body is

$$x \neq y \;\Rightarrow\; (x > y \;\vee\; y > x)$$

which involves both x and y but no global variables. Following Z, Object-Z is a strongly typed language: all variables that appear in the body must first be introduced and typed in a declaration.

A universal quantification evaluates to *true* if and only if its body evaluates to *true* regardless of the value taken by each declared variable (subject, of course, to the restriction that the value of a variable must agree with its declared type). In the above case, the universal quantification is *true* as it is a property of the natural numbers that regardless of the values of the natural numbers x and y, the following is *true*:

$$x \neq y \;\Rightarrow\; (x > y \;\vee\; y > x)$$

As another example, the universal quantification 'the square of any natural number is larger than the number itself' translates into the formal expression

$$\forall\, n : \mathbb{N} \bullet n^2 > n.$$

This evaluates to *false* as its body $n^2 > n$ is *false* when $n = 0$ or $n = 1$. The scope of a variable declared in a universal quantification is the body of the quantification. Syntactically, the body commences immediately after the '•' delimiter and extends to the end of the quantification.

Existential quantification

Consider the predicate 'there is a natural number larger than 5'. This can be expressed formally as

$$\exists\, n : \mathbb{N} \bullet n > 5$$

where '∃' is the existential quantifier (read as 'there exists'). Such predicates are called *existentially quantified expressions* or *existential quantifications*. The syntax of existential quantifications is identical to that for universal quantifications, except that '∃' replaces '∀'. An existential quantification evaluates to *true* if and only if a value agreeing with its type can be found for each declared variable such that the body predicate evaluates to *true*. In the above case, the existential quantification is *true* as taking $n = 6$ results in the body $n > 5$ being *true*. As another example, the predicate 'given any natural number, there is a natural number that is larger' translates to

$$\forall x : \mathbb{N} \bullet \exists y : \mathbb{N} \bullet y > x.$$

This universal quantification evaluates to *true* as the body $\exists y : \mathbb{N} \bullet y > x$, itself an existential quantification, is *true* regardless of the value of the natural number x (just take y to have the value $x + 1$, and then $y > x$ is *true*). Generally, quantifications of either kind can be nested arbitrarily deep. Note that the scope of x extends from the first '$\bullet$' to the end of the entire construct, and the scope of y extends from the second '$\bullet$' to the end of the entire construct.

A.3   Sets

Taking an intuitive and somewhat naive view, a set is nothing more than a collection of elements, or members. A set can be represented syntactically as a list of its elements separated by commas and placed within parentheses, e.g.

$$\{3, 1, 16\}$$

denotes the set whose elements are the numbers 3, 1 and 16. The order in which the elements are listed is not important, and elements are not repeated, i.e. given a set, an element is either in the set or not in the set: there is no notion of the position of the element in the set, or of being in the set more than once. Certain sets that occur frequently are denoted by special symbols:

$\mathbb{N} == \{0, 1, 2, \ldots\}$	natural numbers
$\mathbb{N}_1 == \{1, 2, 3, \ldots\}$	non-zero natural numbers
$\mathbb{Z} == \{0, 1, -1, 2, -2, \ldots\}$	integers
$\mathbb{R}$	real numbers
$\mathbb{B} == \{true, false\}$	logical constants
$\varnothing$	empty set: the set with no elements

where '$==$' indicates that the symbol on the left abbreviates the set denotation on the right.

If X is any finite set,

$$\#X \qquad (\text{hash } X)$$

denotes the number of elements in X, e.g. $\#\{3, 1, 16\} = 3$ and $\#\varnothing = 0$. The number of elements is also called the cardinality of the set.

Membership

If X is a set,

$$x \in X \qquad (x \text{ an element of } X)$$

is a predicate that is *true* if and only if *x* is an element of *X*, e.g.

$$3 \in \{3, 1, 16\} \quad \text{is } true$$
$$7 \in \{5, 8\} \quad \text{is } false$$
$$6 \notin \{2, 7\} \quad \text{is } true$$

where $6 \notin \{2, 7\}$ is syntactic shorthand for the predicate $\neg\ (6 \in \{2, 7\})$. It is important to distinguish between variable declarations and set membership. For instance, in the universally quantified predicate

$$\forall x : \mathbb{Z} \bullet x > 5 \ \Rightarrow \ x \in \mathbb{N}$$

$x : \mathbb{Z}$ declares a new variable x of type integer, while $x \in \mathbb{N}$ is a predicate whose truth value depends upon the value of the previously declared variable x.

Set expressions

Listing all the elements of a set is tedious if the set is large and impossible if the set is infinite. Instead, a set can be defined by a set expression involving a predicate which specifies precisely which elements are in the set. For instance, the set of all natural numbers less than 99 is denoted by the set expression:

$$\{n : \mathbb{N} \mid n < 99\}$$

The general syntactic structure of a set expression is

{declarations | predicate}

where the predicate involves any declared variables and possibly global variables. As another example, the set of even integers is denoted by

$$\{z : \mathbb{Z} \mid \exists k : \mathbb{Z} \bullet z = 2 * k\}$$

where '$*$' denotes integer multiplication.

As sets of contiguous natural numbers occur frequently, if a and b are any natural numbers, the following abbreviation is predefined

$$a .. b == \{n : \mathbb{N} \mid a \leqslant n \ \wedge \ n \leqslant b\}.$$

The set $a .. b$ is empty whenever $b < a$.

Sets may also be defined using set abstraction. For example, the set of even integers greater that 6 can be denoted by

$$\{z : \mathbb{Z} \mid z > 3 \bullet 2 * z\}.$$

The general syntactic structure of a set abstraction is

{declarations | predicate • expression}

where the expression involves variables declared in the declarations and possibly global variables. Such a set abstraction denotes the set of all values taken by the expression as the declared variables range over all possible values consistent with their types and the predicate.

The form 'declarations | predicate' is called *schema text*: it is a template for introducing a collection of typed variables and specifying constraints beyond those imposed by their types.

Subset and power set

If X and Y are sets,

$$X \subseteq Y \quad (X \text{ a subset of } Y)$$

is a predicate logically equivalent to the predicate $\forall\, x : X \bullet x \in Y$, e.g.

$\{3, 1, 16\} \subseteq \mathbb{N}$ is *true*
$2..3 \subseteq 1..5$ is *true*
$2..4 \subseteq 3..5$ is *false*

Notice that $\varnothing \subseteq X$ is *true* for any set X, while the predicate $\{x\} \subseteq X$ is logically equivalent to the predicate $x \in X$.

If X is a set,

$$\mathbb{P}X \quad (\text{the power set of } X)$$

denotes the set of all subsets of X, e.g.

$$\mathbb{P}\{2, 7\} = \{\varnothing, \{2\}, \{7\}, \{2, 7\}\}$$

For any sets A and X, the predicates $A \in \mathbb{P}X$ and $A \subseteq X$ are logically equivalent.

Set operators

There are various operators for combining sets. If $S, T : \mathbb{P}X$, then:

union

$$S \cup T \quad (S \text{ union } T)$$

is the set $\{x : X \mid x \in S \,\lor\, x \in T\}$, e.g.

$$1..5 \,\cup\, 3..7 = 1..7$$

intersection

$$S \cap T \quad (S \text{ intersection } T)$$

is the set $\{x : X \mid x \in S \,\land\, x \in T\}$, e.g.

$$1..5 \,\cap\, 3..7 = 3..5$$

difference

$$S \setminus T \quad (S \text{ subtract } T)$$

is the set $\{x : X \mid x \in S \ \wedge \ x \notin T\}$, e.g.

$$1 .. 5 \ \setminus \ 3 .. 7 = 1 .. 2$$

Cartesian product

If S and T are sets,

$$S \times T \quad (S \text{ cross } T)$$

is the set of all ordered pairs (s, t) such that $s \in S$ and $t \in T$, e.g.

$$1 .. 3 \ \times \ 2 .. 3 = \{(1, 2), (1, 3), (2, 2), (2, 3), (3, 2), (3, 3)\}$$

The set $1 .. 3 \ \times \ 2 .. 3$ can also be denoted by the set expression

$$\{x, y : \mathbb{N} \mid x \in 1 .. 3 \ \wedge \ y \in 2 .. 3\}$$

If $c : S \times T$, $first(c)$ and $second(c)$ are the elements of S and T respectively such that $c = (first(c), second(c))$, i.e. the functions $first$ and $second$ extract the first and second components respectively from an ordered pair. A syntactic alternative for an ordered pair (s, t) is $s \mapsto t$.

Sets and types

In Object-Z as in Z, any set can be used as a type, e.g. an expression of the form

$$\forall A : \mathbb{P} \mathbb{N} \bullet \forall a : A \bullet \cdots$$

is valid. However, a set may not be used as a type within the same declaration list as that which introduces it, i.e. the expression $\forall A : \mathbb{P} \mathbb{N}; \ a : A \bullet \cdots$ is not valid.

A.4   Relations

Given sets A and B, a relation R from A to B has declaration

$$R : A \leftrightarrow B$$

and is some subset of $A \times B$, i.e. $A \leftrightarrow B$ is an alternative denotation for the set $\mathbb{P}(A \times B)$. As an example, consider the relation *factor* where A is the set $3 .. 6$ and B the set $6 .. 9$, and where an element $x \in 3 .. 6$ is related to an element $y \in 6 .. 9$ if and only if x is a factor of y. The relation is formally defined by

$$factor : 3 \mathbin{..} 6 \leftrightarrow 6 \mathbin{..} 9$$

$$\forall x : 3 \mathbin{..} 6;\ y : 6 \mathbin{..} 9 \bullet$$
$$x\ \underline{factor}\ y \Leftrightarrow \exists k : \mathbb{N} \bullet k * x = y$$

This example illustrates the use of an open schema box — a two-dimensional form of schema text. The relation name is introduced and typed in the declaration part (above the horizontal dividing line). The predicate specifying precisely which ordered pairs are in the relation appears in the predicate part (below the horizontal line). In effect, the horizontal line serves the role of '|' in non-boxed schema text and is also read as 'such that'. The 'open' indicates that the quantities defined are accessible within the environment in which the box is placed.

In this case the relation *factor* is the subset

$$\{(3,6),(3,9),(4,8),(6,6)\}$$

of $3 \mathbin{..} 6 \times 6 \mathbin{..} 9$. The term $x\ \underline{factor}\ y$ appearing in the specification is a predicate that is *true* if and only if x is related to y by the relation *factor*, i.e. if and only if $(x,y) \in factor$. The convention adopted here is that identifiers naming relations are underlined when applied as infix operators.

Domain and range

Given a relation $R : A \leftrightarrow B$, the domain of R, denoted $\operatorname{dom} R$, is the set of elements of A related by R to some element in B, i.e.

$$\operatorname{dom} R = \{a : A \mid \exists b : B \bullet a\ \underline{R}\ b\}$$

Similarly, the range of R, denoted $\operatorname{ran} R$, is the set of elements of B which are related by R to some element in A, i.e.

$$\operatorname{ran} R = \{b : B \mid \exists a : A \bullet a\ \underline{R}\ b\}$$

Effectively, dom (respectively ran) is an operator that takes a set of ordered pairs and extracts the set of all elements appearing in the first (respectively second) place of the ordered pairs, e.g. for the relation *factor* defined above,

$$\operatorname{dom} factor = \{3,4,6\} \quad \text{and} \quad \operatorname{ran} factor = \{6,8,9\}$$

Notice that for any relation R,

$$\operatorname{dom} R = \{r : R \bullet first(r)\} \quad \text{and} \quad \operatorname{ran} R = \{r : R \bullet second(r)\}$$

If $R : A \leftrightarrow B$, then $R^{\sim}$ is the inverse relation, i.e.

$$R^{\sim} \in B \leftrightarrow A \quad \text{and} \quad \forall a : A;\ b : B \bullet b\ \underline{R^{\sim}}\ a \Leftrightarrow a\ \underline{R}\ b$$

Restriction

It is often necessary to restrict in some way the domain or range of a given relation: the Z mathematical toolkit contains specific notation to facilitate this. Suppose $R : A \leftrightarrow B$ and $S \subseteq A$ and $T \subseteq B$; then:

domain restriction

$$S \lhd R \qquad (R \text{ with domain restricted to } S)$$

is the relation $\{a : A;\ b : B \mid a \underline{R} b \ \wedge\ a \in S\}$, e.g.

$$4 .. 6 \lhd factor = \{(4, 8), (6, 6)\}$$

range restriction

$$S \rhd T \qquad (R \text{ with range restricted to } T)$$

is the relation $\{a : A;\ b : B \mid a \underline{R} b \ \wedge\ b \in T\}$, e.g.

$$factor \rhd 6 .. 8 = \{(3, 6), (4, 8), (6, 6)\}$$

In both of these cases, the restricted relation still has type $A \leftrightarrow B$.

A.5   Functions

Given sets A and B, a (partial) function f from A to B has declaration

$$f : A \nrightarrow B$$

and is some subset of $A \times B$ with the property that for each element $a \in A$ there is at most one element $b \in B$ with $(a, b) \in f$. As a function is clearly nothing more than a special kind of relation (i.e. $A \nrightarrow B \subseteq A \leftrightarrow B$), all the notation defined for relations in Section A.4 is applicable to functions. Given a function $f : A \nrightarrow B$ and an element $a \in \operatorname{dom} f$, the unique element $b \in B$ with $(a, b) \in f$ is denoted by $f(a)$ and is called the *image* of a under f. Hence the predicates $(a, b) \in f$ and $f(a) = b$ are logically equivalent when $a \in \operatorname{dom} f$. (When no confusion can arise, the term $f(a)$ may be abbreviated to $f\,a$, i.e. the brackets around the a may be omitted.)

As an example, consider the function *pred* that maps each non-zero natural number to its predecessor. This function is formally defined by

$$pred : \mathbb{N} \nrightarrow \mathbb{N}$$
$$\operatorname{dom} pred = \mathbb{N}_1 \ \wedge\ \forall\, n : \mathbb{N}_1 \bullet pred(n) = n - 1$$

A function $f : A \nrightarrow B$ is *total*, denoted $f : A \rightarrow B$, if $\operatorname{dom} f$ is the set A. For example, the function *pred* above could have been declared as the total function $pred : \mathbb{N}_1 \to \mathbb{N}$, in which case the first conjunct (dom $pred = \mathbb{N}_1$) would have been omitted.

A function $f : A \twoheadrightarrow B$ is *one-one* (or *injective*), denoted $f : A \rightarrowtail B$, if distinct elements in the domain map to distinct elements in the range, i.e.

$$f \in A \rightarrowtail B \Leftrightarrow \forall x, y : \text{dom } A \bullet x \neq y \Rightarrow f(x) \neq f(y).$$

Function overriding

When specifying systems, functions are often used to capture the relationship between entities. As a system evolves, the value of such a relationship may need updating from time to time. The function-overriding operator is introduced specifically to facilitate this. Suppose $f, g : A \twoheadrightarrow B$; then

$$f \oplus g \qquad (f \text{ overridden by } g)$$

is the function satisfying the following three predicates:

$$\text{dom}(f \oplus g) = \text{dom } f \cup \text{dom } g$$
$$\forall a : \text{dom } g \bullet (f \oplus g)(a) = g(a)$$
$$\forall a : (\text{dom } f \setminus \text{dom } g) \bullet (f \oplus g)(a) = f(a),$$

i.e. $(f \oplus g)(a)$ for any $a \in \text{dom } f \cup \text{dom } g$ evaluates to $g(a)$ if possible (i.e. whenever $a \in \text{dom } g$) and only evaluates to $f(a)$ when $a \notin \text{dom } g$. The type of $f \oplus g$ is again $A \twoheadrightarrow B$.

As an example, suppose the function $age : People \twoheadrightarrow \mathbb{N}$ gives the age (in years) of each person in a certain town, where *People* denotes the set of all living people (the domain of the function *age* is the set of people living in the given town). If a person p, say, living in the town has a birthday, then the *age* function needs to be updated to a function age', say, where

$$age' = age \oplus \{p \mapsto age(p) + 1\},$$

i.e. the overriding function is the (singleton) function $\{p \mapsto age(p) + 1\}$. As a result, the age of person p is increased by 1 (i.e. $age'(p) = age(p) + 1$), while the age of any other person q in the town is unchanged (i.e. $age'(q) = age(q)$).

A.6   Sequences

In Z, the sequence is the basic data type for modelling linearly ordered structures. A sequence s of elements from a set A has declaration

$$s : \text{seq } A$$

and is a function $s : \mathbb{N} \twoheadrightarrow A$ where dom $s = 1 .. n$ for some natural number n, i.e. seq A is an alternative denotation for the set

$$\{f : \mathbb{N} \twoheadrightarrow A \mid \exists n : \mathbb{N} \bullet \text{dom } f = 1 .. n\}$$

Because a sequence is nothing more than a special kind of function, all the notation for relations and functions defined in Sections A.4 and A.5 is applicable to sequences. A sequence can be denoted by listing its elements in order within angle brackets, e.g.

$\langle b, a, c, b \rangle$ denotes the sequence $\{1 \mapsto b, 2 \mapsto a, 3 \mapsto c, 4 \mapsto b\}$

Notice that, unlike a set, elements in a sequence can be repeated and order is important. The empty sequence is denoted by $\langle \rangle$. The set $\text{seq}_1 A$ denotes the set of all non-empty sequences of A, i.e. $\text{seq}_1 A == \text{seq} A \setminus \{\langle \rangle\}$.

Sequence operators

Because sequences arise frequently in specifications, special sequence operators have been developed. Suppose $s, t : \text{seq} A$; then:

concatenation

$$s \frown t \quad (s \text{ concatenate } t)$$

is the sequence obtained by appending sequence t to sequence s, e.g.

$$\langle a, b \rangle \frown \langle b, a, c \rangle = \langle a, b, b, a, c \rangle$$

More formally, $s \frown t$ is the sequence $s \cup \{n : \mathbb{N}; \ a : A \mid (n - \#s, a) \in t\}$.

head

$head(s)$, in the case when s is non-empty, denotes the element of A that appears in the first place of s, e.g. $head\langle c, b, b \rangle = c$. Formally,

$$\begin{array}{|l}
head : \text{seq}_1 A \rightarrow A \\
\hline
\forall s : \text{seq}_1 A \bullet head(s) = s(1)
\end{array}$$

tail

$tail(s)$, in the case when s is non-empty, denotes the sequence that remains after removing the first element of s, e.g. $tail\langle c, b, b \rangle = \langle b, b \rangle$. Formally,

$$\begin{array}{|l}
tail : \text{seq}_1 A \rightarrow \text{seq} A \\
\hline
\forall s : \text{seq}_1 A \bullet \langle head(s) \rangle \frown tail\, s = s
\end{array}$$

last

$last(s)$, in the case when s is non-empty, denotes the element of A that appears in the last place of s, e.g. $last\langle c, b, b \rangle = b$. Formally,

$$\begin{array}{|l}
last : \text{seq}_1 A \rightarrow A \\
\hline
\forall s : \text{seq}_1 A \bullet last(s) = s(\#s)
\end{array}$$

Glossary of notation B

This glossary lists the notation used in the book. Numbers in square brackets refer to the page where the notation is introduced or where more information can be found. (A glossary of Z notation is included in Hayes, I. (ed) *Specification Case Studies*, Prentice Hall, 1993.)

B.1   Definitions and declarations

Let x, x_k, X, X_k be identifiers and T, T_k be set-valued expressions.

$LHS == RHS$	definition of LHS to be syntactically equivalent to RHS
$x : T$	declaration of variable x of type T
$x_1{:}T_1; \ldots; x_n{:}T_n$	list of declarations
$x_1, \ldots, x_n : T$	declaration of variables $x_1, \ldots, x_n$ of type T
$[X_1, \ldots, X_n]$	introduction of given types named $X_1, \ldots, X_n$
$X ::= x_1 \mid \ldots \mid x_n$	introduction of free type X with introduced identifiers $x_1, \ldots, x_n$ as elements

B.2   Logic

Let P, Q be predicates, D a declaration or list of declarations and t_k terms.

true, false	the logical constants
$\mathbb{B}$	the set of logical constants
$\neg\, P$	logical negation [198]
$P \wedge Q$	logical conjunction [198]

$P \vee Q$ logical disjunction [198]

$P \Rightarrow Q$ logical implication [198]

$P \Leftrightarrow Q$ logical equivalence [199]

$\forall D \bullet P$ universal quantification [199]

$\exists D \bullet P$ existential quantification [200]

$t_1 = t_2$ equality of terms

$t_1 \neq t_2$ iequality of terms

B.3   Sets

Let S, S_k be sets; t, t_k terms; P a predicate; and D a declaration or declarations.

$\varnothing$ the empty set: the set with no elements

$t \in S$ set membership [201]

$t \notin S$ set non-membership [201]

$S_1 \subseteq S_2$ subset [203]

$\{t_1, \ldots, t_n\}$ set containing the values of terms $t_1, \ldots, t_n$

$\{D \mid P\}$ set expression [202]

$\{D \mid P \bullet t\}$ set abstraction [202]

$\mathbb{P} \, S$ power set [203]

$\#S$ set size (cardinality) [201]

$(t_1, \ldots, t_n)$ ordered n-tuple [204]

$S_1 \times \ldots \times S_n$ Cartesian product [204]

$first(t_1, \ldots, t_n)$ term selection [204]

Let X and Y be subsets of S.

$X \cup Y$ set union [203]

$X \cap Y$ set intersection [203]

$X \setminus Y$ set difference [204]

B.4 Numbers

$\mathbb{R}$	set of real numbers
$\mathbb{Z}$	set of integers (positive, zero and negative)
$\mathbb{N}$	set of natural numbers (non-negative integers)
$\mathbb{N}_1$	set of strictly positive natural numbers
div	integer division
$m \mathinner{\ldotp\ldotp} n$	set of integers between m and n inclusive [202]

B.5 Relations

Let X, Y, and Z be sets; $x : X$; $y : Y$; $S \subseteq X$; $T \subseteq Y$; R a relation between X and Y; R_1 a relation between X and Z; and R_2 a relation between Z and Y.

$X \leftrightarrow Y$	set of relations between X and Y [204]
$x \underline{R} y$	x is related by R to y [205]
$x \mapsto y$	x maps to y [204]
dom R	domain of relation R [205]
ran R	range of relation R [205]
$R_1 \mathbin{\substack{\circ \\ 9}} R_2$	forward relational composition [191]
$R^{\sim}$	relational inverse [205]
$R(\!\lvert S \rvert\!)$	image of the set S through the relation R
$S \triangleleft R$	domain restriction [206]
$R \triangleright T$	range restriction [206]

B.6 Functions

Let X and Y be sets; f, g functions; and t a term with value in the domain of f.

$f(t)$ (or $f\,t$)	image of t under function f [206]
$X \nrightarrow Y$	set of partial functions from X to Y [206]
$X \rightarrow Y$	set of total functions from X to Y [206]

$X \rightarrowtail\mapsto Y$	set of partial one-one functions (partial injections) from X to Y [207]
$X \rightarrowtail Y$	set of total one-one functions (total injections) from X to Y
$f \oplus g$	g overrides f [207]

B.7   Sequences

Let X be a set; A and B be sequences with elements from X; and $t_1, \ldots, t_n$ terms of type X.

$\langle\,\rangle$	the empty sequence [208]
$\text{seq}\,X$	set of finite sequences with elements from X [207]
$\text{seq}_1 X$	set of non-empty finite sequences [208]
$\langle t_1, \ldots, t_n \rangle$	sequence listing [208]
$A \frown B$	sequence concatenation [208]
head A	first element of a non-empty sequence [208]
tail A	all but the head of a non-empty sequence [208]
last A	final element of a non-empty finite sequence [208]

B.8   Class and other notation

Let f_k be features; v, v_k variables; op, op_k operation names; $opEx, opEx_k$ operation expressions; *obEx* an object expression; D a declaration; A a class name; and B, C sets of object identities.

$\lceil (f_1, \ldots, f_n)$	visibility list [7]
$\Delta(v_1, \ldots, v_n)$	Δ-list [10]
Δ	secondary variables indicator [14]
INIT	initial schema [8]
$v : \downarrow A$	polymorphic declaration [29]
$v : A_{\copyright}$	object containment [144]
$B \cup C$	class union [117]

$v?$	input variable [9]
$v!$	output variable [9]
v'	value of variable v after an operation [9]
$obEx.op$	operation application [15]
$[v_1/v_2]$	variable renaming [16]
$[op_1/op_2]$	operation renaming [28]
$op \mathrel{\hat=} opEx$	operation name declaration [15]
$opEx_1 \land opEx_2$	conjunction of operations [16]
$opEx_1 \parallel opEx_2$	parallel composition of operations [18]
$opEx_1 \parallel_! opEx_2$	'!' version of parallel composition of operations [178]
$opEx_1 \; [] \; opEx_2$	choice of operations [17]
$opEx_1 \mathbin{\substack{\circ\\9}} opEx_2$	sequential composition of operations [25]
$opEx_1 \bullet opEx_2$	environment enrichment [23]
$\land D \bullet opEx$	distributed conjunction of operations [53]
$[] \; D \bullet opEx$	distributed choice of operations [44]
$\substack{\circ\\9} \, D \bullet opEx$	distributed sequential composition of operations [76]
$\mathbb{O}$	universe of object identities [117]
$\ll ident \gg$	stereotype (UML notation) [37]

Object-Z concrete syntax C

C.1 Notation

The syntax is described in an extended BNF with the following metasymbols:

$=$	produces
$\vert$	alternative
$[x]$	optional x
$\{x\}$	zero or more x's
$\{x\}_1$	one or more x's

Nonterminals ending in *List* have productions according to:

$$xList = x\{,x\}$$

Nonterminal names are typically compound and abbreviated, each syllable commencing with an upper-case letter, e.g. *OpnExpDef*.

Terminal symbols are shown directly as they appear in Object-Z. Metasymbols are larger than terminal symbols of the same shape as seen by:

$$= =, \vert \vert, [\ ]\ [\ ]\ \text{and}\ \{\}\ \{\ \}.$$

C.2 Abbreviations

The following abbreviations are used in the productions listed in Section C.3.

Abbrev	Abbreviation	Invar	Invariant
Ax	Axiomatic	Opn	Operation
Bool	boolean	Pred	Predicate
Dec	Declaration	Prim	Primary
Def	Definition	Sec	Secondary
Des	Designator	Sep	Separator
Exp	Expression	Var	Variable
Gen	Generic		

C.3   Productions

The order of presentation of productions is top down with definitions for non-terminals appearing after their last application (except for recursive definitions).

$$Specification \;=\; Def \, \{Sep\ Def\}$$

$$Def \;=\; ClassDef \;\mid\; NonClassDef$$

$$ClassDef \;=\;$$

┌─ *ClassHeading* ──────────
│ [*Visibility*]
│ [*Inheritance*]
│ [*LocalDefs*]
│ [*StateSchema*]
│ [*InitialSchema*]
│ [*Operations*]
└──────────────────────

$$ClassHeading \;=\; ClassName \, [GenFormals]$$

$$Visibility \;=\; \upharpoonright (NameList)$$

$$Inheritance \;=\; ClassDes \, \{Sep\ ClassDes\}$$

$$LocalDefs \;=\; NonClassDef \, \{Sep\ NonClassDef\}$$

$$NonClassDef \;=\; GivenTypeDef \;\mid\; FreeTypeDef \;\mid\; AbbrevDef \\ \mid\; AxDef \;\mid\; GenDef$$

$$GivenTypeDef \;=\; [NameList]$$

$$FreeTypeDef \;=\; Name ::= Branch \, \{ \mid Branch\}$$

$$Branch \;=\; Name \, [\langle\langle Exp \rangle\rangle]$$

$$AbbrevDef \;=\; Name \, [GenFormals] \;==\; Exp$$

$$AxDef \;=\;$$

│ *Decs*
├───────────
│ [*Pred*]

GenDef =

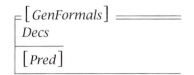

$$
\begin{array}{|l}
\hline
[\textit{GenFormals}] \\
\textit{Decs} \\
\hline
[\textit{Pred}] \\
\hline
\end{array}
$$

GenFormals = [*NameList*]

StateSchema =

$$
\begin{array}{|l}
\hline
[\textit{PrimVarDecs}] \\
[\Delta \\
\ \ \textit{SecVarDecs}] \\
\hline
[\textit{ClassInvar}] \\
\hline
\end{array}
$$

PrimVarDecs = *Decs*

SecVarDecs = *Decs*

ClassInvar = *Pred*

InitialSchema =

$$
\begin{array}{|l}
\hline
\text{INIT} \\
\hline
\textit{Pred} \\
\hline
\end{array}
$$

Operations = *OpnDef* {*Sep OpnDef*}

OpnDef = *OpnSchemaDef* | *OpnExpDef*

OpnSchemaDef =

$$
\begin{array}{|l}
\hline
\textit{OpnName} \\
[\textit{Deltalist}] \\
[\textit{Decs}] \\
\hline
[\textit{Pred}] \\
\hline
\end{array}
$$

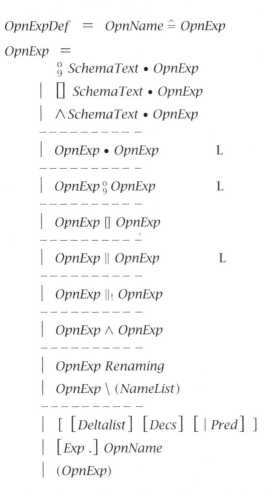

$$OpnExpDef \;=\; OpnName \;\widehat{=}\; OpnExp$$

$$OpnExp \;=$$

$$\qquad {}^{\circ}_{9}\, SchemaText \bullet OpnExp$$

$$\mid \;\;[]\; SchemaText \bullet OpnExp$$

$$\mid \;\; \wedge SchemaText \bullet OpnExp$$

$$\mid \;\; OpnExp \bullet OpnExp \qquad\qquad L$$

$$\mid \;\; OpnExp \,{}^{\circ}_{9}\, OpnExp \qquad\qquad L$$

$$\mid \;\; OpnExp \;[]\; OpnExp$$

$$\mid \;\; OpnExp \;\|\; OpnExp \qquad\qquad L$$

$$\mid \;\; OpnExp \;\|_{!}\; OpnExp$$

$$\mid \;\; OpnExp \wedge OpnExp$$

$$\mid \;\; OpnExp \; Renaming$$

$$\mid \;\; OpnExp \setminus (NameList)$$

$$\mid \;\; [\;[Deltalist]\; [Decs]\; [\mid Pred]\;]$$

$$\mid \;\; [Exp\,.]\; OpnName$$

$$\mid \;\; (OpnExp)$$

Productions are in equal-precedence groups (separated by $----$) and the precedence (binding strength) of groups increases down the page.

Choice composition, '!' version of parallel, and conjunctive composition are associative. Environment enrichment, sequential composition and parallel composition are non-associative and the productions do not impose an order of association. The 'L' indication resolves the ambiguity — it indicates left-to-right association.

$$OpnName \ = \ Name$$

$$Deltalist \ = \ \Delta(NameList)$$

$$SchemaText \ = \ Decs \ [\, | \, Pred]$$

$$Decs \ = \ Dec \ \{; Dec\}$$

$$Dec \ = \ NameList : Exp$$

$$Pred \ =$$

$$\qquad \forall \, SchemaText \bullet Pred$$

$$\qquad | \quad \exists \, SchemaText \bullet Pred$$

$$\qquad | \quad \exists_1 \, SchemaText \bullet Pred$$

$$\qquad | \quad let \ LetDefs \bullet Pred$$

- - - - - - - - - -

$$\qquad | \quad Pred \Leftrightarrow Pred$$

- - - - - - - - - -

$$\qquad | \quad Pred \Rightarrow Pred \qquad\qquad R$$

- - - - - - - - - -

$$\qquad | \quad Pred \vee Pred$$

- - - - - - - - - -

$$\qquad | \quad Pred \wedge Pred$$

- - - - - - - - - -

$$\qquad | \quad \neg \, Pred$$

$$\qquad | \quad Name \, . \, \textsc{Init}$$

$$\qquad | \quad true$$

$$\qquad | \quad false$$

$$\qquad | \quad BoolExp$$

$$\qquad | \quad (Pred)$$

The nonterminal *Deltalist* cannot be written *DeltaList* as the construct represented does not conform to the *List* convention.

Iff, disjunction and conjunction are associative. 'R' indicates right-to-left association.

$BoolExp \;=\; Exp$

$Exp \;=$

$\mu\, SchemaText \left[\, \bullet\, Exp \right]$

$\mid\; \lambda\, SchemaText \bullet Exp$

$\mid\;$ let $LetDefs \bullet Exp$

$\mid\;$ if $Pred$ then Exp else Exp

$\mid\; Exp \left\{ \times Exp \right\}_1$

$\mid\; \mathbb{P}\, Exp$

$\mid\; Exp\; Infix\; Exp$

$\mid\; Exp\; Exp$ R

$\mid\; Prefix\; Exp$

$\mid\; Exp\; Postfix$

$\mid\; ClassHierarchy$

$\mid\; Exp\, .\, Name$

$\mid\; Name \left[GenFormals \right]$

$\mid\; Name \left[GenActuals \right]$

$\mid\; \{ \left[ExpList \right] \}$

$\mid\; \{ SchemaText \left[\, \bullet\, Exp \right] \}$

$\mid\; \varnothing$

$\mid\; (Exp \left\{ , Exp \right\}_1)$

$\mid\; \langle \left[ExpList \right] \rangle$

$\mid\; Number$

$\mid\;$ self

$\mid\; (Exp)$

$$LetDefs \ = \ LetDef \ \{; \ LetDef\}$$

$$LetDef \ = \ Name == Exp$$

$$ClassHierarchy \ = \ [\ \downarrow\ ] \ ClassDes$$

$$ClassDes \ = \ ClassName \ [GenActuals] \ [Renaming]$$

$$ClassName \ = \ Name$$

$$GenActuals \ = \ [ExpList]$$

$$Renaming \ = \ [RenameList]$$

$$Rename \ = \ Name/Name$$

The syntax does not define the details of the productions for

$$Infix, Prefix, Postfix, Number, Name, Sep$$

Elision of end-of-line semicolons, end-of-line conjunction symbols and 'such that' bars in 2-D structures without predicates, is not shown in the syntax.

Further reading D

The purpose of this appendix is to suggest some book references for the reader interested in pursuing issues raised in this book. No attempt has been made to compile a comprehensive bibliography.

Z notation and specification

Davies, J. and Woodcock, J.C.P. (1996) *Using Z: Specification, Refinement and Proof*, Prentice Hall.

Hayes, I. (ed) (1993) *Specification Case Studies*, Prentice Hall.

Potter, B., Sinclair, J. and Till, D. (1996) *An Introduction to Formal Specification and Z*, Prentice Hall.

Spivey, J.M. (1992) *The Z Notation: A Reference Manual*, Prentice Hall.

Both Davies and Woodcock (1996) and Potter *et al.* (1996) present a detailed introduction to logic, sets and relations, explaining the use of the Z notation in the specification of systems and how a specification can be refined to executable code. Hayes (1993) presents a collection of specification case studies using Z. Spivey (1992) provides a comprehensive reference to the Z notation and includes tutorial and mathematical background material.

Object-oriented development

Booch, G. (1994) *Object-Oriented Analysis and Design with Applications*, Addison-Wesley.

Fowler, M. and Scott, K. (1997) *UML Distilled: Applying the Standard Object Modeling Language*, Addison-Wesley.

Gamma, E., Helm, R., Johnson, R. and Vlissides, J. (1995) *Design Patterns: Elements of Reusable Object-Oriented Software*, Addison-Wesley.

Meyer, B. (1997) *Object-Oriented Software Construction*, Prentice Hall.

The four books listed here each consider the general issues involved in object-oriented development. Booch (1994) considers a particular approach to object-oriented analysis and design, giving practical guidance on the construction of object-oriented systems. His graphical notation was one of several such notations which have been unified to the UML notation which is discussed by Fowler and Scott (1997). Gamma *et al.* (1995) explore object-oriented development from the perspective of design patterns. The book by Meyer (1997) offers a comprehensive introduction to many aspects of object technology, covering most of the principal issues, methods and languages.

Object-oriented formal specification

Lano, K. and Haughton, H. (eds) (1994) *Object-Oriented Specification Case Studies*, Prentice Hall.

Stepney, S., Barden, R. and Cooper, D. (eds) (1992) *Object Orientation in Z*, Springer.

Both Lano and Haughton (1994) and Stepney *et al.* (1992) collate contributions from a number of authors exploring various approaches to the object-oriented formal specification of systems. Stepney *et al.* (1992) looks specifically at object-oriented extensions to Z: Object-Z is one such extension.

Java

Horstmann, C. and Cornell, G. (1999) *Core Java 2*, Prentice Hall.

Horstmann and Cornell (1999) is a good introduction to the Java programming language. The Java code for the buttons-toggling puzzle in Section 4.4 was prepared using Java 2.

Index

abstract
  class, 108
  syntax, 183
activity diagram, 89
aggregation, 19
alternating-bit protocol, 79
applicable operation, 11
attribute, 8
  polymorphic, 118
  unprimed, 10
auxiliary
  operation, 24
  variable, 98
axiomatic semantics, 184

base name, 18
basis of class union, 118
binary tree, 148
bingo case study, 51
buttons-toggling case study, 55

Cartesian product, 204
case study
  alternating-bit protocol, 79
  bingo, 51
  buttons-toggling, 55
  credit cards, 4
  geometric shapes, 106
  magnetic keys, 42
  mass transit railway, 127
  retail chain, 151
  spreadsheet, 161
  telephone system, 121

  tic tac toe, 63
  virtual memory, 171
choice operator, 17, 189, 192
  distributed, 44
class, 5
  abstract, 108
  attribute, 8
  constant, 7
  construct, 5
  deferred, 108
  diagram, 33
  feature, 12
  generic, 84
  initial schema, 8
  invariant, 8
  local type, 70
  operation schema, 9
  state schema, 8
  subclass, 23
  superclass, 23
  union, 117
    basis of, 118
    extend, 120
  variable, 8
  visibility list, 7
communication variable, 9
  input, 10
  output, 10
composition
  diagram, 34
  operator, 135
concatenation, 208
concrete syntax, 183, 215

conjunction
    feature, 26
    logical, 198
    operation-schema, 27
    operator, 16, 187, 191
        distributed, 53
    schema, 27
constant, 7
contained, 142
containment, 139
core, 118
correctness, 98
credit-cards case study, 4

deferred class, 108
delta-list, 10
denotational semantics, 161, 183
diagram
    activity, 89
    class, 33
    composition, 34
    genericity, 89
    inheritance, 36
    object, 89
    state, 87
    swimlanes, 89
difference, 204
disjunction, 198
distributed
    choice operator, 44
    conjunction operator, 53
    sequential composition, 76
domain, 205
    restriction, 206
dynamic
    binding, 105
    semantics, 183

empty
    sequence, 208
    set, 201
environment enrichment, 23
equivalence, 199
existential quantification, 200

feature, 12

conjunction, 26
file system example, 140
first, 204
free type, 169
function, 206
    image, 206
    one-one, 207
    overriding, 207
    partial, 206
    total, 206

generic
    class, 84
    type, 84
genericity, 89
geometric shapes case study, 106
Ginger Meggs, 119
given type, 81
global type, 56

head, 208

identity of object, 13
    semantics of, 184
image, 206
implication, 198
inapplicable operation, 11
induction, 95
infix operator, 205
inheritance, 23
    diagram, 36
    multiple, 24
    polymorphic, 31, 105
    semantics of, 192
    single, 23
init, 8
initial
    condition, 8
    configuration, 9
    schema, 8
injective function, 207
input, 10
instantiation, 12
intersection, 203
interval, 202
invariant, 8

property, 95
inverse, 205

Java, 59

last, 208
liveness, 103
local type, 70
logical
    conjunction, 198
    disjunction, 198
    equivalence, 199
    implication, 198
    negation, 198

magnetic keys case study, 42
mass transit railway case study, 127
membership, 201

negation, 198

object
    aggregation, 19
    containment, 139
    diagram, 89
    identity, 13
        semantics of, 184
    instantiation, 12
    universe of identities, 117
one-one function, 207
open schema box, 7, 205
operation
    applicable, 11
    application, 15
    auxiliary, 24
    inapplicable, 11
    input to, 10
    output from, 10
    polymorphic, 118
    promotion, 15
    recursive, 150, 180
    redefine, 28
    rename, 28
    schema, 9
    schema conjunction, 27
operator
    choice, 17, 189, 192

distributed, 44
composition, 135
conjunction, 16, 187, 191
    distributed, 53
infix, 205
parallel, 18, 187, 191
    shriek version, 178, 188, 192
sequential composition, 25, 189,
    192
    distributed, 76
ordered pair, 204
output, 10
overriding, 207

parallel operator, 18, 187, 191
    shriek version, 178, 188, 192
partial
    correctness, 98
    function, 206
polymorphic
    attribute, 118
    core, 118
    inheritance hierarchy, 31, 105
    operation, 118
polymorphism, 29
power set, 203
predicate, 197
primary variable, 14
primed variable, 10
progress, 98
promotion, 15

qualification, 37
qualified expression, 118
quantification
    existential, 200
    universal, 199

range, 205
    restriction, 206
recursive
    operation, 150, 180
    structures, 146
redefine operation, 28
refinement, 59
relation, 204

inverse, 205

rename
    operation, 28
    variable, 16

restriction
    domain, 206
    range, 206

retail chain case study, 151

Russian dolls, 147

safety, 103

schema
    conjunction, 27
    initial, 8
    instance, 8
    open box, 7, 205
    operation, 9
    state, 8
    text, 203

second, 204

secondary variable, 14

self, 43

semantics
    axiomatic, 184
    denotational, 161, 183
    dynamic, 183
    static, 183

sequence, 207
    concatenation, 208
    empty, 208
    head, 208
    last, 208
    listing, 208
    non-empty, 208
    tail, 208

sequential composition operator, 25, 189, 192
    distributed, 76

set, 201
    abstraction, 202
    difference, 204
    empty, 201
    expression, 202
    intersection, 203
    membership, 201
    power, 203

size (cardinality), 201
    subset, 203
    union, 203

signature compatibility, 30

spreadsheet case study, 161

state
    diagram, 87
    schema, 8
    variable, 8

static semantics, 183

stereotype, 37

structural induction, 95

subclass, 23

subset, 203

superclass, 23

swimlanes diagram, 89

syntax
    abstract, 183
    concrete, 183, 215

tail, 208

telephone system case study, 121

tic tac toe case study, 63

total function, 206

type
    free, 169
    generic, 84
    given, 81
    global, 56
    local, 70

UML, 33

Unified Modeling Language, 33

union
    class, 117
      basis of, 118
      extend, 120
    set, 203

universal quantification, 199

universe of object identities, 117

unprimed attribute, 10

variable, 8
    auxiliary, 98
    base name, 18
    communication, 9

input, 10
output, 10
primary, 14
primed, 10
rename, 16
secondary, 14
unprimed, 10
verification, 95
virtual memory case study, 171
visibility list, 7